About the CD-ROM

The companion CD and the software included on it have been designed to run on Windows 95 and NT systems using a Web browser and Internet connection. Because this CD has been produced in HTML, Windows 3.x and Macintosh users may view much of the contents using a browser, but note that all software on this CD is either 95 and/or NT specific.

System requirements for the various types of software vary widely depending on what you download from the CD. Please review all software readme files before installing software directly to your machine.

Recommended System

Pentium PC

Windows 95 or NT operating System

4X CD-ROM drive

16MB RAM

CD-ROM Start Instructions

1 Place the CD-ROM in your CD-ROM drive.

2 Launch your Web browser.

3 From your Web browser, select Open File from the File menu. Select your CD-ROM drive (usually drive D), then select the file called *welcome.htm*.

HOW <u>*to*</u> Program

java

HOW to Program

java

PETER · COFFEE

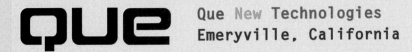

que Que New Technologies
Emeryville, California

Publisher	Stacy Hiquet
Acquisitions Editor	Lysa Lewallen
Development Editor	Renee Wilmeth
Copy Editor	Stephanie Raney
Technical Reviewer	Thomas Feng
Production Editor	Barbara Dahl
Proofreader	Jeff Barash
Cover Design	Megan Gandt
Book Design and Layout	Bruce Lundquist
Illustrator	Sarah Ishida
Indexer	Valerie Robbins
Digital Prepress Specialist	P. Diamond
Software Specialist	Yong Kim

This book was produced on a Macintosh computer system with the following applications: FrameMaker®, Microsoft® Word, QuarkXPress®, Adobe Illustrator®, Adobe Photoshop®, Adobe Streamline™, MacLink®Plus, Aldus® FreeHand™, Collage Plus™.

Que New Technologies
Macmillan Computer Publishing USA
5903 Christie Avenue
Emeryville, CA 94608

ISBN 1-56276-478-0

Manufactured in the United States of America
10 9 8 7 6 5 4 3 2 1

To my children, who needed this book;

To my wife, who was sure I could write it;

To my parents, who always knew when to say, "That sounds like fun. Why not try it?"

And to teachers, who have to tackle the job of turning information into knowledge.

Table of Contents

Acknowledgments

I could write another book about the process, and the people, who put me in a position where I could even think about writing the book that's in front of you now.

Twenty years ago, James Lyman took time away from teaching high school physics to let "The Computer Bums" club learn things in the only way that stays with a person: by getting our hands on the hardware and finding out what didn't work.

Blaine Bocarde and Bill Mock didn't settle for accurate spelling and punctuation, but demanded that their English students learn to write. I didn't know that high school was the last time that I'd have the chance to do it: I was lucky that they never settled for less.

Eight years later, when personal computers started sneaking into The Aerospace Corporation, I was once again lucky enough to meet the right people at the right time. Gary Jackson, Dennis Persinger, Lorraine Junge, and I had to invent the art of managing microcomputers in a technical organization. Max Weiss gave us the blocking we needed to move that ball down the field.

Since then, the editors at PC Week have put me in the rare position of keeping up with this stuff as my job—instead of trying to do it, as so many others must, in addition to "regular" work. I never put in such ridiculous hours in any other business: not in oil, not in defense, not even in software development. But I never learned so much, either.

Finally, thanks to the team at Que New Technologies, who asked the impossible—but then, with a lot of hard work, made it possible after all. My editors went the extra mile to give me every chance to polish, extend, and correct this work before it went out to face the world.

For what is good in this book, the reader should thank many people; for any defects that might remain, the thread stops here.

Introduction

The world has plenty of programming languages that let a programmer solve any problem, at the cost of learning to think like a computer.

The world has plenty of other tools that let a creative person use a computer to solve one kind of problem, but only that kind of problem and often on just one kind of computer.

The Java programming language can be used for any kind of problem, on any kind of computer: It can express the mathematical formulas of FORTRAN, or the parallel tasks of Ada, or the high-level "object-oriented" abstractions of Smalltalk—all with a syntax and a conceptual approach that make Java a strong head start for learning the C++ language that dominates new commercial projects.

Before Java, there was no *single* language that a programmer who really loves languages could recommend to anyone wanting to make computers do something original and useful.

But Java is that language, and this book is that recommendation: It's the book that I tried to find when I wanted to teach the language to others. I wrote it because there was no quicker way to get it.

I'll use this book to teach my own three sons. I can hope for no greater reward than seeing every reader use this book to teach just one other person that computers are the brain's power tools.

Java Technology

Java vs. Other
Programming Tools

Java's Value to
Builders and Users
of Information Systems

Chapter 1
Brewing a Revolution

During 1996, a new approach to computing swept through the many worlds that are built out of online information. It knocked down the walls between different varieties of personal computer, letting any program run without conversion on any kind of machine. It splintered the concept of an information appliance, reshaping bulky beige boxes into far more convenient devices. It energized worldwide networks, adding live and interactive content to static online archives. It elevated users' expectations for home, education, and entertainment services delivered by mass-market multimedia hardware. It carried programmers, and would-be programmers, to higher levels of creative power by doing low-level chores that once consumed scarce and costly time and energy.

The name of this new approach is Java: a name that covers many different kinds of technology, both familiar and novel. Java does many things that have been done before, but generally does them better; Java also combines cababilities that previously existed only in separate tools, creating a blend that turns many speculative notions into deliverable products.

More than a programming language, Java is also the name of a rapidly growing community of skills and resources for which the Java language is a unifying tool.

The Language Java is a programming language, one whose written appearance is much like that of the C++ language that seemed destined for dominance before Java came along. As we'll see, writing programs in C++ required laborious attention to error-prone details that the Java technology handles on its own.

Writing programs in Java frees the programmer to focus on what the program is doing, instead of on the hardware resources that are being used. Advanced features of the Java language make it easier for the programmer to make the computer adjust to the user, instead of the other way around.

The Virtual Machine Java is also a *virtual machine:* that is, a program that simulates one kind of computer while actually running on something else. If you've ever used a DOS emulator on a Macintosh or a Unix workstation, or even run a DOS window under Windows or OS/2, you've used a virtual machine.

A Java virtual machine program treats Java programs as its data. It carries out Java operations using the "native instructions" of the operating system and the hardware of the host computer, which might be anything from a handheld device to a mainframe.

Java isn't the first attempt to make a language portable by using this approach, but is a breakthrough in trying to do it with low-cost hardware. Where other virtual machines have demanded megabytes of memory, Java runs well in a fraction of that space.

The Worldwide Library   The fast-growing, worldwide collection of Java programs can run on any new kind of computer, as soon as a matching version of the virtual machine program is written for that type of system. Vendors and users don't have to recompile programs for different computers, as they do when programs are written in C++ or in most other languages. Every version of the virtual machine accepts the same Java code at the front end, and turns it into the operations of the underlying computer at the back end.

The end user's library card is an Internet connection. The reading lamp is a Java-enabled browser. By adding more interactive power to the World Wide Web, augmenting the Web's graphical access to Internet resources, Java itself aids users in finding examples of the ways that Java can meet their varied needs.

The Hardware   Why not eliminate the middleman? As Java's popularity grows, it's becoming commercially attractive to build Java machines in hardware. When the Java program issues its instructions, they'll go directly to the instruction unit of a Java microchip instead of being translated by a software virtual machine.

Such chips will soon be available at various levels of price and performance. They're on their way into everything from appliances to workstations. They'll give the programmer greater return on the investment of time that goes into writing a program, and give the user greater leverage in applying software tools to a wider range of tasks.

What Java Can Do for You

Taken all together, Java is a technology that performs many kinds of computer-based tasks quite well. Does that sound a little lukewarm? Well, it is, because there's no single thing that Java can do that can't be done as well (or better) with some other programming language.

Java's strength is its balanced mixture of established fundamentals (like economy and speed) with leading-edge innovations (like transparent access to network-based resources). For any type of programming project, it's easy to find another language that would solve the problem just as well as Java, but it's also easy to see why Java should be considered no matter what the task.

▶ If you wanted an operating system, or a mass-market word processor, you might write it in C or C++ for the fastest possible performance in the smallest amount of memory. But you'd better sell a lot of copies to spread the high cost of the project, because you'll spend a lot more time writing that program than you would with Java's more modern facilities on your side.

▶ If you wanted an expert system, like a credit risk analysis tool or a medical diagnostic aid, you might write it in Lisp, OPS5, Smalltalk, or some other "dynamic" language. But you'd better have a lot of money for hardware, because that program will need a computer with four or five times the raw processing power that you'd need to do the same things (with a little more programming effort) if you wrote the program with Java.

▶ If you wanted a program that does simple things like processing lists of numbers, you might write it in BASIC or REXX because these languages are so similar to English. But you'd better know at the beginning what kind of computer your users will have, because dialects of BASIC differ considerably from one kind of computer to another; REXX, though well standardized, is available on relatively few computer systems. By contrast, vendors of different kinds of computer are all bending over backwards to make sure that they can run the standardized language of Java.

Hitting the Sweet Spot with Java

Java programs run quickly, without adjustments for different dialects (surpassing BASIC on both criteria), and without requiring a cumbersome recompilation to run on a new kind of computer (as needed with C or C++). Java's tools use much less memory than Lisp, OPS5, or Smalltalk. And Java is a new, modern language, designed to meet today's demand for programs that are attractive and fun to use (much more so than REXX).

Java is not burdened by the need to stay compatible with earlier versions of a language, a need that already interferes with the technical evolution of languages like C++, FORTRAN, or COBOL. These languages have to retain clumsy or error-prone remnants of their earliest versions to ensure that users won't have to go through a costly process of auditing and rewriting old, already-tested programs.

No one wants to repeat the furor that arose when a standard-setting committee proposed some useful modernizations of COBOL, only to find themselves individually and collectively sued by companies who had not participated in the process and who claimed that their products had been deliberately crippled by the proposed changes. So old, "legacy" languages have a hard time being born again. They inevitably show their age.

For these reasons, Java has been embraced by companies that write software for finding information and using services on the Internet and the World Wide Web. Such content providers need to serve users who are equipped with every known kind of computer, and who have high expectations for the entertainment value of the content they're paying to receive.

That Internet connection, in turn, has propelled Java with amazing speed to the fastest, broadest acceptance ever achieved by any new programming language. One year after Java first appeared, half of the corporate software developers surveyed by the industry newspaper *PC Week* expected to be using Java within the next twelve months. At that time, this placed Java behind only Microsoft Visual Basic and (generically) C++ as the third most ubiquitous tool of the leading-edge developer.

This happened even as Java's strengths were propelling a surge of interest in programming among Internet users who had previously been more like publishers than programmers.

In short:

▶ If you make computers, Java gives you a way of being sure that any new computer you make will immediately run a large amount of software.

▶ If you use computers, Java lets you choose a computer based on overall price and performance, without being locked in to the kind of computer that happens to run the software you already own.

▶ If you create Internet content, Java gives you a way of packaging "live" material—with complex behaviors, as well as text and pictures—so that it's usable by any kind of computer.

▶ If you use the Internet, Java makes it a source of programs as well as data. Java makes the Internet less like a library, where luck determines whether you'll find the facts that you need, and makes it more like a consulting service, ready to do new work to answer precisely the questions that you want to ask.

For these reasons, the ability to run Java programs is becoming a common feature of any modern personal computer. No matter what you want to do, knowing Java will make it easier for you to do it better—with any kind of computer that happens to be around.

Summary

In this chapter, we described

▶ How Java combines a language, computer architecture, and worldwide library of reusable software.

▶ How the Java language offers a unique mix of strengths.

▶ Why Java is becoming a common capability of modern computers.

Java Tools

Integrated vs. Separate Tools

Using Tools to Speed Your Work

Choosing Tools That Match Your Java Goals

Chapter 2
Choosing Your Tools:
Picking a Java Development System

In this chapter, you'll learn what tools it takes to write, generate, and run a Java program. You'll discover what benefits you get from using integrated versus separate tools. You'll also get a look at how different tools interact with the Java language to speed your work.

To use Java on your computer, you'll need the following software tools:

▶ Editor: A program that can create and edit text files of Java language commands. Such a file, which a person can read, is called a program's *source code* (*source* for short). You are the editor program's source of input; a source code file, whose name will usually end with .java, is the editor's output. That source code file will be the input, in turn, to the next tool: the compiler.

▶ Compiler: A program that translates the source code file into the *bytecodes* (a file whose name ends with .class) that are actually used as instructions by the Java virtual machine. The compiler's input is source code; its output, the bytecodes, will become the input to the next tool, the interpreter.

▶ Interpreter: A program that reads the bytecodes and follows their instructions. The interpreter might be something that you have to start from a menu or a command line; it might be part of your Internet browser; it might even be built into your computer's operating system.

The interpreter's input is the bytecodes produced by the compiler or obtained from some other source; its output is determined by the program that's being executed.

Additional tools that you might want to have are:

▶ Debugger: This lets you step through a program slowly and see exactly what is happening as it runs—including things that don't normally show up on the screen.

▶ Resource editor: This lets you do things like draw a push button on the screen and automatically get the Java code that will make it a part of your program's display.

▶ Configuration manager: Sometimes called a version control system, this lets you save and catalog versions of your work, and lets you restore a previous working version if you make a change that has unexpected effects. This is needed more often by large teams than by individual developers.

BTW   *Do feel free to skip anything in this chapter that looks irrelevant to your situation. The Java examples in this chapter are only here to illustrate the use of various types of Java development tool. Subsequent chapters don't depend on this one to introduce any aspects of the language.*

The Java tools that you'll find on this book's CD-ROM will support you while you master the concepts of programming in general, and programming Java in particular.

Even if you already have a Java development system that you prefer (or that you've been told) to use, read this chapter anyway: it will explain the boundaries and the interactions of the tools that make up that system.

Java tools create behaviors for your computer, in the same way that a word processor creates documents or a graphics program creates pictures. A simple word processor and graphics tool are included with many computer systems (for example, WordPad and Paint on Windows 95 machines): in the same way, it's becoming common for many well-equipped personal computers to offer basic tools for running Java programs.

To understand your tools is to lay a crucial foundation: once you know what each tool does, you'll develop a solid feel for the task of translating high-level Java source code into low-level computer operations. From that foundation, you'll start to build a mental image of your own Java applications.

The Source Code Editor

Your source code editor may be just a plain word processor, like Windows 95's WordPad, though like WordPad it has to offer the option of saving text without any hidden formatting codes (which won't be ignored, and can't be understood, by the compiler).

If your word processor offers a command with a name like Save As or Export, then it probably has a way to save your files as raw text (Figure 2.1). You can write Java code, save it in a file, and be ready for the next step that we'll discuss in the section on compilers later in this chapter.

When writing anything but the simplest programs, many people find it helpful to move one step up the food chain to a so-called *syntax-aware* editor like Mansfield Software Group's KEDIT for Windows. An editor with Java syntax awareness will automatically scan the file, even while you're making changes, for the distinctive patterns of the Java language.

The editor screen will then color the different words and symbols in the file to help you keep track of how everything fits together (Figure 2.2).

Most editor products that are aimed at programmers have awareness for many languages. The editor program figures out what language is being used based on the source code file name's extension. For example, Java language files usually have a name like *MyProgram.java*, and that *.java* signals the editor to use Java's rules for analyzing the file. Even Macintosh tools tend to follow this convention for Java development.

To determine if a given programming editor has syntax support for Java, you can check the product literature to see if Java is specifically mentioned on the list of supported languages. If it's not there, check to see if the product's language support can be extended by downloading a

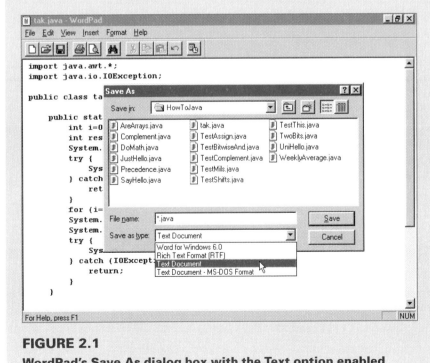

FIGURE 2.1
WordPad's Save As dialog box with the Text option enabled

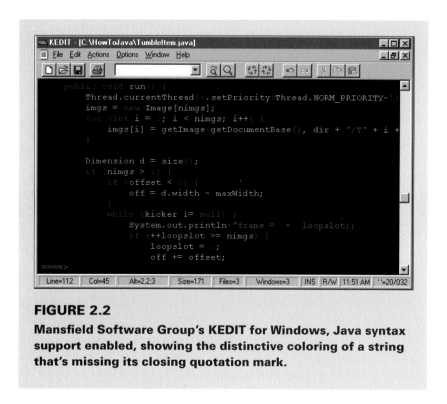

FIGURE 2.2

Mansfield Software Group's KEDIT for Windows, Java syntax support enabled, showing the distinctive coloring of a string that's missing its closing quotation mark.

parser or *lexer* file (two common names for this capability) for Java: if so, check with the vendor to see if such a file for Java is available from the vendor through some facility such as a Web page or electronic bulletin board.

Finally, some editors can extend their language support through user modifications, with procedures that range from the obvious to the obscure.

What do you get from a syntax-aware editor? Their major benefit is in calling attention to common mistakes that often occur when revising a program.

For example, when a Java program needs to put some words on the screen, the programmer puts those words between quotation marks to tell the program that those words are "literal" data. If the programmer leaves out the closing quotation mark, the program won't work as it should, because every symbol out to the end of the line will be treated as data instead of being processed as instructions.

A syntax-aware editor can use distinctive colors to alert the programmer, before a mistake like this wastes a lot of time.

When you're using a separate editor of this kind, and you finish (or think you've finished) writing the Java-language description of your program, you save the Java source code file and move on to the next tool in your collection. We'll discuss this in the section on compilers.

Integrated Environments

As with any other language, the most advanced tool for developing with Java is an integrated environment, like Symantec's Café or Microsoft's Visual J++ (Figures 2.3 and 2.4). Integrated environments combine into a single product a complete set of tools for creating and running a program—easier to buy, install, and use than a similar set of tools from different companies.

An integrated environment begins with a source code editor, usually one with syntax awareness. In addition to editing individual source code files, an environment typically adds some facility for defining a project that includes several related files. Opening the project makes all of its files available, usually through some kind of graphical view, and often with some way of showing the relationships between what's defined in those various files.

The tools of an integrated environment are usually connected behind the scenes. For example, if you try to run a program after you've changed its source code, but you haven't saved those changes, most integrated environments will warn you and will offer to save the file and rebuild your program before it runs. Figure 2.5 shows such warnings as they appear in two different environments.

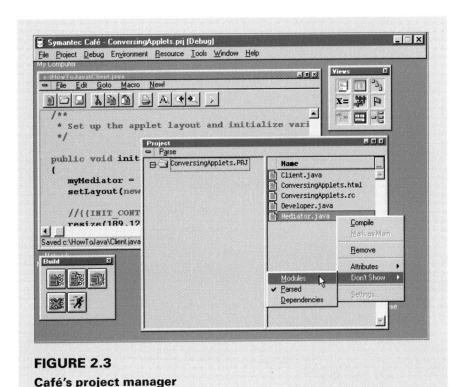

FIGURE 2.3
Café's project manager

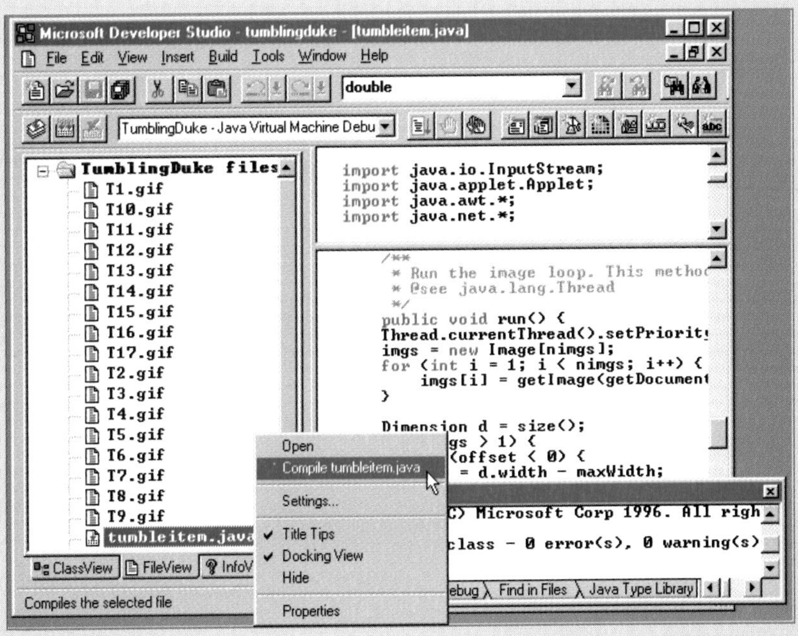

FIGURE 2.4
Visual J++'s FileView

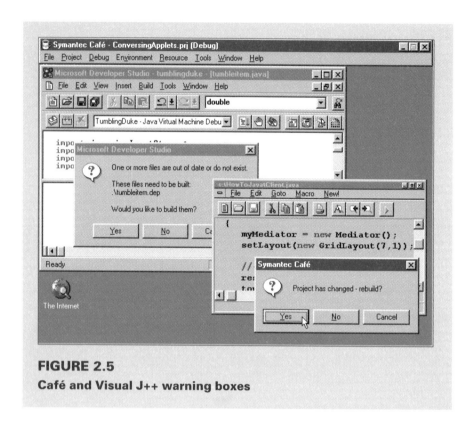

FIGURE 2.5
Café and Visual J++ warning boxes

The Java Compiler

No matter what you use to write your program, it won't be able to run until it's been translated from source code into Java bytecodes. Bytecodes are the tiny operations that the virtual machine actually performs.

For example, when you write a Java command to add two numbers, it looks something like this:

```
i = j + k;
```

The Java bytecodes for this operation look something like,

```
load j
load k
add
store i
```

The Java language lets you write, and think about, your program in the former notation that's much easier to read. The Java compiler breaks that source code into the latter format of step-by-step instructions that the Java machine (whether virtual or hardware) can use.

There are times when it makes sense to work with those "machine instructions" directly, as when writing arcade-style games where the speed of the final program is the player's top priority. For most kinds of program other than games or utility software, programmers usually find it more productive to work with a high-level language, even though this means a noticeable delay due to compilation before the program can be tested. Compilers used to yield programs much slower than those devised in hand-crafted machine language, but this difference is much smaller today than it used to be.

Making the Connection

If you're using a separate editor and compiler, you'll need to figure out how to tell the compiler where to find the source code file that should be processed. On a DOS or Unix system, you just make sure that the compiler program is in a directory that's part of your PATH environment variable. This lets you go to the directory that contains your source file and run the compiler with a simple command. Three examples, using three different Java compilers, appear in Figure 2.6.

On the Macintosh, tools like Metrowerks Java work with the Mac's graphical desktop, so that you can just drag the icon for your source file "into" the icon of the Java compiler to start the process as in Figure 2.7.

If you're using an integrated environment, you'll usually be able to click on a menu or an icon to build the currently open project: the environment will know the locations of the project's files and will pass them to the compiler (Figure 2.8).

Right from the Beginning

No matter how you do it, compiling is an important step because the Java language gives the compiler many ways to detect common programming errors.

For example, suppose you were going to do some calculations with a number whose value you planned to change so that you could see the results of different assumptions. Suppose you

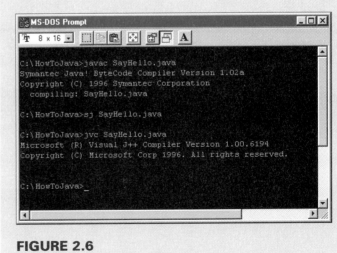

FIGURE 2.6
DOS screen showing compilation commands and compiler's responses

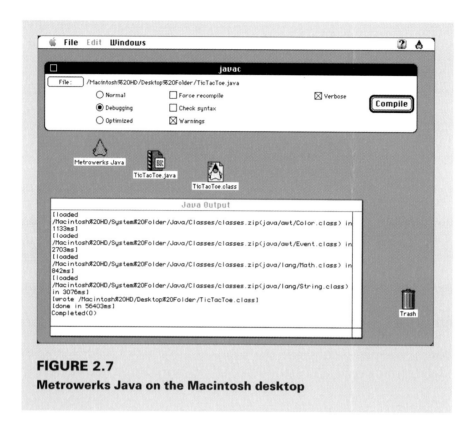

FIGURE 2.7

Metrowerks Java on the Macintosh desktop

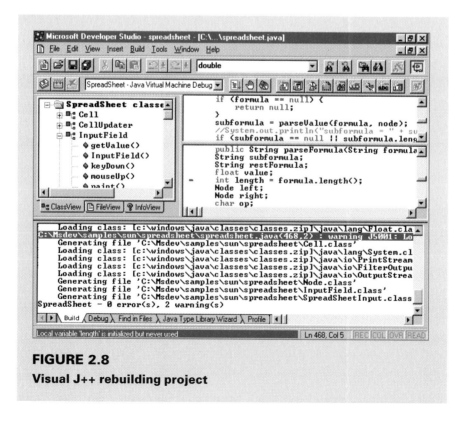

FIGURE 2.8

Visual J++ rebuilding project

gave that number the name, *myNumber*, and suppose that you told Java that this number would always be an exact value like 1 or 17. You'd do this with something called a declaration, which in this case would look like:

```
int myNumber;
```

Declaring that this number is an exact value (an integer) would let Java use the simplest method it has for storing numbers: that is, the electronic equivalent of simply counting on its fingers.

Later on, though, you might want to give myNumber a value like 2.3. If you just wrote "myNumber = 2.3," the Java compiler has to make a decision. Should it come as close as it can to doing what you ask? Or should it ask you to think again?

 Some programming languages would take the first approach, truncating the value 2.3 to the next smaller integer, 2. Your program would run, but it would not do what you wanted.

Java, however, will complain at the time that you compile your code, with an error message such as "Cannot implicitly convert" (Figure 2.9). This kind of error detection is one of Java's strongest features.

If you use a separate editor and compiler, though, you'll have to read the compiler's output to determine the nature and location of each error, then open the editor to find and fix the mistakes. This is quite time-consuming.

An integrated environment will usually present the error messages in a window; if you double-click on an error message, the environment will take you directly to the error's location in your source code editor window (Figure 2.10). This is a whole lot quicker.

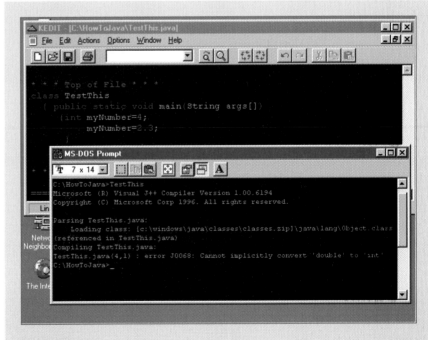

FIGURE 2.9
DOS window showing javac compiler error message

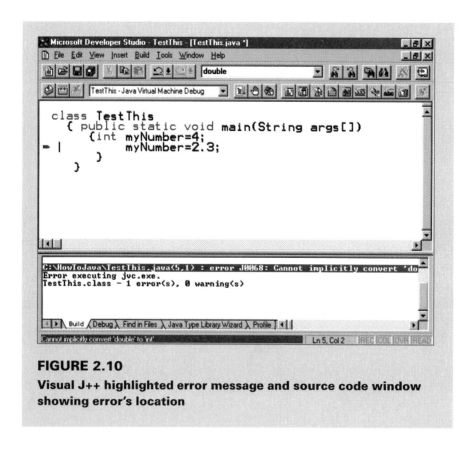

FIGURE 2.10

Visual J++ highlighted error message and source code window showing error's location

The Java Interpreter

When it's time to run your Java program, there are four common ways to do it.

The simplest way is in a text-mode window, such as a DOS window under Windows 95 running an interpreter program like the Sun JAVA utility (Figure 2.11).

This works fine if your program only needs text-based interaction with the user. Such programs are sometimes called *console* programs, because this approach recalls the old-fashioned typewriter-style consoles on the earliest computers. A console session can print output from the machine and accept keyboard input from the user, and that's all. But that will be enough for our first several study projects.

The next step up, in both creative freedom and programming effort, is running your program with the graphical enhancements that users expect to see on a Web page or other graphical presentation. A program that works in this mode is harder to write than a console application, though many integrated environments provide an automatic start-up tool that creates the framework for such a program.

When you want to run a program of this kind, you might use something called an applet viewer, or your program might be what's called a stand-alone application (Figure 2.12). The details will vary considerably from one kind of computer to another, or depending on which Java tools you're using.

The most sophisticated option is to embed your Java program in a Web page (Figure 2.13), defined by the HTML markup language that's described in *How to Use HTML 3* by Scott Arpajian (Ziff-Davis Press, 1996). Such a page may contain several Java programs, all sharing the computer's facilities. We'll see in Chapter 16 how we can put our programs on the Web.

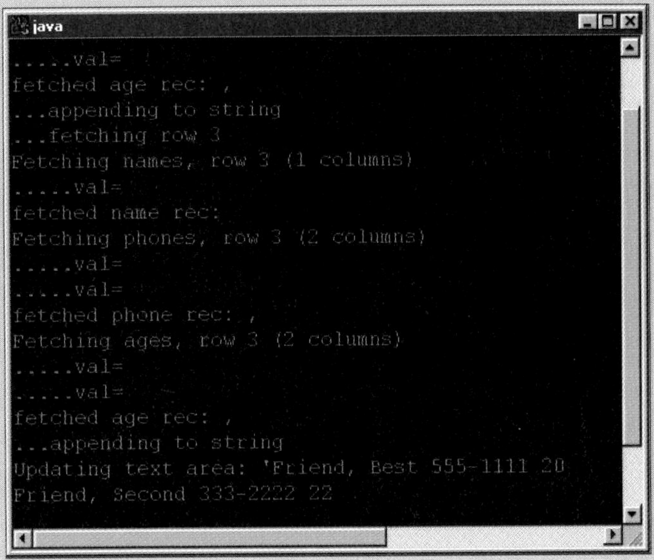

The fourth way to run your program is "in the debugger," as it's called, where your program is contained by a middle layer of software. Your program is in an adolescent phase, not as easily changed as when it's just Java source code in an editor window; not as free to run at full speed, or with its full powers, as when it's a stream of Java bytecodes that's directly driving the Java virtual machine.

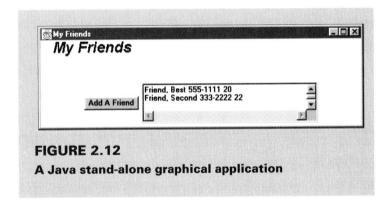

FIGURE 2.11
DOS session running a Java console application

FIGURE 2.12
A Java stand-alone graphical application

The debugger is something like a simulator: it lets you do things like examine the values of different pieces of data at various stages of the program's operation, confirming that you haven't forgotten vital steps in the task your program must perform (Figure 2.14).

Depending on which Java tools you're using, you may be able to use the debugger's facilities while viewing your program in its full Web-page context; even the simplest debuggers, however, will support programs running in dedicated text or graphics windows.

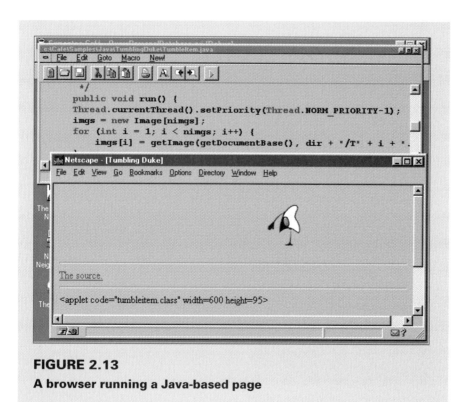

FIGURE 2.13

A browser running a Java-based page

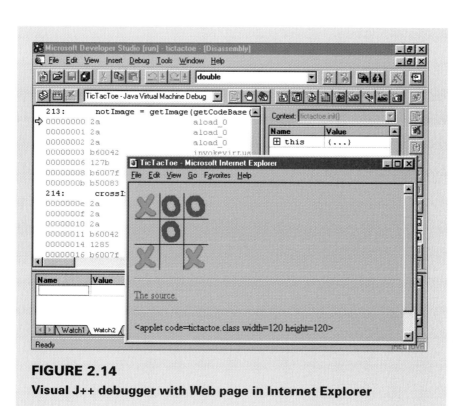

FIGURE 2.14

Visual J++ debugger with Web page in Internet Explorer

A program runs much more slowly in the debugger than it does in its normal mode, and a program that's been built with internal debugging information may also take up more disk space and use more memory than a "release" version. In some languages, a program built for debugging may also be more vulnerable to attack by a malicious program such as a "worm."

For these reasons, integrated development environments usually provide convenient facilities for defining named groups of option settings. It's common, for example, for an environment to create any new project with provisions for defining debug and release option sets.

With some languages, such as C or C++, developers on the ragged edge of intricate programming have to allow for another effect: the debug version of a program won't put things into the computer's memory at exactly the same locations as the release version, because debugging information is embedded among the normal instructions and data that make up the program.

 When a program exhibits errors in normal operation, but those errors disappear under the debugger, life gets hard. But this annoying behavior is almost impossible to create with Java, since Java has no facilities for direct manipulation of specific memory addresses. Java achieves the same purposes with higher-level solutions, as we'll see when we look at Java's arrays and other classes.

What to Buy?

As this book is being written, new Java products and new versions of the first-wave products are appearing every few weeks.

Symantec's Café is really two different products, one for Windows 95 and one for the Macintosh (Figures 2.15 and 2.16). They have similar capabilities but differ in the details of their operation. Both have been early to offer significant features, such as graphical views of the relationships between different libraries of Java code.

These libraries, called packages, are described in general in Chapter 10; the six standard packages that give Java much of its personality are each covered separately in Chapters 11 through 16. You can also create or share more specialized packages to accelerate the writing of new programs by reusing previous work.

If you want to support users of both Windows and Macintosh, Café is an excellent choice.

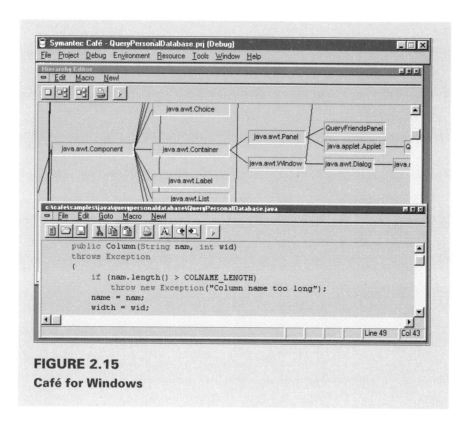

FIGURE 2.15
Café for Windows

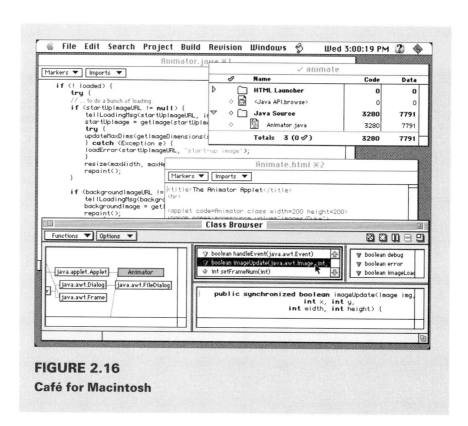

FIGURE 2.16
Café for Macintosh

Metrowerks is a respected toolmaker for Macintosh software developers, and their Discover Programming With Java is an attractively priced package with thorough tutorial materials. This product combines a Java compiler with Metrowerks's language-independent integrated environment, CodeWarrior (Figure 2.17).

Metrowerks will also be offering tools aimed at the Java Operating System, JavaOS, that Sun Microsystems plans to promote for Java applications such as intelligent appliances, and Metrowerks plans to become a Windows toolmaker at about the time that this book will appear in print. For developers with goals that span many different platforms, Metrowerks is surely worth a look.

Microsoft's Visual J++ is in some ways a more advanced product than the ones described above, in particular thanks to its low-level facilities for exploring Java's bytecodes: a capability that's useful to both the professional developer and the serious student.

The Visual J++ environment can be a little overwhelming, compared to those of Café and CodeWarrior, but features that aren't needed can be hidden from view.

Borland International has been giving demonstrations of a Java tool with the code name of Latte, aimed at corporate developers who want to use Java to give Web pages flexible access to corporate databases. Powersoft, makers of the client/server tool PowerBuilder, also plans to add Java capabilities to its Windows C++ tool called Optima++. Like Visual J++, both of these products will only be available for Windows.

At the opposite extreme of openness is Java WorkShop from Sun Microsystems, which is written in Java and therefore works wherever Java works. This product was released just weeks before this book was completed, limiting our ability to comment on its success. During early previews, however, Java WorkShop was praised for the superb integration of its tools, embedded in the same

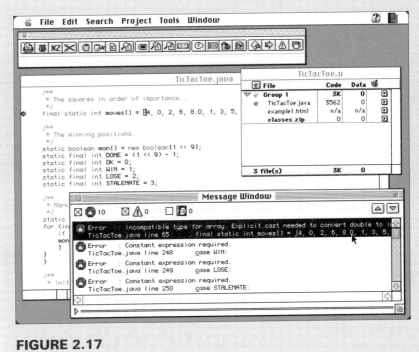

FIGURE 2.17
Metrowerks CodeWarrior for Java

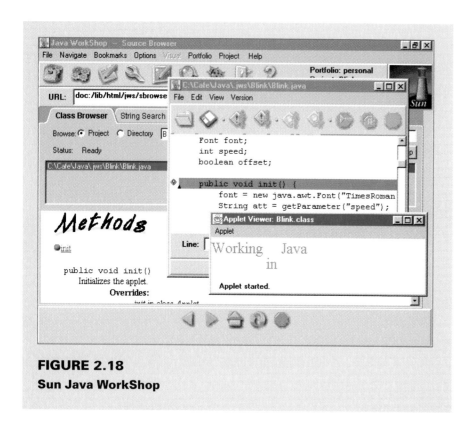

FIGURE 2.18
Sun Java WorkShop

kind of Web-browser environment that will host most Java applications when they're delivered to users (Figure 2.18).

Java WorkShop also has exceptional features for enabling teams of programmers to publish and share work with each other. It requires a fast computer with plenty of memory to give satisfactory performance. But for the person who's using Java with no experience in programming, and whose only need for Java is due to ambitions for creating rich Web content, Java WorkShop may be the perfect Java environment

Summary

In this chapter, we explained

▶ How the editor, compiler, and interpreter combine to create a Java development system.

▶ How separate tools use the computer's file system to pass work from one to another under your control.

▶ How integrated development environments coordinate work flow, testing, and error correction during program development

Anatomy of a
Program

Your First Java
Program

Making Your
Programs "Listen"

Writing Your Programs
to Be Readable

Chapter 3
Your First Java Program: Hello!

In this chapter, you'll learn what elements are present in the simplest Java program, and what role these elements will play in more complex projects. We'll also examine how a basic Java program interacts with the computer and the user.

You're sitting at your computer. It's been equipped, as discussed in the previous chapter, with

▶ An editor program that lets you create files `.java` of Java source code.

▶ A compiler program that turns human-readable source code into `.class` files of computer-readable bytecodes.

▶ A Java interpreter program that acts on those bytecodes to produce the desired behavior.

Let's start using the Java language to tell that computer what to do.

When we start a conversation with a person, we begin by getting that person's attention. When that person says "Hello," we know that we're connected and ready to exchange information and ideas.

That's how we start to converse with a computer as well: by writing a program that makes the machine say "Hello."

This may seem silly, but even the most seasoned programmer writes this kind of program when approaching an unfamiliar computer or programming language. This isn't kid stuff: it's the foundation of using any combination of language, software, and hardware to do anything that we can describe with specific instructions.

In later chapters, we'll build on this foundation to explore graphics, user interaction, and other complex tasks. Right now, we'll stick to the simplest version of "Hello," which looks like the following code.

```
class SayHello
   { public static void main(String args[])
      { System.out.println("Hello");
      }
   }
```

For a program that does so little, you may wonder why it needs to say so much. Every word and symbol in this short text has a vital meaning, however, as we'll soon see.

You'll note that we've printed some of the words above in blue, and "Hello" in red. We're doing this for the same reason that it's done by a source code editor with Java syntax awareness: it helps us see our program as an interaction between the facilities of the Java language (in blue), the literal data that our program will contain (in red), and the other things whose names we devise to make our intentions clear.

Specifically, we will use blue to denote a *reserved word* in the Java language. When something is a reserved word, it cannot be used as an *identifier*—that is, as a made-up name for some piece of data or behavior. If you're writing a program that manipulates public key and private key values in a data encryption program, for example, you can't use the names *public* or *private*, despite the intuitive appeal. They are both reserved.

Java's reserved words, with a summary of their purpose, appear in Appendix B.

Do note that some of Java's reserved words don't have any function: they're just reserved to make sure that you won't use them, since they might prove seriously misleading or because they might be annexed by future refinements to the language.

For example, the reserved word *goto* (pronounced "go to") looks a lot like an instruction to transfer control from one place in your program to some other arbitrary point. Java, like many modern languages, specifically excludes this feature, because its misuse makes programs hard to read: the language makes *goto* a reserved word so that the very idea becomes unmentionable.

Note also the oddly decorative variety of paired punctuation marks, including (), [], and {}. This isn't like algebra, where we use different marks so that nested groups can be distinguished. In fact, you'll notice that we have two levels of {}, one nested within the other.

These marks have different functions, with () indicating that the things between are used as input to a piece of the program; [] indicates that we're looking up a value in a collection of values, called an array; {} indicates that a group of statements in our program should be considered as a single idea, so to speak, when the program is running. All of these notions will be explored more rigorously later on.

Why is there so much packaging around this little gift? In BASIC, our entire program would just be

```
print "Hello"
```

So there had better be good reasons for all that other stuff. And there are, as we'll soon see.

It's Alive!

Let's put your Java tools to work. Using your stand-alone source code editor, or the editor that's built into your integrated environment, create a new file called *SayHello.java*.

If you're using an integrated environment, there may be an automated process for creating a project workspace or a new application. In that case, follow whatever directions came with your development system for creating a new, text-mode, stand-alone, console application.

Once you're looking at a blank area on the screen that's ready to accept your keyboard input, type in the program exactly as it appears above. Every punctuation mark is required, and Java is sensitive to the difference between capital and lowercase letters. Enter the program just as it's shown.

Depending on your tools, the next step is either to save the file and run the separate compiler with a command like `javac SayHello.java`, or to build the project using the linked tools of your environment. Do that.

Run the program. If using separate tools, you'll give a command like `java SayHello`. You'll probably get some copyright notices and other flotsam before you get your Hello. But there it is, right there on the screen, and it's there because you told your program to put it there.

Feel free to play around with your program. (Doesn't that sound great, "your program"? Enjoy the sound of that phrase.) Break a few rules. Change some punctuation. Spell something wrong. Get a feeling for the kinds of error messages that result, and for the process of connecting the error message back to the place where you made your "mistake." It's much more fun to learn this stuff when you're making mistakes on purpose, than to try to deduce the meanings of error messages when you don't know what you did wrong.

When you're ready, come back to this point and we'll figure out why all that bubble wrap is surrounding our 'println("Hello");'.

Anatomy of a Program

If your editor program has Java syntax awareness, you'll notice that different words in the program above appear in different colors on your computer's display. These color codes lead us toward understanding the reasons why our Java program has so much more verbiage than a comparable program in BASIC. Let's go through our Java program, a piece at a time.

class

What is a class? Think of the formal names that are given to different kinds of living things. From the most general to the most specific, we can identify any life form by its kingdom, phylum, class, order, family, genus, and species.

We're using *class* in just this sense of the word: a Java class defines a set of characteristics. From one class, we can derive more specialized classes, sharing those characteristics and adding other attributes.

In the real world, members of the class *mammalia* have characteristics that every schoolchild can recite. Mammals have hair, have warm blood, and produce milk for their babies. The order *carnivora* has additional characteristics, like sharp teeth. The family *felidae* has whiskers and tails. The genus *panthera* is big cats that roar; the species *leo* is, well, lions.

Java classes are like that. There are general classes and subclasses, and there are instances of those classes—just as there are many individual lions.

Those real-world lions have different weights and ages: in Java, we call such things *instance variables*, since every instance of the class has its own values for these attributes.

Since Java classes can form as many levels as we like, we won't give each level its own name: there's no such thing as a Java species. We'll just call everything a class: a vitally important word, and note that it appears on your screen (if your editor has Java syntax awareness) in a distinctive color.

That's because `class` is a reserved word in the Java language. If you'd rather call each level a family instead of a class, that's simply not an option. Java insists on `class`.

SayHello

The name of our class, `SayHello`, is colored differently: depending on your editor, it may have a special color as an identifier, or it may just have the default color that's given to anything that isn't special to Java.

That's because this is an arbitrary name that you can make up yourself. Our code samples leave identifiers black, as noted above.

Notice that we used an initial capital letter for the name of our class: this is a common practice. Notice also that we used another capital letter in the middle of the name, where we're starting what would normally be a new word: this enhances readability, given that we can't use a space without confusing the compiler. This use of embedded capitals is also common practice.

Our class `SayHello` is about as simple as a class can get. Its one behavior is described by something called a method, which begins in this case with a jaw-breaking phrase, `public static void main()`.

public static void main(...)

Ignore, for now, the stuff inside the parentheses. We'll get to that in a moment.

Let's take apart the rest of this phrase, going from right to left, since the words on the left all modify our declaration of a method named `main()`.

main()

Normally, we can give a method almost any name we like, and we'll usually choose something that describes the reason for using it. But the name, *main*, is special.

It means what it says. When we invoke this class (a Javaesque way of saying "run this program"), this method will be the only thing on its little mind. It will execute this method before it does anything else.

void

This means that our `main()` method won't give anything back to any other program that might have brought `SayHello` to life. `SayHello` will arise, put its output on the screen, and die.

Only the user who's watching the screen will see any evidence of its short (but productive) existence.

static

Usually, things in Java get done by instances of classes. In this case, however, the only thing we want our class to do can be done without creating any instances. The class definition is simply there: a piece of behavior, ready to perform when needed, hence the description `static`.

public

This means what it says, that we aren't trying to hide this piece of program from any other programs.

Later on, we'll see that a complicated program might want to conceal the details of exactly how something gets done, forcing other programs to ask for that operation by an indirect and tightly controlled process. By hiding those internal details, the person in charge of a program remains free to make internal changes, without breaking other programs that were tightly coupled to the original approach.

String args[]

String is a class that's defined as part of the Java language system. It lets us do operations on *string variables*, which is a programmer's way of talking about pieces of information that "string together" a group of simpler pieces of information.

Specifically, strings are usually sequences of letters that we're assembling because people want to enter information from keyboards or read output on the screen as words.

This phrase, String args[], means that SayHello will come to life with a little bundle of data inside it. That bundle is named *args*, short for *arguments*, and it's what programmers call an array: a container, so to speak, made up of numbered compartments.

What will go inside these compartments? Anything that you type as part of the command that starts the program. Do note, however, that those values will be stored merely as strings of characters, with no meaning as numbers or anything else.

No such meaning will be assigned until you tell Java to analyze and interpret those sequences of letters, numerals, and punctuation marks.

How many compartments will there be? As many as the Java interpreter needs to hold the number of things that you type.

Let's experiment with this. Make the following change to your SayHello class, inserting the two lines that refer to args[0] and args[1]:

```
class SayHello
{ public static void main(String args[])
{ System.out.println("Hello");
  System.out.println(args[0]);
  System.out.println(args[1]);
  }
}
```

Recompile. Run your program, this time using a command like

```
java SayHello and another thing
```

If you're using an integrated environment, you might need to enter *and another thing* in a dialog box that invites you to provide "parameters" or "arguments" for your program.

If you entered this as shown, you should have gotten the output

```
Hello
and
another
```

What happened to *thing*? We didn't ask to see it, so the program didn't display it. Now try running the program with only one argument:

```
java SayHello arguably
```

Your output will look something like,

```
Hello
arguably
java.lang.ArrayIndexOutOfBoundsException
```

What happened? We asked to see the contents of two compartments, numbered 0 and 1, but the Java interpreter only found one argument when it ran the program. Therefore, it only created one compartment: compartment number 0. (This is a good time to notice that computer people start counting at 0, not 1. It happens a lot. You'll get used to it.)

When we asked to see the contents of a compartment that didn't exist, Java didn't just show us whatever was in the computer's memory at the place where that compartment would have been—though this is exactly what would happen if we were doing this in the C language.

When we tried to do this in Java, we got the computer equivalent of the warning, "There's no there there." Java is intrinsically safe, and this is a good example of its careful design.

System.out.println()

By now, you've figured out that this expression displays whatever's inside the parentheses as a line of output to the Java console (which is usually a window on our screen). But why does it say such a simple thing in such a laborious way?

---

println()

The `println()` part is easy: it's a contraction of *print line*, and it means that Java will automatically start a new output line after putting out the thing we asked to see. If you want to build a long line of output from several smaller items of information, we can do that very easily.

Let's try that now. Let's further modify our `SayHello` class to tell us more about the arguments that it's printing.

```
class SayHello
    { public static void main(String args[])
        { System.out.println("Hello");
          for (int whichArg = 0;
                  whichArg < args.length;
                  whichArg++
               )
              { System.out.println(whichArg
                          + ": "
                          + args[whichArg]); }
        }
    }
```

This extended version of `SayHello` does three new things. First, it looks at an attribute of our array, `args`, by asking the array for the value of an instance variable (a piece of descriptive data) called `length`. This tells our program how many compartments the array contains. (We'll talk about instance variables when we discuss object-oriented programming in Chapters 8 through 10.)

Then the program goes from one compartment to another, using a Java instruction called a `for` statement, whose details we'll explore in Chapter 7.

Lastly, our program uses the symbol "+" (which you might think is only for numbers) to stick several strings together into a single longer string. That string then becomes the argument to `System.out.println()`.

Will Java use + in this way with numbers, or will it add them as you might expect? We'll find that the answer is "that depends" when we look at data types and operations in Chapters 4 through 6.

Recompile the program. Run it with any number of parameters that you wish. For example,

```
java SayHello I could do this all day
```

will produce the output,

```
Hello
0: I
1: could
2: do
3: this
4: all
5: day
```

Experiment. Try inputs like,

```
java SayHello "And how many arguments is this?"
```

What did you think the output would be from this command (*with* the quotation marks)? Were you right?

Well, now we understand `println()`. It seems like a simple name for a useful function, so you may wonder why it's been cluttered up with that `System.out` that's stuck in front.

This prefix is there to tell our program where it can learn the meaning of `println()` (which is *not* a reserved word), and what it is that's actually receiving and carrying out that instruction.

out

As it's used here, the symbol "out" is the name of something called a stream. You could think of a stream as a pipeline that carries data from one place in your Java system to some other place.

We didn't set up this stream: we got it from another class, `System`, that Java thoughtfully provides to take care of common chores like this.

So `System.out.println()` means "apply the method called `println()` to the stream called `out` that's owned by the `System` class." By now, you're getting used to reading from right to left—aren't you?

"Hello"

This is the only symbol in our program that we haven't explained. In programming, we call something like this a literal.

When it encounters a literal, the Java compiler isn't expected to understand it, or interpret it, or do anything but treat it as a chunk of information: something that needs to be parked in memory until we tell the program to use it for something.

And This Was a Simple Program!

Kind of impressive, isn't it? To realize how many things you were doing, just as part of making your computer hold up its end of a very brief conversation?

It's kind of a good news-bad news joke: the bad news is, even this little program demanded that we assemble a four-piece jigsaw puzzle:

▶ **Name** We had to tell the computer, "Here is a program; this is its name." We did this with the statement, `class SayHello`.

▶ **Basis** We had to use the tools of our programming language to say, "This is what you already know (or may assume to be true); this is what I want you to do."

   Our program included `public static void() main` and `"Hello"` as items in this category: they defined facts to be carried in the program itself, and contracts that our program should make with the rest of the system. `Public` is a contract to respond to requests by other programs; `void` is a contract that says, in effect, "but don't expect a receipt."

▶ **Input/Output** We had to tell our program, "This is how to find out the other things you need to know; this is where I want the results to go." We used `args[]` to capture input at the time that the program ran, and `println()` to send out results.

▶ **Do It!** We had to tell the computer, "Here is my program. Run it." Depending on your setup, you did this with either a menu command or a click of the mouse in your integrated environment, or with an entry on the command line of a text-mode console window.

The Good News

But our joke has a good news piece as well. That good news is that any other program we write, no matter how complex the task, is just an elaboration on these four basic ideas.

If you can write a program that says "Hello"—and you can!—you can write a program to do any other task that you can describe as a series of specific instructions.

People Read Programs, Too

In our program that says Hello, we used a lot of punctuation marks like [], (), and {}, as well as an occasional semicolon. These are called *delimiters*.

Java really doesn't care about things like line breaks, margins, indentations, and the like as long as the delimiters are there. For example, SayHello could just as well be written,

```
class SayHello{public
static void main(String
args[]){System.out.println(
  "Hello");}}
```

This is, of course, much harder for the human reader to understand. That brings us to a critical point in programming: that programs will be read by people, as well as by machines.

Every person who writes programs for any length of time will develop personal preferences for the use of white space and line breaks. SayHello could have been written,

```
class SayHello {
    public static void main(String args[]) {
        System.out.println("Hello");
        }
    }
```

This style puts the opening { mark at the end of the line that names the piece of the program to be enclosed; it indents the lines of that piece of program by three spaces from the column where that name begins; and it gives the closing } that same indentation. You'll like this style if you often make changes near the beginning of a {}-enclosed block of code, since the opening { mark never gets in the way.

Another style would be,

```
class SayHello
  {
  public static void main(String args[])
    {
    System.out.println("Hello");
    }
  }
```

This style uses more lines, but some people prefer the way that it puts the enclosing {} marks out in the open: this makes the entire line serve as a delimiter, making it easy to scan down the page and get a sense of the modular organization of the program. You might like this style if you often have to read other people's programs.

If you have a section of your program that you want to squeeze into the smallest number of lines, you might go to the opposite extreme with a style like,

```
class SayHello
    { public static void main(String args[])
        { System.out.println("Hello");}}
```

This style relies entirely on the different levels of indentation to show the structure of the program. If you rarely have to read other people's programs, the compactness of this style can be an advantage.

For the individual programmer, it's a matter of personal preference: all of these programs do the same thing. For the corporate programmer, there's often a "house style" that's promoted—and sometimes even enforced—to make it easy for code to be reviewed with minimal confusion. In many computing environments, you'll find "pretty printer" utility programs or editor commands that format code automatically into any desired style.

The key point is this: only the human reader cares. Indentation and extra white space have no role in the behavior of Java programs.

A Final Comment

No pretty-print utility can help the readability of your code as much as you can, by inserting comments that explain what you were thinking when you wrote it and what you meant for the program to do.

There are three ways to put comments into Java code, giving you a chance to explain your intentions—not only to another programmer who might have to work with your program in the future, but also to yourself when you come back to that program days or weeks after you first wrote it.

The most common comment marking is the double slash, //. This says, "the rest of this line is a comment."

The next most common way to mark comments is to begin the comment with the symbol /* and end it with the symbol */. This lets you embed a comment in the middle of a line: for example,

```
index /* this will never be less than zero */ = startPosition;
```

Note that we've introduced our fourth and final source-code color, green, to indicate a comment.

Another use for /* */ markings is to "comment out" a large section of code, for example, to remove a time-consuming section of a program when you're trying to test other sections—but this is a bad idea.

Why? Because these comments can't be nested. If you had a piece of code such as,

```
i = 1;
j = 4; /* this never matters */
k = 7;
```

you might try to disable the entire section by marking it,

```
/*  i = 1;
    j = 4; /* this never matters */
    k = 7;
*/
```

But the first */, at the end of the second line, ends the comment as far as the Java compiler is concerned. (Mistakes like these used to be much more common before syntax-aware editors were widely used. Today, commented text will usually appear in a distinctive color, and you'll get an immediate visual cue if your markings don't mean what you intended.)

Are you allowed to do this?

```
/*  i = 1;
    j = 4; // this never matters
    k = 7;
*/
```

Yes. If your original, "never matters" comment had been marked using the // notation, the enclosing /* */ that you added later would have done what you expected.

Do you have better things to do than keep track of this kind of cleverness? Probably. So don't get involved in this kind of self-defeating tap dance through the rules.

Today's high-powered programming editors make it easy to put a // at the beginning of every line in an entire section of your program, and to remove it later when you want that code re-enabled: a better approach, since it leaves no possible doubt as to which lines of code are relevant.

There's one more way to mark comments in Java programs. A comment that begins with the special symbol group, /**, and ends with */, will automatically be extracted and incorporated into instructions for your program's operation if you use one of the utility programs that's been created for this purpose. Even if you never use one of these utility programs, this marking calls the reader's attention to comments with a high-level explanatory purpose, so use this wherever it's appropriate.

Don't Say the Same Thing Twice

When you write your comments, don't say in English what you just said in Java. Don't write code like,

```
startValue = 3; // set the variable startValue to 3
```

That's an extreme example, but such things do appear in too many programmers' work. Better would be something like,

```
startValue = 3; // already handled 0, 1, and 2
```

Write the Java Last

Comments aren't just decorations or explanations that you add after the fact, when you're asking yourself, "I wonder if anyone will understand this?"

They can be even more valuable if you write them first, before you write any Java at all. When you're thinking about how you want to tackle a task, there's nothing to stop you from writing a description of your approach in the form of Java comments, then going back and filling in that outline with the statements that the Java compiler will actually use.

With useful comments, our Hello program might look like,

```
class SayHello        // Remember, names are case-sensitive
    { public static void main(String args[]) // No input expected
        { System.out.println(
                        "Hello" // Meant for text-mode output
                    );
        }
    }
```

Can You Stop What You Start?

Before you run a program that you've never tested before, it's really a good idea to find out how to stop a program that's flown away to Neverland. Otherwise, you'll wind up doing something drastic like rebooting your computer, quite possibly losing some work in progress and definitely wasting a lot of time.

For example, if you wrote a program that was supposed to stop when some value got to 10, but you forgot to put in the command that added "1" to your counter, that program might run forever if you didn't know how to interrupt it. Some operating systems let you do this with the key combination Ctrl-Break, some use Ctrl-C, some use Command-period.

Go for It!

With that warning duly issued, we turn you loose to experiment with `SayHello`. As trivial as it is, it gives you the chance to see what happens when things are working normally, and even to try making little changes here and there and seeing how the system responds.

Milestones

Specific milestones that you should aim to reach, before you go on, are

▶ If you're using an integrated environment, investigate its facilities for creating a new project. `SayHello` will be a stand-alone application, not an applet, and it will be a console application, not a graphical one. Find out how to get your environment to set up the skeleton of such a project.

▶ If you're using separate editor and compiler programs, find out how to create a new file and how to make your editor treat it as a Java file (if your editor has Java syntax awareness). Find out how to make your Java compiler usable from the directory where you want to keep your source code files.

▶ Type in the program. Notice, if your editor has syntax coloring, the different colors that are used for different words and symbols. Look at the options settings for your editor and find out what those colors mean. If you don't like them, change them to suit your preferences.

▶ Compile the program. If you get error messages, read them and figure out what caused them. If you don't get error messages, try changing the program to introduce deliberate "mistakes" and see if the resulting messages are useful. This will help you figure out the meaning of error messages later on, when your mistakes are spontaneous instead of contrived.

▶ Run the program.

Congratulations. You're a Java programmer.

Summary

In this chapter, we showed

▶ That the simplest Java program still reflects Java's object-oriented design.

▶ That Java programs can embed data directly or obtain it from the user when the program runs.

▶ That you can write your programs to be understood more easily by other programmers.

Chapter 4
Just the Facts, Ma'am:
More about Data

In this chapter, you'll learn how facts get represented in a computer's hardware; we'll also demystify why fast computers sometimes do dumb things.

In Chapter 3, we wrote a program that contained one piece of *literal* data (the word *Hello*). Later in that chapter, we extended the program to take user input when it started, and to display that input as a list of numbered items. This began to move us in the direction of creating Java programs that add interactive content to your presence on the World Wide Web.

With this first taste of programming power, it's tempting to rush right off and build an animation or a game to enliven your Web page. But this is like trying to learn guitar by starting with a Vivaldi concerto. We'll understand the instrument much better if we start with notes and chords, and master these basic elements before we put them together in complex ways.

So it is with Java. We're going to use the next several chapters to master the notes of data, the chords of expressions, the tempos and dynamics of statements, and the compositional forms of classes and objects before we try to write a concerto of our own.

Can You Count on Your Computer?

In our Chapter 3 examples, both "Hello" and the additional user inputs were a single kind of data: a kind that's called a *character string*, or just a *string*, for short. We deliberately introduced Java by writing a program that didn't do math.

We did this because computers have a reputation for being just like calculators, only bigger and more automatic. Early computers, even the first mechanical designs that used spinning wheels rather than electrons, were conceived for math-intensive tasks like aiming the guns of battleships.

Until recently, only a handful of experts knew about other reasons for writing programs: Reasons like analyzing a piece of writing, for example, to see if it could be identified as the work of a particular author based on distinctive patterns in the choice and use of words.

But with the advent of low-cost microchips, today's computers spend far more time dealing with patterns than with simple numbers. Computers focus cameras, recognize spoken words, and give online updates on the whereabouts of shipments in transit. Arithmetic, though still important, is not the central purpose of most software sold today. Spreadsheets are useful, but so are spelling checkers and online library catalogs.

The "number cruncher" stereotype persists, in part, because computer science is treated by many schools as a branch of mathematics. Many people assume that this means numbers are the most important kind of data.

Let's kill that stereotype right now. Computers don't manipulate numbers: They manipulate symbols, which may represent numbers or may represent anything else.

A number is an idea, one that our brains can manipulate to understand concepts like, "5 times 1/5 equals 1." We know that this is true, on a fundamental level: No person would ever suggest that 5 times 1/5 was really 0.99609375. But the most common ways of representing numbers as symbols, within the limits of practical computer hardware, can easily lead to such errors.

It is possible to write computer programs that do error-free conceptual mathematics, based on fundamental principles like, "For any x, $x * 1/x = 1$." Any process that we can describe in detail to another person, we can describe to a computer as well. Working with symbols, instead of numbers, does not have to mean accepting peculiar errors as the price of a computer's speed.

It's much more efficient, though, and therefore much more common, to accept the limits that come with doing ordinary arithmetic on primitive symbols that represent specific numbers. This uses much less memory, and much less time, than it takes to manipulate general ideas like, "for any x."

We operate on those symbols using rules that yield correct results, within a limited range of values and with known margins of error.

We also manipulate symbols that aren't meant to represent numbers at all, though we operate on those symbols using rules of logic that resemble those of arithmetic.

The point to remember is that programs, in general, are not just recipes for lengthy calculations. Programs, in general, are sets of rules for creating groups of symbols, for comparing those symbols to each other, for doing operations on those symbols, and for generating symbols that communicate something useful to a human user or a computer-controlled machine.

Most of the time, convenient features and behaviors of a language like Java will let us think about our ideas and ignore the low-level details behind the symbolic facade. But the programmer who understands the hidden limits will have a head start on dealing with those rare occasions when those limits do become a problem. Failure to understand those limits is a major reason why carelessly written programs produce inaccurate results.

My Computer Floweth Over

If computers really worked with numbers, not symbols, then programs would always do obvious arithmetic correctly. For example, let's write a program that has the same overall structure as our SayHello example from Chapter 3, but make it do some arithmetic instead of just printing out a word.

```
class DoMath
 { public static void main(String args[])
    // any arguments provided will be ignored
   { byte aNumber = 100;
     anotherNumber = 100;
     byte addThem = (byte)(aNumber + anotherNumber);
     System.out.println(addThem);
   }
 }
```

Create this source code file, compile it (with a command like javac DoMath.java), and run it (with a command like java DoMath).

It didn't work, did it? You got a ridiculous result. Try the same thing with 10 and 10, though, or even 50 and 70, and this program does just what you'd expect.

When we asked Java to stuff the value 200 into a byte—a representation that held values like 20 or 120 with ease—we got exactly what we asked for. But what we got was the result of manipulating bytes (that is, symbols) rather than the result of doing real math on real numbers.

Don't Byte Off More Than You Can Chew

Why is Java being so stupid? Any bright six-year old can tell you that 100 plus 100 equals 200, but Java doesn't know enough to treat this problem as 1 plus 1 with a pair of zeros on the end.

When we tell Java, for example, that `aNumber = 100`, what are we really doing? To begin with, notice that we didn't just make up a name and give it a numeric value. Programming isn't as easy as your first algebra class, where you could just say, "Let X be the number we start with: X equals 100."

We first told Java that `aNumber` was the name of a byte-type piece of data. This told Java to use a particular set of rules for operating on that symbol.

What's a byte? It's the somewhat humorous nickname for a group of eight bits. *Bit*, in turn, is a contraction of *binary digit*, where *bi* is used in the same sense as *bi*plane or *bi*cycle: A decimal digit can take on values zero through nine, but a binary digit can only take on values zero or one.

We could just as well say "X or O," or "A or Z": there's nothing magic about using zero and one. This convention makes it easier, however, to understand the rules for manipulating binary symbols, since some of those rules resemble those of ordinary arithmetic.

Why limit ourselves to a binary system? Why not just make computers work with values from zero to nine, so that math on computers would look more like the base-10 math that most modern civilizations normally use?

It comes down to hardware and the cost of representing information. And this is not a computer-age discovery: the basic ideas are almost fifty years old.

The Power(s) of Two

In 1948, Norbert Wiener first looked at the ways that complex systems (like people) do complex tasks (like picking up a pencil).

> *If you think that picking up a pencil is easy, take a break from reading this book and do it, then sit down and write an exact, step-by-step description that you could use to program a robot to perform this "simple" task with equal reliability. Come back when you're convinced that this is hard. You'll be back soon.*

Wiener invented the much-hyped word, *cybernetics*, based on a Greek word meaning *steersman*, to represent the idea that systems can tackle complex tasks by applying a single powerful technique: That is, by comparing where they are to where they want to be.

Cybernetic systems use the difference between their current state and some desired state to create an error signal, also called feedback. Other parts of the system use that feedback signal as an instruction to do something that will make that error get smaller.

When the difference gets smaller than some target value, the system is where it originally wanted to be. The system "steers" through a series of corrective maneuvers, hence the origin of *cybernetics* and related words like *cyberspace*.

To build machines with similar, self-guiding behavior, Wiener needed to figure out the most reliable and least expensive way to represent information using electronic hardware. In two pages and six equations, he showed that the cheapest way to do this is with simple devices that only have two possible states.

You could think of each device as being an electrical switch that can be either on or off: It's obvious that such a switch is cheaper than a more complex device, like a light dimmer, that can take on many values in between these two extremes.

With these two-valued devices, we can express some important ideas. To begin with, we can "write" a simple "program" by connecting a battery, a light, and an on-off switch in series with each other. Only when the switch is closed will the light be connected to power, and glow.

This is a program expressed in hardware. The switch is our input device, the light bulb is our output device. The program is,

```
if (theSwitch==closed) {bulb=on;}
```

That double equal sign, ==, is not a typographical error. It's a Java safety feature.

When you see ==, you know that Java is comparing two values but is not changing either one. When you see =, you know that Java is changing the value that goes with the name on the left to match the value on the right. We'll discuss this more in Chapter 5.

The (), {}, and semicolon (;) characters also have important meanings, as we'll discuss in later chapters. We're using them now to get ourselves used to the appearance of correctly written code.

Now, let's get back to our light switch. At its lowest level, even the most complex computer has some elements that are just about this simple, known as *hardwired logic*. It's the building block of more complex programs as well.

For example, suppose we had two switches, wired end-to-end with each other and in series with the battery and the bulb. Both switches have to be closed before the light will get any power. This is the program,

```
if (switch1==closed && switch2==closed) {bulb=on;}
```

where **&&** is an operator (as we'll discuss in Chapter 5) that means *and*.

What about *or*? Suppose that instead of being wired end-to-end, our switches were wired side-by-side so that turning on either switch would connect the bulb. This would be the program,

```
if (switch1==closed || switch2==closed) {bulb=on;}
```

where || is an operator that means *or*.

Finally, suppose that our circuit is wired like a pair of switches at opposite ends of a corridor. If the light is off, and either switch is flipped, the light will go on. If we then flip the other switch, the light will go back off. The light goes on when the two switches are in different states, and goes off when they're in the same state—no matter what that common state may be.

This arrangement is equivalent to the program,

```
if ((switch1==closed && switch2==open)
         ||
    (switch1==open   && switch2==closed))
      {bulb=on;}
```

This kind of thing happens quite often in practical computer programs. It's used, for example, in a simple animation technique that lets us move an object across a background, without redrawing the entire background for every new position. We put the moving object where we want it, leave it there long enough to be seen by the viewer's eye, then make the object go away and restore its background (like flipping the switch at the other end of the hall) and repeat the process at the moving object's next position.

This operation is called an *exclusive or*. It's exclusive in the sense that the or operation will only accept one true value, not one or more such values as in the ordinary *inclusive or* that we saw before.

With this new phrase in our vocabulary, our program is written more easily as:

```
if (switch1==closed ^ switch2==closed)
   {bulb=on;}
```

where ^ is the operator for *exclusive or,* sometimes written *xor*.

Now imagine this program, not as a circuit with switches, but as a set of math problems using binary arithmetic with ones and zeroes:

Both switches open	Ø + Ø	Switch 1 closed	1 + Ø	Switch 2 closed	Ø + 1	Both switches closed	1 + 1
	——		——		——		——
	Ø		1		1		10

We're seeing that two-valued hardware devices, like switches, can represent logical expressions, and that this kind of logic also looks like arithmetic using the base-2 instead of our more familiar base-10 system. Closing both switches is like saying, "1 + 1 = 0, carry a 1," though we haven't described the hardware for that "carry."

We could finish our description of this "two-bit adder" in hardware, but let's not: let's do this in Java instead.

Boola Boola

To do that, let's learn about the type of data that Java defines for simple, two-valued concepts (like a switch that's open or closed, or a light bulb that's on or off).

Do we have to make up some rule like "1 = true, 0 = false"? Arbitrary decisions like this can easily lead to confusion and errors, which Java seeks to avoid.

We don't want to do that, and fortunately we don't need to. For simple tasks, Java defines a simple data type with what may seem a peculiar name: a `boolean` data value, which can only have the values `true` and `false`.

We learned before that a two-valued symbol can be represented by a single binary digit, so why not just call this data type a bit? The name *Boolean* honors the work of George Boole, who developed a notation for operating on logical expressions of truth and falsity in the 1800s—long before Norbert Wiener showed that this was an ideal way of representing information in electronic circuits.

As part of its goal of program clarity, Java reserves the words `true` and `false` as `boolean` literals. Just as you can't say something silly like "1 = 2," Java won't let you use `true` as a name for something else.

In Java, true means `true` and `false` means false—unless of course, either word is enclosed in quotation marks and appear in character strings, as in the expression

```
String answerIfRight = "true";
```

which is perfectly all right. But be sure you understand that the character string "true" has no particular meaning in Java. The reserved word `true`, written without quotation marks and in lowercase letters, has an intrinsic meaning. The character string could just as well be "definitely" or "For Sure!" as far as Java is concerned.

Let's see if we can borrow these reserved words by giving them other meanings:

```
class BreakRules
 { public static void main(String args[])
   { byte true = 50;
```

```
        byte false = 70;
        byte addThem = (byte)(true + false);
        System.out.println(addThem);
        }
    }
```

These are pretty silly ways to use these words, but we can try this quickly by changing our DoMath example.

Java will not compile this. You can almost sense the indignation in the compiler's error messages.

If you really want to use these words, just use a different capitalization. Java doesn't care about True, fALSe, or any other variations. Only true (all lowercase) and false (ditto) are reserved.

But you should wonder if you're just outsmarting yourself, going to a lot of effort to create a program that's likely to confuse somebody—maybe even yourself.

The boolean data type is the tool that we want for writing our two-bit adder program in software, rather than trying to wire it up with switches. Here it is in Java.

You'll see some aspects of the language that we have not yet explained, such as one part of a program invoking another part by name and getting a result *returned* to the place where that named method was invoked: we'll examine these facilities in more detail in Chapter 7.

```
class TestTwoBits
 {public static void main(String args[])
   // Set up and runs the test cases
   {boolean open = false;  // define names for
   boolean closed = true; // states of "switches"

  System.out.println("");    // print a blank line
  System.out.println("Both switches open");
  System.out.println(twoBitAdd(open, open));
  // call another method and print what it returns
  System.out.println("");
  System.out.println("Close switch 1 only");
  System.out.println(twoBitAdd(closed, open));
  System.out.println("");
  System.out.println("Close switch 2 only");
  System.out.println(twoBitAdd(open, closed));
```

```
        System.out.println("");
        System.out.println("Both switches closed");
        System.out.println(twoBitAdd(closed, closed));
        System.out.println("");
    }

    public static String twoBitAdd(boolean switch1,
                                   boolean switch2)
    // this method breaks out the logical operations
    {boolean onesBulb = (switch1 ^ switch2);
     boolean twosBulb = (switch1 && switch2);

     return bulbDisplay(twosBulb)
        // calling yet another method
        + "   " // + appends Strings
        + bulbDisplay(onesBulb);
    }

    public static String bulbDisplay(boolean turnBulbOn)
    // the display of a "bulb"
    {if (turnBulbOn) return "XXX";
     else            return "---";
    }
}
```

As noted above, this example has a more complicated structure than those that we've done before. We're doing some things, like analyzing the switch states, more than once, and we don't want to write identical code for each of the four test cases or for each of the two "light bulbs" that have to be controlled in each test case.

We therefore take those repeated operations and put each of them into its own method. This is sometimes called "factoring out" operations.

The main() method sets up the four possible test cases. For each case, main() calls the twoBitAdd() method to do the logical operations that decide whether each of the light bulbs is on or off.

The twoBitAdd() method then calls the bulbDisplay() method whenever it needs to decide how we will represent a particular light bulb on our display.

Back to the Byte

Now that we've mastered the mechanics of single bits, as represented by `boolean` values, let's look at what we can do with bits in bunches. Let's compare binary (base 2) numbers to their more familiar representations in base 10 in Table 4.1.

You'll notice a pattern here. Every time that we hit a new power of 2 (2, 4, 8, 16, and so on), we need one more bit to represent the resulting value in binary. We can represent the values 0 and 1 (two values) with one bit, 0 through 3 (four values) with two bits, and 0 through 7 (eight values) with three bits.

The pattern continues: If we start counting at 0, we can represent 2^n different values in a binary number made up of n bits.

The binary notation for any sizable number is a long, hard-to-read string of ones and zeros. We can make life easier by writing values in what's called *hexadecimal*, or base 16, as shown in Table 4.2.

Hexadecimal notation lets us write values 0 through F (0 through 15 in the base-10 column of the table) with a single digit (where A, B, C, D, E, and F are now digits). When we get to 16 in the base-10 column of the table, we carry a 1 into the "16's" position of our hexadecimal number, and restart the 1's position of that hex representation at 0.

Just as 99 (base 10) equals 9 * 10 + 9 * 1, FF (base 16) equals 15 * 16 + 15 * 1. That adds up to 255 (base 10), or 1 less than 2 to the 8th power.

We know that in binary, 1 less than 2^n will be written as n 1s: 3 (one less than 2^2) was 11, 15 (one less than 2^4) was 1111. This means that 255 (one less than 2^8) will be written in binary as

We can compare this with the table above to see that it is the same thing as FF in hexadecimal.

This is where we've been heading since the first time we used the word byte. Here it is: An 8-bit group, able to hold 256 different values that can be written 00000000 through 11111111 in binary or 00 through FF in hexadecimal.

TABLE 4.1	THE BASE-10 AND BASE-2 SYSTEMS	
Base 10	**Base 2**	**Power of 2**
0	0	
1	1	2^0
2	10	2^1
3	11	
4	100	2^2
5	101	
6	110	
7	111	
8	1000	2^3
9	1001	
10	1010	
11	1011	
12	1100	
13	1101	
14	1110	
15	1111	
16	10000	2^4

What's Your Sign?

At this point, a little alarm should be going off in your mind. Wait a minute, you're thinking. We just established that a byte can hold 256 different values. But our `DoMath` class at the beginning of the chapter did something ridiculous when we asked a byte to hold the number 200. Why couldn't that size 200 value be properly represented in that size 256 space?

Some programming languages can define a byte-type piece of data that would hold this value. That's because these languages define *unsigned* numbers: Values that can't be less than zero, and therefore don't need any way to provide a minus sign.

TABLE 4.2 BASE-10, BASE-2, AND HEXADECIMAL SYSTEMS

Base 10	Base 2	Power of 2	Hex	Power of 16
0	0		0	
1	1	2^0	1	16^0
2	10	2^1	2	
3	11		3	
4	100	2^2	4	
5	101		5	
6	110		6	
7	111		7	
8	1000	2^3	8	
9	1001		9	
10	1010		A	
11	1011		B	
12	1100		C	
13	1101		D	
14	1110		E	
15	1111		F	
16	10000	2^4	10	16^1
17	10001		11	

Java doesn't do this. When the programmer has to keep track of the difference between signed and unsigned numbers, mistakes get made. Java seeks to prevent this. All of Java's number-type values are *signed* values, in which the first bit of the number's binary symbol tells you if the number is positive or negative.

A leading bit of 1 means a negative value, and that leading bit is sometimes called a sign bit. The format of a negative number is something called a *twos complement* of the positive value: This is produced by taking the positive value, changing each 1 to a 0 and vice versa, and then adding 1.

```
                    Base 2        Base 10
                    00001000         8
swap the symbols    11110111
add 1               11111000        -8
```

Does this make sense? Let's try adding the result to a larger positive value, using binary arithmetic, and see if we go past zero and back to the world of normal-looking binary numbers.

```
    11111000        -8
  + 00001010      + 10
  ----------      ----
  (1)00000010      +2 (discard carried bit at left)
```

At the left-hand end of our answer, we get a leading 1 after carrying all the way across, but this extra bit will be thrown away (which is why we show it in parentheses).

We now see how half of the possible values of a byte (all the values that start with a 1) will be used by the negative numbers. This means that Java's byte type will only be able to represent the 256 values (including 0) that range from -128 through +127. So 200 is too big.

Try making some changes to our DoMath class and confirming that this is how byte types behave.

Obviously, practical computer programs need some way to count to larger values. But before we look at the more ambitious numeric types, let's look at non-numeric uses of binary symbols.

On Beyond Numbers

Remember, we said that computers operate on symbols, and that numbers were just one of the many kinds of information that we can represent with those symbols. What else could we do, for example, with an 8-bit byte?

Well, we can give a separate code number to each of the digits 0 through 9, each of the uppercase letters *A* through *Z*, each of the lowercase letters *a* through *z*, and still have 194 codes left over. We can have codes for symbols like +, -, <, >, and everything else that we need for expressing common arithmetic operations. We can give codes to punctuation symbols like the period, the comma, the apostrophe, and all of the other symbols that we've needed so far to write our various Java programs.

This means that we can represent our program source code, or other text like an everyday document, in a file containing a stream of bytes.

Who decides what code numbers are going to be used for each of these symbols? There's more than one standard, but the standard most commonly used for many years has been the American Standard Code for Information Interchange.

That's abbreviated ASCII, pronounced "Askee," and the full set of values appears in Appendix B.

Some of those ASCII codes have rather quaint assignments. Code number 7, for example, is known as "bell," and was initially used to ring the bell on the mechanical typewriter-style terminals originally used with computers.

If you're using a DOS or OS/2 computer, you can see that this old convention is still around: Go to a command line display and type the word *ECHO*, followed by a space, followed by Ctrl-G (hold down the Ctrl key while typing the letter). You'll see ECHO ^G as your input. Hit the Enter key, and you'll hear a beep from your machine—unless it actually has a bell!

Know the (Uni)code

But ASCII, which only defines 7-bit codes (values 0 through 127), doesn't begin to provide the number of symbols that are needed to represent the written forms of the world's many languages. Even ISO-Latin-1, an 8-bit superset of ASCII, can't handle the Hiragana and Katakana alphabets in Japan, the Cyrillic alphabet in Russia, plus the Greek, Arabic, and many other scripts that are used in other countries.

We want our programs to use identifiers (the names of classes, variables, and other parts of the program) that have meaning to the programmer. We want our programs to have comments that the programming team will understand. So Java needs an internal character representation with world-class range.

What Java uses to meet this need is a standard called Unicode, which defines 16-bit codes for a huge variety of symbols.

Java's internal representation for Unicode symbols is the data type *char*, short for *character*—and usually pronounced, therefore, with a hard "k" like "karat" instead of a "ch" sound like "charming."

The char data type is a 16-bit (2-byte) chunk of data, which can hold 2^{16} different codes: that's 0000000000000000 through 1111111111111111 in binary, or 0000 through FFFF in hexadecimal, or 0 through 65,535 in decimal.

With so many different codes to choose from, Unicode gives us huge flexibility in writing programs that say what they mean to the programmer as well as to the user.

If your programming environment can handle it, you can use symbols like π or Σ to express common mathematical terms in their standard form in program identifiers and comments, as well as rendering programs and comments (and handling user input and output) in the scripts used by languages other than English.

Note also that you can use any Unicode character in your Java programs, even on a computer that doesn't provide them on the keyboard. This is done with an *escape sequence*, a code that tells a computer to assign a special meaning to a group of symbols.

To put a Unicode character into your Java program, use the sequence \u followed by the four-digit hexadecimal code for that character. You can put such a sequence anywhere that Java would normally expect an ordinary letter or digit.

For example, the lowercase ASCII letters *a* through *z* are represented by the Unicode values 61 through 7A (remember, this is hexadecimal, where the digits are 0 through 9 *and* A through F).

This means that

```
class SayHello
 { public static void main(String args[])
    { System.out.println("H\u0065l\u006Co");
     }
  }
```

will do exactly the same thing that this program did when "Hello" was our argument to println().

From Bytes to Longs: Consistency Counts

We've already learned a lot in this chapter. We've learned how to represent the simplest facts that programs can manipulate, involving matters of truth and falsity (for which we use boolean values). We know how to "count on our fingers" using

That figure of 65,535 Unicode values is unwieldy, and it gives us a good chance to introduce another piece of programmer-speak. It's easy to remember that 2^{10} is the base-10 value 1,024 ("two to the ten is ten twenty-four"). This is close enough to 1,000 that programmers call it a k, from the metric abbreviation for *kilo*—as in *kilometer*, one thousand meters. With this convention, 65,536 is referred to as 64k.

By analogy, 1 kilo times 1 kilo equals 1 Mega, from the metric abbreviation for a million. A megabyte is not a million bytes, but is 1,024 times 1,024 or 1,048,576 bytes.

This pattern continues with the giga- ($1,024^3$), tera- ($1,024^4$), and even peta- ($1,024^5$) prefixes that are starting to show up in discussions of 21st-century computers.

bytes. We know how to do our ABC's (not to mention our ä ß ç's) using char-type data, with Unicode enabling a cosmopolitan approach to naming and describing our work.

There's more. There are plenty of times when we'll want to count more than 127 things, so it's clear that we need more than 8-bit byte-size numbers. Java also defines the 16-bit short, the 32-bit int, and the 64-bit long.

Other languages, such as C and C++, also use names like *short*, *int*, and *long* for various data types, but Java offers a vital advantage. Java defines the behaviors of its named data types in terms of precisely specified formats, no matter what hardware is being used.

By contrast, C and C++ allow an int (for example) to be the "natural size" for an integer on a given type of processor, meaning that a program may behave one way on one type of computer but do something different on another type of machine. A programmer may need to use the C or C++ *sizeof* (size of) operator to find out what's happening under the hood, and adjust things based on the result. Java programs won't exhibit this variability, and don't have to be so cautious.

Do note, though, that we said Java specifies *behaviors*, not physical representations. If a certain type of processor works more efficiently with 32-bit chunks of data than with smaller units (as is the case for many modern chips), a Java implementation is free to represent bytes and shorts internally using such 32-bit "words." But it must carry out its computations *as if* it were working with 8- and 16-bit entities, respectively.

Experiment with our DoMath class, changing the types of aNumber, anotherNumber, and addThem to short, int, or long, and changing the values that you assign to aNumber and anotherNumber. Confirm that these data types behave as expected, in terms of the largest value that each will hold without complaint. Experiment with negative values as well.

Floats and Doubles: Precision Is the Point

Is there anything left to discuss? Well, yes: the entire universe of everything that's too big, or too small, to count.

That universe includes all of the numeric values that lie between -1 and 1, in the fractions—and the fractions of fractions—that represent things like the size of an electron.

It also includes the huge values that represent things like the number of different books that could be written by a million monkeys with a million typewriters over a period of a million years.

There are languages, such as Smalltalk, Lisp, and REXX, that can handle enormous numbers as strings of digits that can be as long as your computer's memory can hold. But this flexibility comes at the expense of speed.

Java takes a different approach, called *floating point* computation. You're used to fixed point numbers, like the numbers we write to represent dollars and cents: We write these numbers with two digits to the right of the decimal point, and round off smaller fractions to the nearest penny.

Floating point numbers are like the ones in your hand-held calculator. Take your calculator and multiply 1 million by 1 million. Your calculator probably displays the result in a form that means "1 times 10^{12}." This is also known as *scientific notation*.

Your calculator can probably enter numbers directly in this form with a key like "EE" or "EEX," for example, by entering "1 EEX 12."

Floating point numbers are flexible, but they're not exact. On your calculator, enter 1 times 10 to the 12th power, add 1, and subtract the initial value of 1 times 10 to the 12th.

You might expect the answer to be 1, but it probably comes back as 0. If this doesn't happen, try starting with 10 to a larger power, such as 15 or 20.

You'll reach a point where your calculator tells you that for a large enough X, $(X + 1) - X = 0$. This is obviously wrong, but it's the unavoidable result of finite precision—an artifact of using convenient but limited symbols to represent real numbers.

How accurate can Java's math be? The Java `float` data type is a 32-bit representation that provides a sign bit (as we've discussed before), an 8-bit exponent field (used to represent a power of 2), and a 23-bit significand field (used to represent the significant figures of the number). The Java `double` data type is a 64-bit word: a sign bit, 11 bits of exponent, and 52 bits of significand.

With more bits of exponent, a `double` can represent both larger and smaller numbers than a `float`; with more bits of significand, it can represent values that are spaced more closely together.

Specifically, a `float` can represent either positive or negative values from about 8.43 times 10 to the -37 through 3.37 times 10 to the 38, with an accuracy equivalent to about 7 decimal places. A `double` can represent positive or negative values from about 4.19 times 10 to the -307 through 1.67 times 10 to the 308, with an accuracy equivalent to about 16 decimal places.

Arrays

What we've discussed in this chapter so far are the Java simple types: the `boolean`, `byte`, `char`, `short`, `int`, `long`, `float`, **and** `double`.

We can use these data types to represent individual values, or we can define groups of values (all of the same data type) that are called arrays.

We already saw one array in Chapter 3, the `args[]` array that was automatically created to hold any additional input that the user gave when invoking a Java program. Arrays are useful for many other things. For example, a program that kept track of daily observations for a period of one week might define an array of seven values to represent the observations on each day.

Let's see how this might work.

```
import java.io.*;
// This gives us the use of pre-written input methods
class WeeklyAverage
 {public static void main(String args[])
                    throws IOException
// "throws IOException" warns that errors might occur.
// Anyone using this class might have to handle those
// errors, as we'll discuss in Chapter 11.
   {String DayNames[] = {"Sunday", "Monday", "Tuesday",
                         "Wednesday", "Thursday",
                         "Friday", "Saturday"};
// This defined an array and its contents in one step
    float dailyNumbers[] = new float[7];
    float sumOfNumbers  = 0;
       // we'll add our inputs to this
    DataInputStream userInput
            = new DataInputStream(System.in);
// a DataInputStream is a predefined facility that's
// described in Chapter 12
    String inputAsEntered;
          // this will capture whatever the user types
    for (int whichDay = 0;
            whichDay < 7; // this loops over the days,
            whichDay++)   // asking for input
   { System.out.println("Please enter the value for "
                    + DayNames[whichDay]
```

```
                              + ":"
                              );
        // Now get the input...
        inputAsEntered = userInput.readLine();
        // ...convert the string of input to
        //  a "float" and place that value in our array
        dailyNumbers[whichDay] =
               Float.valueOf(inputAsEntered).floatValue();
        // Accumulate a running total
        sumOfNumbers = sumOfNumbers
                   + dailyNumbers[whichDay];
     }
  // We're done getting input. Time to report.
  System.out.println("The values this week were:");
  for (int whichDay = 0;
           whichDay < 7;
           whichDay++)
   { System.out.println(DayNames[whichDay]
       + ": "
       + String.valueOf(dailyNumbers[whichDay]));
  // we turn our numbers back into strings so we
  // can print them
    }
   System.out.println("");
   System.out.println("The average for the week was "
                   + String.valueOf(sumOfNumbers/7));
        // compute and print the weekly average...
   }         // ...and we're done with "main()"
 }          // ...and done with "WeeklyAverage"
```

Hardtops and Convertibles

We've seen that when we try to make a Java data type hold something that just won't fit, we bump our heads against the top. It's painful.

But Java isn't fanatic about this "type purity." If we put a value of one data type into another data type that's more than large enough to hold it, we'll get what's called *implicit conversion*. For example,

```
int    anInt   = 231;
double aDouble = 1.75;
int    aSum    = anInt + aDouble;
```

will not work, but,

```
int    anInt   = 231;
double aDouble = 1.75;
double aSum    = anInt + aDouble;
```

will do just what you would expect.

Do note, though, that we can still trip ourselves up with implicit conversions that distort our calculations. For example, a long (64-bit integer) data type can count values up to 9,223,372,036,854,775,807, exactly. That can also be written as $9.223372036854775807 * 10^{18}$, accurate to 18 decimal places. A double can hold larger values, and will therefore accept an implicit conversion, but the double is only accurate to about 16 decimal places.

So the following code,

```
long   aBigLong   = 100000000000000000L;
                    // that's 17 zeros, with an L
                    // at the end to say it's a long

double aBigDouble = aBigLong; // implicit conversion

System.out.println(aBigLong   + 1 - aBigLong);
System.out.println(aBigDouble + 1 - aBigDouble);
```

will produce the output,

```
1
0
```

In terms of real math, the first result is what we'd expect. In terms of finite precision, floating-point math, the second is something we have to learn to expect (or rather, perhaps, learn to avoid).

A final example of useful and intuitive conversion occurs when we mix strings with numbers. For example,

```
String greeting = "Hello";
int anInt       = 231;
double aDouble  = 1.64;
System.out.println(anInt + greeting + aDouble);
```

will produce the output 231Hello1.64. Java automatically converts the numbers to their string representations so they can be concatenated with the value that was specified as a string.

If you look back at our `WeeklyAverage` example, you'll see two places where we explicitly converted numbers to strings using `String.valueOf()`. This was not necessary: It was done to make our intentions clear, at a point where we wanted to emphasize the differences in data representations.

Remove those enclosing `String.valueOf()` invocations, and verify that Java will convert those numbers to strings without being told to do so.

What's Next

In our examples throughout Chapters 3 and 4, we've used a growing vocabulary of operators: That is, punctuation marks or groups of marks that Java treats as instructions to act in different ways on different kinds of data.

We've added and divided numbers with + and /, we've done logical operations on `boolean` values with &&, ||, and ^, we've concatenated strings with + (an overloaded operator), and we've incremented our way through repetitive loops with ++.

These operators, and others yet to be seen, influence Java programming style—as do the operators of any programming language—making certain ways of writing a program more natural than others. We'll look at Java's operators more fully in Chapter 5. We'll see how a program declares its intentions to use certain types of data in those operations in Chapter 6.

Our programs have followed fairly simple paths, in general moving from the beginning straight through to the end—with occasional looping, or with side trips through helping methods like `bulbDisplay()`. Java has many ways of controlling the path through a program to make complex operations both clear and efficient: We'll look at these in Chapter 7.

Summary

In this chapter, we showed

▶ That programs are sets of rules for manipulating symbols.

▶ That Java gives programmers a large vocabulary of built-in symbol types.

▶ That programming languages resemble hard-wired logic circuits, but with far more flexibility.

▶ That programs written without regard to symbols' limitations can return misleading or inaccurate results.

▶ That Java automates some conversions between different types of symbols to produce intuitive and convenient results from concise notations.

Boolean and
Bitwise Operators

Relational
Operators

Active Assignment
Operators

Arithmetic Operators

Chapter 5
We'll Have to Operate

In this chapter, you'll learn how Java programs describe operations on data. We'll also cover how internal data formats can affect operations' results and how Java decides what to do first in a complicated set of instructions.

We can talk about a programming language in much the same way that we talk about a "human" language. Literal data values like `2.718` or `"Hello"` are like nouns; variable names, like `greeting` in the statement

```
String greeting = "Hello";
```

are like pronouns.

But if we want to make anything happen, we need some verbs as well. That brings us to this chapter's topic: Java's operators.

We've seen some of these already in the previous chapters' examples. In order of their appearance, we've seen the operators described in Table 5.1.

We didn't choose these operators as introductory examples. They were chosen as a side effect—so to speak—of devising typical problems to illustrate basic ideas.

But even this haphazard collection makes a vital point about operators. Some operators do something (for example, "assign a value" or "increase the value of a variable"), while others merely "return" something (for example, "return exclusive OR of two values").

It's crucial to keep track of the difference between these two types of operators. The "doing" operators produce *side effects:* They don't just return a value, they leave behind a change in the state of the data. The "returning" operators merely describe what they find.

Notice also that an operator can mean different things, depending on where it's used. For example, as we saw in the previous chapter, + is a smart little thing: It adds numbers, but it also concatenates Strings—even persuading any non-String operands to provide their String representations.

TABLE 5.1   JAVA'S OPERATORS: WHAT WE'VE SEEN SO FAR

Chapter/Example	Operator	Behavior
Chapter 2		
i = j + k;	+	Return sum of two numeric values.
	=	Assign a value to a variable, and return that new value as the value of the assignment. For example, the compound expression (j=3)+(k=4) leaves j and k with the values 3 and 4 while itself returning 7.
Chapter 3		
whichArg < args.length	<	Compare two numeric values, returning `boolean` `true` if the first is less than the second.
	. ("dot")	Apply the method, or retrieve the instance variable, named after the period, in the context of the object named before.
whichArg++	++	When used in postfix position, increase value of operand by 1 *after* returning current value (while ++whichArg changes whichArg *first*).
whichArg + ": "	+	Return concatenation of two Strings. If one operand is not a String, use that operand's printable form in building the String that's returned.
Chapter 4		
if (switch==closed)	==	Return `true` if identical, `false` if not.
switch1 ^ switch2	^	Evaluate two `boolean` or integer-type values and return an XOR of the results.
switch1 & switch2	&	Evaluate two `boolean` or integer-type values and return an AND of the results.

Booleans and Bits

Now that we've got the big picture, let's look at the details. We started Chapter 4, our exploration of data, with the most basic types of value: the `boolean` and the `byte`. Let's follow this path with operators as well, looking first at the ones that work with those fundamental types.

! — Logical Complement Inverts True/False

This operator returns the opposite of a `boolean` value. For example, `!true == false`. For no good reason, this operator is often called *bang*, or (more reasonably) read aloud as *not*.

~ — Bitwise Complement Flips All Bits

This operator returns the result of changing every 1 in the binary symbol of an integer-type number to a 0, and vice versa. This symbol is called a *tilde* (pronounced, "tilldee").

This operator *can't* be used on a boolean, even though that type may seem a lot like a one-bit integer. Java does *not* allow us to casually mix the booleans true and false with the numeric values one and zero, as many other languages do permit.

We can use ~ to explore Java's internal representation of integers. In Chapter 4, we said that Java represents a negative integer by the twos complement of the matching positive integer. This is calculated by taking the bitwise complement and adding one. Let's prove that this is how this part of the Java language works.

```
class TestComplement
  { public static void main(String args[])
      { byte aPositiveNumber = 76; // an arbitrary value
        System.out.println("This should be -"
                          + aPositiveNumber
                          + ": "
                          + ( ~aPositiveNumber + 1 ));
      }
  }
```

It doesn't matter if you use another value in place of that 76, as long as it's a positive number no larger than 127. The program will still produce consistent results, confirming our earlier description of how Java represents a negative-valued byte.

Test this same example with simple types short, int, and long if you wish. All of them work the same way.

& — Boolean AND Seeks Truth in Pairs

The & operator has meaning for both booleans and integers. When used with two boolean operands, & returns true if both of its operands evaluate to true.

Later in the chapter, you'll meet an operator called *conditional AND*, which also operates on boolean values. What's the difference? The simple AND always evaluates both of its operands, while the conditional AND might not—for a perfectly logical reason, as the alternative name *logical AND* suggests.

If one of those operands is itself an expression containing an operator that produces a side effect, then this difference is important. From Table 5.1, for example, recall that an assignment expression using the = operator returns the value as-signed, with the side effect of performing that assignment.

Let's look at the effect of using an assignment expression, with a boolean value, as an operand to a simple AND.

```
boolean oneThing = false;
boolean anotherThing = false;
boolean andWhat = oneThing & (anotherThing = true);
System.out.println(oneThing
                    + " " + anotherThing
                    + " " + andWhat);
```

The last statement prints,

```
false true false
```

The program evaluates both of its operands before doing an AND on the re-sults. Evaluating the second operand, which is an assignment expression, per-forms the assignment. This changes the value of anotherThing as a side effect. When anotherThing is printed, we see its changed value.

What would happen if we used == instead of =?

```
boolean andWhat = oneThing & (anotherThing == true);
```

The output becomes,

```
false false false
```

because now the value of anotherThing is merely being *compared* against true. It is *not* being reassigned.

Now restore the = operator, but change the simple AND to a conditional (or log-ical) AND:

```
boolean andWhat = oneThing && (anotherThing = true);
```

The output is, again,

```
false false false
```

because the conditional AND, finding that the first operand was false, didn't bother to evaluate the second operand. There was no way that the AND could come out true, no matter what the second operand might be: Conditional AND doesn't waste time evaluating operands that can't affect results, so anotherThing never got reassigned.

What about this business of = having a side effect, while == does not? This gives us expressions like (x = x + 1), which doesn't look right at all.

Some languages try to make assignments more obvious by using the operator :=, which is supposed to look like the ← that's used in the algorithm publication language ALGOL. (Most keyboards don't have that left-pointing arrow, which does convey the notion of "put the value on the right into the place that's named on the left.") Using := for assignment leaves the = sign free for comparisons.

How can we remember the C/C++/Java convention for = and == ? Perhaps it will help to think of = as an impatient "Make it so!," and think of == as a more relaxed "I was just wondering."

At least Java, with its clear and enforced distinction between boolean values and integers, makes it harder to use the wrong operator by accident.

This behavior is also termed short-circuit evaluation, since the operator returns its result without making the rest of the trip to the end of the statement. It can be quite useful, as we'll discuss below.

For the moment, the moral of the story is that Java does what it's told to do. Understand what you're asking for, and you won't be surprised when you get it.

& — Bitwise AND Finds Matching 1's

The & operator returns the result of applying AND to each matching pair of bits in each of two integer-type values. Like ~, & can be used on any of the four simple integer types.

Here's a practical example. We'll use a byte to represent a group of eight questions on a medical history form, and another byte to represent a patient's answers.

We'll put a 1 in the questions byte for every question that requires an interview if the answer is Yes; we'll put a 1 in the answers byte for each Yes answer to a question. (We call something like questions a *mask*, because it will mask the bits that don't matter when we AND it with another piece of data.)

No interview is needed unless at least one matching set of question and answer both get the value 1. If there's at least one such set, then the bitwise AND will produce a result with at least one nonzero bit. The value of that byte will then be nonzero.

We can use the `!=` (not equal) operator to compare the result against zero. Here's the code:

```
class TestBitwiseAnd
  { public static void main(String args[])
    { byte questions
            = 0x49; // 0x means hex; 49 = 0100 1001
      byte answers
            = 0x27; //                 27 = 0010 0111
                  // bitwise AND is      0000 0001
      System.out.println("Interview needed: "
                + ((questions & answers) != 0));
    }
  }
```

What we're doing in this program is the calculation,

```
questions & answers
```

which means

```
      0 1 0 0 1 0 0 1
AND   0 0 1 0 0 1 1 1
      ---------------
      0 0 0 0 0 0 0 1
```

The answer is not zero, and the expression

```
((questions & answers) != 0)
```

will evaluate (and be printed) as `true`.

| — Boolean OR Takes Truth Where It Can Find It

Like the simple Boolean AND, the simple Boolean OR always evaluates both of its operands. It returns `true` if either of its operands evaluates to `true`. We'll see `||`, the conditional (logical) OR, below.

| — Bitwise Inclusive OR Finds Any 1s

When applied to integer types, | does pairwise inclusive ORs on the corresponding bits in each operand. For the same two values that we used to demonstrate & above,

```
questions | answers
```

would be

```
    0 1 0 0 1 0 0 1
OR  0 0 1 0 0 1 1 1
    ----------------
    0 1 1 0 1 1 1 1
```

^ — Exclusive OR Finds Truth in Differences

We used this operator in one of our earliest examples, `TestTwoBits`. It can be applied to `boolean` operands, evaluating both and returning `true` if they yield different values.

There's obviously no such thing as a conditional XOR: We always have to look at both operands before an XOR's value can be known.

As a bitwise operator, with our current test case values `questions` and `answers`, `^` would appear in an expression like this:

```
questions ^ answers
```

and would perform the calculation,

```
     0 1 0 0 1 0 0 1
XOR  0 0 1 0 0 1 1 1
     ----------------
     0 1 1 0 1 1 1 0
```

Note that XOR is a reversible operation. If we take the result of `questions ^ answers`, and perform a second XOR with `questions`, we get

```
(questions ^ answers) ^ questions
```

which would be

```
     0 1 1 0 1 1 1 0
XOR  0 1 0 0 1 0 0 1
     ----------------
     0 0 1 0 0 1 1 1
```

This result is the original value of `answers`.

This behavior of XOR is useful in animation, for example, when we want to draw a figure on a background, then remove it before we draw it at a new position: (`figure ^ background`) draws the figure, (`figure ^ background`) `^ figure` returns the original background.

<<, >>, and >>> — Bit Shifts Work Like "Moving Lights"

Imagine one of those electric signs, where letters appear to move across the sign as lights are turned on and off. The light bulbs don't move—it's their on/off state that moves, so to speak, from one bulb to the next along each row.

Shifting bits in a binary symbol works the same way. Each bit takes on the value formerly held by the bit to its right or its left, depending on the direction of the shift.

Bit shifts are an easy way to extract a single bit from a binary symbol. For example, the expression (i & 16) >>> 4 extracts the fifth bit (counting from the right) of integer i's internal representation. This is how it works:

```
0101 1101   a byte-type integer
0001 0000   binary symbol for 16
---------
0001 0000   bitwise AND
0000 0001   shift right by 4, fill from left with 0s
```

We call 16 a *mask*, as explained above: The bitwise AND with 16 masks all bits whose values aren't of interest. The composite operation is called a *mask and shift*. We wind up with a value of 1 or 0, equal to the fifth bit from the right in the original byte.

Bit shifts also have an arithmetic meaning. Under the hood of your computer, bit-shifting is part of the process of integer multiplication or division. For example,

```
       0000 1101   binary symbol for decimal 13
  (00)0011 01??   shift left by two
       0011 01??   discard extra bits at left
       0011 0100   fill bits at right with 0s
          3    4   equivalent hexadecimal symbol
       x 16   x 1  multiply by powers of 16
       ---------
         48    4   decimal value components
       ---------
            52     add to get value of new number
```

This operation produced a value of 52, which is four times our original value of 13: exactly what we should get when we multiply by 2, then multiply by 2 again (shifting left twice).

Don't try to second-guess your compiler by using your own sequence of shifts and adds, instead of just using the multiplication (*) or division (/) operators that we'll discuss below. The compiler will do this just as well as you can.

But this arithmetic meaning of a bit shift is the reason why there are two right-shift operators, >> and >>>. We just looked at the low-level behavior of <<, which shifts bits to the left, discarding the bits that get pushed off the left end and filling in the space at the right with 0s. Here's another example:

```
int shiftThis = -64;
System.out.println(shiftThis << 2);
```

This produces the output

```
-256
```

which is 2^2 times -64, a power of 2 for each left shift, as you'd expect.

If a left shift changes the value of the leftmost bit, we've overflowed the limits of that data type, and we'll wrap around to the opposite end of its range of values. Java does what it's told.

Will either of our right shift operators yield intuitive arithmetic results? Let's try both:

```
System.out.println(-64 >> 2);
System.out.println(-64 >>> 2);
```

This produces the output,

```
-16
1073741808
```

The >> operator produced the expected arithmetic result: shifting right twice divided a number by 4. We call >> an arithmetic right shift.

The >>> operator produced a result that is arithmetically bogus, because it ignored Java's twos-complement representation of negative numbers. The >>> filled from the left with 0s, while >> filled from the left with the starting value of the leftmost bit (this is called "extending the sign bit").

So we don't use >>> to do arithmetic: We use it for the logical operation of extracting a bit, as in our first example in this section. The >>> operator is called a logical right shift.

Testing...

We've spent a lot of space on the bitwise operators, because their functions aren't familiar from everyday experience. Other, more familiar operators won't need such thorough explanation.

For example, Java has a complete family of relational operators for comparing numeric values. These return `boolean` results, as you'd expect, and are written in programs as shown in Table 5.2.

Remember, we use `==` to perform a comparison, which doesn't have any side effects. Java will try to keep you from getting confused about this, as we can see from this example:

```
class TestAssignment
  { public static void main(String args[])
      { int aValue = 1;  // first time used, type needed
        System.out.println(aValue =  0); // false?
        System.out.println(aValue == 0); // true?
        aValue = 1;
        System.out.println(aValue == 0); // surely false
      }
  }
```

The output from this program is

```
0
true
false
```

We see that the expression, `aValue = 0`, does not return a value of `true` or false, but rather changes the value of `aValue` and returns that new value as the value of the expression. If we try to say something like,

```
if (aValue = 0)
```

when making a decision about what to do in a program, we'll get an error, because 0 is neither true nor false: in Java, 0 is 0, a number, with no Boolean interpretation.

TABLE 5.2   JAVA'S RELATIONAL OPERATORS

Operator	Meaning
>	Greater than
>=	Greater than or equal to
==	Equal to (when comparing non-numeric values, better thought of as "identical to")
!=	Not equal to
<=	Less than or equal to
<	Less than

This makes Java much stricter than C, BASIC, or other languages that let 0 be the equivalent of false, and any nonzero value be the equivalent of true.

&& and || — Conditional (Logical) AND and OR Are Just Lazy

There are three more operators in this testing group. The first two are the conditional (or logical) AND and OR, written `&&` and `||`, as opposed to the simple bitwise AND (`&`) and OR (`|`). We don't need to belabor these: We discussed their effects above, contrasting them with their simple counterparts.

These operators are notable for their short-circuit behavior, which doesn't bother to evaluate the second operand unless its value can affect the result. This behavior can be used to make programs faster and more reliable.

For example, suppose that two values need to be compared. Suppose that one of them is easily determined, while the other requires a remote database lookup.

Our program may run more quickly if we put the "cheap" expression first: depending on the value of that expression, that time-consuming lookup might not be needed.

We can also use short-circuit evaluation to keep our program from trying to do the impossible. For example,

```
int p=3;
int q=0;
System.out.println((q != 0) && (p/q > 1));
    // prints false, p/q ignored
System.out.println((q != 0)  & (p/q > 1));
    // aborts due to division by 0 in p/q
```

?: — Conditional Ternary Has Fans and Foes

Some people dislike this last testing operator, the *conditional ternary* ("three values"). This operator evaluates its first operand, and evaluates/returns the second operand if that result is `true`; it evaluates/returns the third operand if the first operand evaluates to `false`.

Suppose, for example, that a company has a savings plan in which the company contributes 50 percent of the first $1000 of an employee's contribution. This can be expressed with the ternary ?: operator as

```
double employerMatch = employeeAmount >= 1000.00
                           ? 500.00
                           : employeeAmount * 0.5;
```

Many people find this hard to read. Parentheses around the conditional test can help.

Like the conditional AND and OR, ?: omits evaluation of irrelevant operands. For example,

```
int a=0, b=0, c=0;
int d = a==0 ? b=1 : c=2;
System.out.println(c);
```

produces the output 0. The third operand, whose evaluation would have reassigned c, was ignored since the first operand evaluated to true. Again, parentheses would surely improve the readability of this code, even if they aren't required.

...and Twiddling...

Let's look now at the operators whose main purpose is their side effects. We've already seen the basic assignment operator: that is, the = sign. Java also uses this in a large family of *active assignment* operators, which condense common operations into more concise expressions.

For example, it's common in programs to use a variable to accumulate a running total, as in our WeeklyAverage class in Chapter 4. You'll recall that we accumulated the running total of our daily observations so that we could later compute the average, using the expression

```
sumOfNumbers = sumOfNumbers + dailyNumbers[whichDay];
```

Java lets us say this more concisely as

```
sumOfNumbers += dailyNumbers[whichDay];
```

This generalizes to any operator that does arithmetic or bitwise operations on a pair of values. For example, to double a value, we could write

```
i = i * 2;
```

or we could write, more compactly,

```
i *= 2;
```

It is important to note that this doesn't merely save space in the program. These active assignments also have a useful property. They are defined, internally, so that the expression that describes the target of the assignment will only be evaluated once.

What does this mean? Well, suppose we wanted to introduce some random fluctuations into a series of values so that we could simulate a stream of real-world, noisy data. We might write a little helping program that produced a random number, then use that random number to choose a compartment in an array of undistorted data. We would then alter the value in that randomly chosen compartment with some simulated noise.

If our values are in an array called valSeries, and our random number generator program is named aRandom(), then we might write something like:

```
valSeries[aRandom()] = valSeries[aRandom()]
                          * (1 + noise);
```

But when we look at this more carefully, we realize that each reference to valSeries[aRandom()] will use a new random number. Unless we get lucky, we won't store the distorted value in its original location. We'll store it in *another* randomly chosen location that might be anywhere in the array. This is not what we want.

We could write,

```
int placeToChange = aRandom();
valSeries[placeToChange] = valSeries[placeToChange]
                              * (1 + noise);
```

But this is hard to read. We have to look carefully to see that we are only working on one piece of data.

Additionally, the computer will have to figure out the location of valSeries [placeToChange] twice, each time going to the beginning of the valSeries data structure and counting up to the desired location. This is inefficient.

If we write, instead,

```
valSeries[aRandom()] *=  (1 + noise);
```

we'll get exactly what we wanted. The method aRandom() will be called only once to decide which value gets distorted, and the location in memory to be modified will only have to be calculated one time.

Using +, * and the other bitwise and arithmetic operators that we've described, we can now create the active assignment operators +=, -=, *=, /=, &=, |=, ^=, <<=, >>=, and >>>=. Their functions all follow the pattern illustrated above using += and *=.

...and 'Rithmetic

We've saved for last the operators whose values are most familiar from everyday experience: the arithmetic symbols +, -, *, /, and one new operator: %.

With any type of number,

▶ + is addition

▶ – is subtraction

▶ * is multiplication

▶ / is division

But division requires discussion.

If we are using integer data types (byte, short, int, or long), then division in general will not produce an exact result. For example, 5/2 is not an integral ratio.

Like most programming languages, Java handles such cases by truncating—that is, by chopping off the fractional part of the result.

Java truncates toward zero: for example, 13/2 is 6 and -13/2 is -6. This means that math with integer-family values doesn't follow your everyday expectations: (13/2)*2 will be 12, not 13.

Our new operator, %, is now easily defined in terms of integer division. % is the *remainder* operator: 13%2 is 1, -13%2 is -1. For integer-family values p and q, (p/q)*q + p%q will equal the original value of p.

Another warning about division: Remember that under the hood, Java is working with a finite number of bits and is working in base 2, not base 10.

Even in base 10, you know that a number like 1/3 cannot be written as an exact decimal fraction with any finite number of digits. If you allow yourself five decimal places, 1.00000/3.00000 = 0.33333; (1.00000/3.00000)*3.00000 = 0.99999.

Well, base 2 is even more finicky. In base 2, you can only represent fractions that are negative powers of 2, like 2^{-1} (1/2) and 2^{-3} (1/8), and fractions that are sums of such powers (like 3/8 or 77/128). Some fractions that can be represented exactly in base 10, like 1/5 (0.2), cannot be represented exactly with any finite number of bits in base 2.

Java uses a set of formal rules for floating-point math, based on an extremely detailed standard called IEEE-754-1985. This usually yields impressively accurate results, and it takes a little effort to construct a test case that doesn't behave "naturally."

Here, however, is one such case:

```
(float)(1.0/5.0) * 5.0 - 1.0
```

This returns, not 0.0, but 0.0000000149012.

Note, though, that this was a sort of floating-point entrapment: It only happened when we forcibly *cast* the quotient, 1/5, to a reduced-precision float while letting

What Is the IEEE, and What Does It Have to Do with Java?

IEEE is the Institute for Electrical and Electronics Engineers, a professional organization. Among its other activities, the IEEE develops technical standards that let different manufacturers agree to follow non-proprietary rules. In the same way that a Sony CD player can plug into a Kenwood amplifier, IEEE standards let buyers evaluate and combine a wide range of products from many sources, rather than being locked into a single company's solutions.

The IEEE standard for floating-point math is a comprehensive rule book that defines the number of bits to be used, the range of values to be represented, and the manner in which computations will be performed for a variety of floating-point data types of varying precision. It devotes special care to extreme cases, such as the handling of infinities.

The statement,

```
System.out.println(1/0);
```

cannot be compiled because division by zero is not defined for integers. But this statement,

```
System.out.println(1.0/0.0);
```

will produce an output reflecting the assignment of an infinity value. Java can continue computations with infinities, following common sense rules such as "anything times infinity equals infinity."

Another special value is NaN (Not a Number): multiplying an infinity by zero yields a NaN.

Java will do its best to produce reasonable results when such values arise in floating-point operations. There are also methods that let a program inquire if a particular value is an infinity or a NaN, making it possible to handle these situations as the programmer thinks best. We'll see these in Chapter 11.

the literals 5.0 and 1.0 use the more precise `double` format (which they used, by default, because they contained decimal points and we did not specify `float`).

We cruelly devised this example to show why you should not use the identity operator (==) with floating-point values like `floats` or `doubles`. If such a test happens to work in one or more test cases, that's just luck. It's not reliable for all legitimate input.

Instead, decide how nearly equal your values need to be, then have your program make its decision by subtracting one value from the other and seeing if the difference is smaller than your tolerance. This makes your program say what it really means, which is always a good idea.

If you're working with fractional values such as dollars and cents, and you want to make exact comparisons without the risk of rounding errors, you may want to do your calculations in pennies or perhaps in tenths of a cent (using an integer-family data type).

When you want to print your results, put in the decimal point by character string manipulation. For example, if you've been working in mils (tenths of a cent), you could generate your output like this:

```
System.out.println("Please pay "
                + costMils/1000
                + "."
                + Math.abs(costMils%1000));
```

The `Math.abs()` that we wrapped around `costMils%1000` is an absolute value function, which keeps us from getting a second minus sign after the decimal point if `costMils` is less than zero. We're getting that function from a package (a library of Java classes) called Math: We'll learn more about packages in Chapter 10, and more about package Math in Chapter 11. Note also the use of our integer division and integer remainder operators in this brief example.

Before you apply such techniques, however, be sure that you understand the behavior of integer data: remember, integer operations don't round off values. Any fractions at the end are just ignored.

And don't rush to make a lot of work for yourself. Floating-point math in Java is quite accurate, and there's rarely any need to reinvent the floating-point wheel. Just remember to avoid exact equality tests on floating-point values, and you'll almost always get the expected results.

But if simple math seems to be yielding strange results, consider the possibility of hidden rounding problems. It pays to know what's under the hood when your program starts making strange noises.

Keep Your Priorities Clear

In our various fragments of code, you may have noticed our frequent use of parentheses. These have more than one meaning.

Parentheses enclose the arguments to a method, as in `main(String args[])`. They enclose the name of a data type if we want to coerce (or cast) a value of one type into another: for example, `(long)(price*1000)` will force a floating-point price in dollars and cents into an integer-type equivalent in tenths of a cent. Parentheses also modify the precedence—that is, the sequence of execution—of operators. For ordinary arithmetic, precedence in Java follows the rule that's often taught by the name of My Dear Aunt Sally (Multiply, Divide, Add, Subtract): From left to right, Java does multiplications and divisions first, then additions and subtractions. So `7*4-4` is `28-4`, not `7*0`; `7-4*4` is `7-16`, not `3*4`.

This is normal usage, and you probably wouldn't bother to type in the parentheses to make these read `(7*4)-4` or `7-(4*4)` in your code. But you and the future readers of your programs may not be so familiar with the order of precedence for shifts and logical operations. Parentheses will clarify what you mean, even if they aren't needed to get what you want.

For example, what is the value of this?

```
5 << 3 & 9 ^ 13
```

Shifts have higher precedence than the bitwise AND, which in turn outranks the bitwise XOR. So this is equivalent to

```
((5 << 3) & 9) ^ 13
```

This should therefore return the value,

```
0000 0101     5
0010 1000    << 3
     &
0000 1001     9
- - - - - - - - - -
0000 1000
     ^
0000 1101     13
- - - - - - - - - -
0000 0101    == 5
```

Test this for yourself.

But perhaps you wanted

```
(5 << 3) & (9 ^ 13)
```

If so, you can put in the parentheses and get it.

```
0000 0101   5        0000 1001   9        0010 1000
        << 3                    ^                    &
-----------          0000 1101   13       0000 0100
0010 1000            ----------           -----------
                     0000 0100            0000 0000
```

The ranking of precedence for Java's most often used operators is shown in Table 5.3 (see also Appendix A). On each line of the table, precedence is equal: operators of equal precedence are applied from left to right.

For example, $7*4/3$ means $(7*4)/3$ and $8|5|9$ means $(8|5)|9$.

There is one exception to the precedence rule for operators on the same row of this table. That exception is for the assignment operators, whose evaluation goes from right to left: $i*=j+=k$ means $i*=(j+=k)$, or $j=j+k$; $i=i*j$.

With the assignment operators, intuition can be misleading. If you see the $*=$ and think, "This is like a multiplication," you'll be wrong if you think that this makes the expression equivalent to $(i\ *=\ j)\ +=\ k$.

TABLE 5.3   PRECEDENCE IN JAVA

Precedence group	Operator	Comments
postfix	[] () ++ — .	
prefix	++ — + - ~ !	
type cast	()	
multiply/divide	* / %	
add/subtract	+ -	
shift	<< >> >>>	
ordering	< <= >= >	
equality	== !=	
bitwise AND	&	Like multiplication: 1 & 0 == 0
bitwise XOR	^	Like addition: 1 ^ 0 == 1
bitwise OR	|	Like addition: 1 | 0 == 1
logical AND	&&	
logical OR	||	
assignment	= *= /= %= += -= <<= >>= >>>= &= ^= |=	

Besides, what would this even mean? (i=i*j) is not the name of a place in the computer's memory, so how can (i*=j) be the target of the second assignment operation? When it comes to assignments, there has to be a value on the right-hand side and a name of a location in memory on the left. This is easily remembered.

What's Next?

Knowing both data and operators, we know enough Java to tell a story: We have both nouns and verbs.

But our work won't be very dramatic, because the plot of any program will always be the same. Changing the values of data will be like changing the cast of the play without writing any new scenes.

To add some interest, we need to be able to set the scene and to tell different stories that suit the personalities of different actors. In other words, we need to learn how Java lets us declare our intentions for using data, and how we can change the path that a program follows depending on the values of data and on the actions of the user. These are the facilities of the language that we'll examine in Chapters 6 and 7.

Summary

In this chapter, we showed

▶ That Java has a variety of symbols that get turned into operations on data.

▶ That some operators alter data, while others just analyze it.

▶ That some operators are best understood in terms of operations on bits.

▶ That operators are applied in order, by fixed precedence, in ways that may not give the expected results unless we control this effect.

Building
Statements

Declaring Data

Implicit
Conversion

Type Promotion

Using Arrays

Modifying Strings

Chapter 6
Anything to Declare?
Data Declarations, Types, and Structures

In this chapter, you'll learn how Java programs are built from statements. You'll see how Java differs from *non-procedural* languages: You'll learn how declaration statements describe a program's plans for using data and how simple data types form a promotable hierarchy. We'll cover the data declaration rules that guard against common programming errors, and the literal data values that default to certain types—and how to override those defaults. You'll also learn more about arrays: how groups of data values can be defined and named using arrays, how arrays behave as self-aware objects, and how characters can be grouped into arrays or strings for operations on text—as well as how pieces of text are modified and combined.

When you're learning something as complex as a new programming language, it's easy to wind up feeling like a blind man meeting an elephant. In the classic tale of six such men, none of them could see the whole animal; each formed a strong but misleading impression of its nature, based on the first part of the whole that he encountered.

The blind man who bumped into a tusk said that an elephant was hard, thin, and sharp; the one who bumped into a leg said that an elephant was soft, fat, and rough. But neither of them had gotten to the body of the beast. Neither the tusk nor the leg is the essence of an elephant.

Nor could any of those men form any idea of how an elephant behaves in the real world. None of them had the slightest inkling, for example, of stampedes.

We've tried to avoid putting you into a similar situation. Our first look at Java, in Chapter 3, explored a complete program that actually did something. We took that program apart to understand, at least in principle, the role of each piece, before we discussed the details.

We made sure that you knew, so to speak, that there were four legs before we started to talk about knees and toenails.

Then we started to go into depth. In Chapter 4, we looked at the "legs" of data that support a Java program. In Chapter 5, we examined Java's operators, the "tusks" that a program uses to dig out results.

Now that we understand those elements better than we did in Chapter 3, we're going to step back and look at how they fit together to produce something that can really run. And not just run in a straight line, but run through a changing environment while making quick decisions on the way. This is our goal for Chapters 6 and 7, before we build on that base to make richer use of Java's object-oriented facilities in Chapters 8 through 10.

When we get to Chapters 11 through 16, we'll be using everything that's come before to apply the standard libraries of classes—called *packages*—that come with the version of the Java language that runs on any particular kind of computer.

That's when we'll be able to write programs that protect themselves against abnormal situations; that split themselves into pieces, able to take turns using the system's resources; that wrap themselves in bordered windows and appear on your desktop with a graphical user interface; and that embed themselves in a Web page, drawing information from that environment, to enliven the content of your presence on the Internet. But that journey has to take place one line at a time.

I Have a Prepared Statement...

A Java program, like programs in any procedural programming language, is a series of *statements*. In some languages, like COBOL and Smalltalk, a statement ends with a period; COBOL actually calls its statements sentences, with typical expressions like MULTIPLY X BY X GIVING X-SQUARE.

Java follows a more common convention for modern programming languages, with a notation that fits a lot more meaning into a given amount of space with a lot less typing: Java would express the preceding idea as:

```
xSquare = x*x;
```

Rather than using a period, Java ends each statement with a semicolon.

Note that we said, "*ends* each statement." Some languages use a semicolon as a statement *separator*, which would mean that your final statement wouldn't need a semicolon at the end.

Java uses the semicolon to mark an *end* of a statement, not a separation between one statement and the next. Why make such a big deal about this little piece of punctuation? Because those semicolons mean a lot.

For example, Java defines a looping statement called `for`, which repeats a series of operations with variations—as you've seen before, and as we'll explain more fully in Chapter 7.

We might write a program that included the statements,

```
int i;
for (i = 0; i < 3; i++)
   System.out.println(i);
```

These would produce the output

```
0
1
2
```

Note that this fragment, though it takes up three lines, contains only two statements: The declaration of the variable `i`, and the `for` statement that looped through several values of `i` and used each one in a repetitive operation. Two statements: two semicolons.

Suppose that we got confused about this, and thought we needed a semicolon at the end of the first line of the `for`:

```
int i;
for (i = 0; i < 3; i++); // ends the for statement:
   System.out.println(i); // this is now separate
```

This fragment produces only the output,

```
3
```

because the `for` statement was ended by that first semicolon.

The `for` statement now had an empty body: It counted from 0 through 2, and quit when `i` reached the value 3. All of this happened *before* the program went on to the piece of code that printed the value of `i`.

The indentation of the source code, with the `println()` call indented from the `for`, makes it clear that the programmer meant to have the `println()` inside the loop. But indentation has no meaning to a Java compiler. As far as the compiler was concerned, the `println()` call was *not* a part of the `for` statement, and the `println()` did not take part in the looping behavior as planned.

Sometimes, Java can tell you at compile time where a semicolon was expected. If you try to compile this:

```
class TestThis
  { public static void main(String args[])
    { int thisNumber=3
      }
    }
```

you will get an error message from the compiler, something like:

```
TestThis.java:3: ';' expected.
    { int thisNumber=3
                      ^
```

or something more refined if you're using an integrated development environment.

But there are other situations, like the `for` loop and `println()` sequence farther above, in which a program is valid either way. It just does different things.

For this and similar reasons, programmers joke about needing a DWIM function, meaning "Do What I Mean": Ideally, you could wrap a DWIM() around your entire program and have all your simple mistakes fixed automatically.

Java has not achieved this level of mind reading, nor has any other language. There *is* a function called DWIM in some dialects of Lisp, but it only fills in enough missing punctuation to guarantee that the program will run. It doesn't guarantee that the program will do what the programmer planned.

Give the Compiler a Clue

Proper programming style can give Java a little help in figuring out your intentions and give the compiler a fighting chance to warn you of likely errors.

For example, we would have gotten a compiler error that would have led us straight to our mistake if we had written,

```
for (int i = 0; i < 3; i++);
  System.out.println(i);
```

Here, instead of declaring our counter variable *outside* the `for` statement, we declare it within the loop control expression. That variable, `i`, then ceases to be defined when the loop completes. The `println()` call then tries to use what is now an undefined variable. The compiler complains:

```
TestThis.java:4: Undefined variable: i
         System.out.println(i);
                            ^
```

If the only thing you want to do with a variable is count your way through a loop, and perhaps to use that counter value in some way within the loop, it's good practice to make that variable *local* to that loop. It keeps the declaration close to the place where the variable is used, and frees the memory required by that variable as soon as its job is done.

You're less likely to become confused; the compiler is more likely to discern any errors that you make; the user is less likely to run out of system resources.

Is There Any Other Way to Write a Program?

There are other kinds of programming language, in which a program is a list of rules to be applied rather than a list of actions to be taken. In such a *non-procedural* language, running a program means handing that list of rules to a general purpose program called an engine: The engine compares the rules to the known facts and uses some built-in strategy to decide which rule the engine should next apply to deduce additional facts.

Applying (also called *firing*) a rule will generally change the state of the system. The engine then examines its new state of knowledge and decides what to do next. This continues until some desired end state is reached, or until the engine can't find anything else to do.

A rule-based system might hold a rule like this:

```
if typeOf(x) is Customer and paymentStatus(x) is Late and
billingGroup(x) is not Urgent
then set(billingGroup(x),Urgent)
```

and it might hold a fact like this:

```
Customer({Doe, John}, Late, Normal)
```

Matching the descriptive portions of its rules against its current facts, the engine would find that this fact matches this rule. It would fire this rule, with the result of changing this customer's billingGroup. The updated fact would now match another rule that fires to send out second-notice bills.

For a task like this, a rule-based language is clearly not helpful. But a language like this is ideal for the kinds of problem that are solved by expert system programs.

Expert systems are programs devised for tasks, such as medical diagnoses, that are best approached by collecting the knowledge of human experts in the form of separate (and sometimes approximate) rules, rather than trying to write a precise, sequential "recipe" for solving the problem.

This approach has been successfully used for tasks that range from prospecting for precious metals to configuring complex computer systems. Rule-based programs, also called *declarative* programs or *production systems*, are commonly written in languages designed for this purpose, such as Prolog and OPS5.

But the inference engine that drives such a language tends to be a large, memory-intensive program with unpredictable performance. For most of the things that we do with computer programs, a procedural language like Java remains the preferred approach.

Well, I Declare!

We've seen Java's simplest kind of statement many times in our sample programs so far. This type of statement is called a *declaration*.

We use a declaration to tell Java the name of a piece of data, or a multivalued *data structure*, and to specify the type of that data. This lets the compiler reserve space in memory to hold that data's value (or values), and in a *strongly typed* language like Java it tells the compiler what rules to use when operating on that data.

For example,

```
int aValue;
```

tells the Java compiler that a 32-bit value will be stored, and that any value assigned to the name aValue must be type int and will be representable by and manipulated by those rules.

From then on, we can just say things like:

```
aValue = 32;
```

without repeating aValue's data type. If we forget that type and try to say something like

```
aValue = 32.1;
```

we will get an error at the time we compile our program, since the value 32.1 cannot be represented by an int.

Note: We did not say that the value assigned to aValue had to *be* of type int, only that it had to be something that could be *represented* by an int. An 8-bit byte can clearly be represented, with bits to spare, by a 32-bit int; so can a 16-bit short, while any of these integer types can fit into a 64-bit long. A 32-bit float has a big enough range of values to represent the value of any integer type; a 64-bit double can represent any of the other simple types.

Java practices *implicit conversion* to let a value of one type be assigned to any wider ranging superset type. For example, the following is perfectly all right:

```
int  i = 27;
long j = i ;
```

But the following will produce an error:

```
short j = 17;
byte  k = j ;
```

When you're trying to figure out if an implicit conversion is allowed, don't make the mistake of merely counting bits. For example, even though a char is 16 bits, such a value cannot be assigned to a 16-bit short.

This is because a char is an unsigned type, whose equivalent numeric values range from 0 through 65,535; a short, by contrast, uses half of its range (the bit strings beginning with 1) to accommodate negative values, and can only hold positive values up to 32,767.

We can see why this matters with the following test program:

```
class TestThis
  { public static void main(String args[])
    { int i;
      char j = '\uFFFF';          // = sixteen 1s
      i = j;            // represent the value
      System.out.println(i);
      short k = (short)(j); // copy the bits
      System.out.println(k);
    }
  }
```

which produces the output 65535 for the value of i, but -1 for the value of k.

Replace the value FFFF with 7FFF in the program above, and confirm that the value is now correctly represented by either an int or a short.

You can, however, put any `char`'s value into an `int`: Once this is done, that value loses its "`char`"acteristics, as in the fragment:

```
char i = 'A';
int  j =  i ;
System.out.println(i);
System.out.println(j);
```

which yields the output,

```
A
65
```

The number 65 is both the ASCII and the Unicode value for *A*.

Implicit conversion is related to another behavior called *type promotion*. If you mix values of several types in a single expression, for example, by multiplying a `byte` by an integer literal, the result is promoted to the most all-encompassing type that appears anywhere in that expression.

You may have to do an explicit conversion to get the result squeezed back down to the type that you wanted to use to represent the result. It is up to you, in such a case, to make sure that this *cast* operation will not discard significant bits.

For example, in class `java.lang.Math` (which we'll examine in Chapter 11), the function `pow(x,y)` raises the value x to the power y. This function is defined to accept `double` arguments and return a `double` result.

Implicit conversion will let us write,

```
int  i = -5;
byte j =  2;
System.out.println(Math.pow(i,j));
```

and get back the output

```
25
```

But that doesn't mean we can make an assignment like:

```
int k = Math.pow(i,j);
```

Such a statement will produce the error message,

```
Cannot implicitly convert 'double' to 'int'
```

We can, however, write

```
int k = (int)Math.pow(i,j);
```

and further exploration confirms that k winds up with the correct value. It's just up to the programmer to be sure that such casts are valid.

Unless otherwise stated, Java will treat a numeric literal with no decimal point as an int; a number with a decimal point as a double. When combined with automatic type promotion in mixed expressions, this can yield perplexing behaviors such as:

```
short i = 32;
short j = 2 * i;
```

returning the compiler error message,

```
Incompatible type for declaration. Explicit cast
needed to convert int to short.
    short j = 2 * i;
              ^
```

It doesn't even help to cast that literal value to a short, like this:

```
short j = (short)2 * i;
```

because all operations on int or short values promote their results to type int. The entire result must be cast back to a short, if that's what's wanted, like this:

```
short j = (short)(2 * i);
```

Using a long anywhere in an expression will make the result a long: A numeric literal has this type if it ends with a letter L (or l, but this looks like a 1 in most fonts and really should not be used). An integer literal is assumed to be written in base 10 unless it begins with a 0 (indicating that the number is written in base 8) or a 0x (indicating base 16).

A floating-point literal will be of type float if it ends with f or F; a literal double can be tagged with a trailing d or D if one wishes to be explicit.

A Language Can Be Too Helpful

By requiring that data be declared, Java avoids a common problem in languages such as BASIC that aren't so formal. In BASIC, merely using a name automatically allocates the memory to hold that item's value.

This sounds very convenient, but a misspelled name won't set off any alarms. It will simply be treated as the name of a new piece of data. Mysterious problems ensue.

The author once had to break the bad news, for example, that another engineer's cost estimates during the prior year had been low by tens of millions of dollars, because that engineer had misspelled the name of a variable at a vital point in his program. This happened in the summary section of a BASIC program that calculated subsystem costs, then added up those numbers to get a grand total.

The misspelled name was treated as a new item, which BASIC silently gave a value of zero and added to the rest of the subtotals.

Oops.

That cost-estimating error might have been noticed more quickly if BASIC did not automatically initialize new variables. In the case of numbers, a newly named variable in BASIC gets the value 0 until that's changed by an assignment.

Some languages live at a different extreme of bad behavior. In these languages, declaring a variable without giving it a value just connects that variable name with a location in the computer's memory.

The contents of that memory are left as they were, containing whatever bits might have been stored there by some previous use of that space. In many cases, this produces unrepeatable behavior, an early clue that something's wrong.

But Java won't cause either of these problems. The Java compiler will refuse to compile code that uses a variable whose name and type have not been declared, and it will refuse to compile code that operates on a variable with no value—except, of course, for the operation of giving that variable an initial value, which is called *initialization* rather than assignment.

Initialization can take place in the declaration statement, as in:

```
int i = 72;
```

or it can take place at any later time, as in:

```
int i;
System.out.println("I'm doing things that don't use i");
i = 33;
```

Arrays of Options

Arrays, as you've seen in some previous examples, must also be declared. But an array is not a simple type whose size is always the same: an array can have any length. How is this handled?

Java actually allows two formats for declaring an array: For example, if we're declaring and initializing an array that can hold seven strings (like our `dailyNumbers` example in Chapter 4), we could say,

```
float dailyNumbers[] = new float[7];
```

or we could say

```
float[] dailyNumbers = new float[7];
```

There's a good argument for either format. The first format shows us `dailyNumbers[]` to help us remember that we'll always use this name with a *subscript* (a number inside the brackets, telling us which slot of the array we want to use).

The second format shows us `float[]` to help us remember that the type of the thing named `dailyNumbers` is array of `float`, rather than just plain `float`.

What do we mean when we say that `dailyNumbers` has the type *array of float*? Isn't `dailyNumbers` just a convenient way of referring to a set of related `float` values by similar names? Or is `dailyNumbers` some kind of object in its own right, with those numbered slots being just a part of its personality?

Let's use our versatile `println()` method to find out. Here's some code that we can use to investigate.

```
class AreArrays
{ public static void main(String args[])
  {
     int[] someInts = new int[3]; // [] in the type
     int moreInts[] = new int[7]; // [] in the name
     float[] someFloats;          // Not initialized
     byte andBytes[]= new byte[4];
  /* System.out.println(someFloats);
  If this weren't a comment, the compiler would abort
  since someFloats does not yet name anything
  */
     System.out.println(someInts);
     System.out.println(someInts[0]);
     System.out.println(andBytes);
     System.out.println(andBytes[3]);

  // System.out.println(someInts[-2]); // Not OK
  // System.out.println(someInts[3]);  // Likewise
```

```
    someFloats = new float[10]; // Now it has a value
    System.out.println(someFloats);
    System.out.println(someFloats[2]);
  }
}
```

The output from this program looks something like the following, with the hexadecimal values varying from one Java environment to another:

```
[I@4296f8   //array of ints
0                              //one slot of that array
[B@42cba0   //array of bytes
0                              //ditto
[F@42cd44   //array of floats
0                              //ditto
```

This is interesting. When we tell `println()` to show us an array, without asking for any one component of that array, we get a name that looks as if it's telling us what kind of compartments the array provides: I for `ints`, B for `bytes`, F for `floats`. When we look at the slots of that array, we see neatly initialized values.

Do some experiments with other data types: see what you get. Now try declaring an array name with one data type, then assigning that name an actual array (created, as shown above, using `new`) of some other type. What happens?

Bumping into Objects

We're getting our first taste of something tremendously important to Java: the fact that it is an object-oriented language.

Specifically, we're seeing that an array is an object. This means that it is a data structure that owns its own data, but operates on that data using methods that are defined for the entire family of similar objects.

An array like `someFloats` is a named thing: When we apply the postfixed operator, `[]`, to that named thing, with a number between those brackets, we cause that thing to look up one of its internal pieces of data and return that value.

Our array object knows what it is: If we try to create an actual array of non-`float` values, and stuff that array down the throat of the `someFloats` object, `someFloats` will reject it.

We can use other operators on an array: operators like the `.` operator, which lets us look up the components of an object or invoke its methods. Any array, for example, has a component variable named `length`, which we consulted in our extended `SayHello` example in Chapter 3, using the syntax `args.length` to determine the number of arguments that our program had received as runtime parameters.

So a Java array is more than just a convenient shorthand notation for referring to any one of a group of related values. This makes Java's arrays significantly different from those of, for example, C or C++.

To emphasize this, we'll use the format

```
<value type>[] <name> = new <value type>[<size>];
```

to declare and initialize our arrays from now on.

What about the Garbage?

If we say,

```
int[] changesSize = new int[5];
```

and then, later on, we say

```
changesSize = new int[7];
```

then what happens to the size-5 array of `int` that used to be connected to the `changesSize` name?

In a more labor-intensive language, we would have to keep track of when we were done with a piece of memory, and write statements telling the compiler that such memory could be reused. Errors in such statements are a major cause of program bugs.

Java, however, does something called *garbage collection*. This automatically recognizes chunks of memory that are no longer connected with any part of a program. Such memory is then returned to the pool that's available for other requirements.

An Array Knows Its Limits

If an array can tell us (in its `length` attribute) how many spaces it has, does it also pay attention to that limit? Is an array that smart? Or is it up to the programmer to check the size of an array before trying to fill it with a certain number of values?

Given Java's safety-first design, you can probably guess the answer. Specifically, if we ask an array to do something in a compartment, but we give a compartment number that's not valid for that particular array, Java will protect us. We won't just get whatever happens to be in the computer's memory, at the location where that compartment would have been if it existed.

Instead, we get a well-defined error behavior. That's part and parcel of the object-oriented philosophy.

An array will also size itself, if we tell it what to hold when we create it. We can initialize an array with a literal value when we declare it, for example, by writing

```
int[] smallOddNumbers = {1,3,5,7,9};
```

and get an array of int, with length 5, that contains these values.

Arrays of Arrays

What if we want to think in terms of an array that has more than one dimension? For example, we might want an array that corresponds to a chess board, letting us look at the square in a given column of a given row. A given compartment would hold the name of the piece (if any) that's sitting on a given square.

We can define something that works like an 8-by-8 array of chessboard squares with:

```
String[][] chessBoard = new String[8][8];
```

Note that we said this works *like* an 8-by-8 array. It isn't. It's an array of eight arrays, each of which has eight String components.

Does this difference make a difference? Yes, because this one-line declaration format (yielding a square or rectangular array) is merely a convenient shorthand for this:

```
String[][] chessBoard = new String[8][];
chessBoard[0] = new String[8];
chessBoard[1] = new String[8];
chessBoard[2] = new String[8];
chessBoard[3] = new String[8];
chessBoard[4] = new String[8];
chessBoard[5] = new String[8];
chessBoard[6] = new String[8];
chessBoard[7] = new String[8];
```

For a square or rectangular array, the one-line format makes our purpose clear and is easier to write. It should be apparent, however, that we can have something that acts like an array of any shape if we're willing to spell it out like this.

For example, suppose we want a triangular array: That is, one in which each row has one more column than the one before. We could do this with something like:

```
int[][] triArray = new int[100][];
triArray[0] = new int[1];
triArray[1] = new int[2];
triArray[2] = new int[3];
//...and so on through...
triArray[99] = new int[100];
```

If we have a table of values that's symmetric around its diagonal—for example, a table of the distances between cities, like the one found on many road maps—then we can cut our memory usage almost by half with this approach.

After all, if New York is city number 50, and Chicago is city number 17, then it's necessarily true that `distanceBetween[17][50]` == `distanceBetween[50][17]`. Why bother storing the upper-right half of the rectangle—that is, the part in which the column number is larger than the row number?

Our program can be written to accept a request that would fall in that region of a rectangular array, but to answer such a request from the mirror image location in the triangular array that we actually create.

This will make our triangular array "look" rectangular to the program that uses it as a source of data. This is an example of *encapsulation*, in the lingo of object-oriented programming, and we'll explore this at greater length in Chapters 8 through 10.

It would get pretty tedious to write code like the example above if we wanted a triangular array with dozens or hundreds of rows. But we can make Java do more of the work, more concisely for a large number of rows, with something like:

```
int triSize = 100;          // could be any int value
int[][] triArray = new int[triSize][];
for (int triRow=0; triRow < triArray.length; triRow++)
    triArray[triRow] = new int[triRow+1];
```

This is yet another example of the `for` statement that we'll explore in Chapter 7.

As with a one-dimensional array, we can also initialize an array of arrays with a literal statement of the contents, as in:

```
int[][] triArray = { { 0 },
                     { 3, 0 },
                     { 5, 42, 0 }
                   };
```

Stringing Along

Since we're talking about declaring data, we should consider the choice between different data types that can be used in similar ways. Specifically, this is a good time to note the many ways in which character strings are like arrays, and also the important ways in which they are different.

The character string is not a primitive data type in Java. This makes it unlike byte, boolean, char, and the longer types of number, and you'll note that in source code listings we do not give String the color that denotes a reserved word in the definition of the language. We give it, rather, the initial capital letter that denotes the name of a class.

The class String is defined in a *package* of standard classes (a concept that we'll discuss in Chapter 10) named java.lang, which we'll discuss in detail in Chapter 11. This package has the unique behavior of being automatically available to any Java program, without the explicit import statement that's normally required.

We can assume that class String is always available to our programs, and that we can create String objects and apply their vocabulary of methods whenever we like.

Like a simple data type or an array of a simple type, an instance of String must be declared. Most commonly, you'll see this done by assigning a literal string to an instance of the String class, as in:

```
String helloString = "Hello";
```

Now, this is a lot like saying

```
char[] helloArray = {'H', 'e', 'l', 'l', 'o'};
```

(This is only the second time that we've used char literals in an example, so we'll note again that they are delimited with single-quote marks (' ') instead of the regular quotation marks (" ") that surround a character string.)

We can ask either the string or the array to tell us its length: in this case, `helloString.length()` and `helloArray.length` both return the value 5.

Why are there parentheses in `helloString.length()`, but not in `helloArray.length`? Because `length()` is a method of the `String` class, but `length` is an instance variable of an array object.

An *instance variable* is a piece of data that's kept on hand by each instance of a class: for example, by each separate array that belongs to the class of all arrays.

An array has an unchanging length, determined when the array is created with `new` or when it is sized to match a literal array value that's supplied in an assignment expression. Each array's length is stored with its "personal effects," so to speak.

A *method* is a little piece of program that's defined for an entire class of objects, and that any object in that class can apply to itself on demand. As we'll learn in Chapters 8 through 10, it's impossible to tell from the outside whether a method is looking up a value that's already been supplied or computed, or performing that computation when that value is needed. A method can even do something really smart, like waiting until the first time that a value is requested to compute it and store it, and then simply looking it up on any subsequent request.

Is there any good reason why we should have to remember to apply the *component access* expression `.length` to an array, while applying the *method invocation* `.length()` to an instance of `String`? There doesn't seem to be any compelling rationale. It's the way that Java was defined.

There are other ways in which a `String` and a `char[]` are similar but not the same. We can ask either of these data structures to tell us what character is located in a particular position: strings, like arrays, start counting positions at zero, so `helloString.charAt(1)` and `helloArray[1]` each return the `char` `'e'`.

Note that `'e'` (a char) is not the same thing as `"e"` (a `String` of length 1).

Like an array, a `String` enforces its size. Like `helloArray[-1]` or `helloArray[7]`, a request for the value of `helloString.charAt(-3)` or `helloString.charAt(6)` will trigger Java's automatic safeguards (which we'll study in Chapter 11).

Don't Tangle My String

If a `String` and a `char[]` are so much alike, why define them as separate types of data? There are some vital differences in what we can do with each.

An instance of `String` cannot be changed after it's created. The `charAt()` method can only look at a position in a string, it cannot be used to assign a new `char` to that position.

By contrast, it's perfectly all right to say something like:

```
helloArray[0] = 'J';
```

to make `helloArray` now contain `{'J', 'e', 'l', 'l', 'o'}`.

Why are instances of `String` made impossible to change? Because this lets Java share a single physical string of `chars`, stored in the computer's memory, among more than one variable.

For example, if we have

```
String fourthOfJuly
        = "We hold these truths to be self-evident";
String fourthWord
        = "truths";
```

then it is possible for the Java system to connect the name, `fourthWord`, with the exact same bytes that already hold the `char` values `'t'` `'r'` `'u'` `'t'` `'h'` `'s'` in `fourthOfJuly`. This technique can reduce our need for memory.

If we could edit `fourthWord`, then `fourthOfJuly` would also be changed. For reasons of application robustness in general, and system security in particular, Java therefore makes `Strings` read-only.

Is there any way to turn the character string `Hello` into `Jello`? Yes, in fact there's more than one way to do this.

We can assemble a new character string, keeping what we want from the old one:

```
helloString = "J" + helloString.substring(1,5);
```

where the first parameter to the `substring()` method is the first position that we want (start counting at zero!), and the second parameter is the position after the last one that we want.

Think of `substring(p,q)` as saying, "Starting at position p, up to but not including position q." If this seems a strange way of doing things, just notice that the length of the substring is the second value minus the first value.

We could also turn `helloString` into a `char[]` (an array of characters), modify one slot in that array, and turn the array back to a string:

```
char[] makeJello = helloString.toCharArray();
makeJello[0] = 'J';
helloString = String.valueOf(makeJello);
```

where the `valueOf()` method of the `String` class is smart enough to take an array of `char` as an argument and produce a matching instance of `String`. (If that temporary array, `makeJello[]`, is locally defined, then Java will be able to garbage-collect it later.)

The third way to make `Hello` into `Jello` is to use the class `StringBuffer`. This defines a data structure that can be used to assemble and edit strings, using a large vocabulary of available methods and automatic behaviors.

You probably won't bother with a `StringBuffer` unless complex string manipulations are a major part of your program's total workload. For the first time in this book, therefore, we're going to say that something in Java is beyond the scope of what we'll cover.

If you want to go farther with this, a reference book for experienced programmers (like Ken Arnold and James Gosling's *The Java Programming Language*) can take you to the next level.

For now, however, this is all we'll say about declarations and various data structures until we get deeper into object-oriented topics later in the book.

Summary

In this chapter, we showed

▶ That tiny details of punctuation can affect a program's behavior.

▶ That Java's declaration rules and array behaviors protect against common kinds of programmer error.

▶ That automatic type conversions may require adjustments to produce results of desired types.

▶ That arrays of arrays offer flexibility in grouping data.

▶ That arrays of characters and strings of characters differ in the details of what they can do, despite their similar overall functions.

Chapter 7
Express Yourself: Using Statements

In this chapter, you'll learn how Java's conditional statements express a program's logic. You'll also learn how statements can choose between alternative actions, and how statements can combine several actions. We'll then cover how statements can interrupt a process and reevaluate their options.

In Chapter 6, we looked primarily at declarations. These set the stage for the performance of our program, but they don't offer much in the way of a plot. It's time to raise the curtain and say, "Action!"

The simplest kind of active statement is an *expression statement*. We've used many of these in examples so far. There are two kinds of expression statements: assignments and increment/decrements.

The fragment:

```
int i;
int j;
i = 5;
j = 6;
```

consists of four statements: two declarations and two initial assignments *(initializations)*.

A statement can also be formed from an *active assignment* expression, simply by adding a statement-ending semicolon at the end:

```
i += j;
```

which in this case leaves i with the value 11.

Increments were explained in the table near the beginning of Chapter 5. Continuing the example above,

```
j++;
```

is a complete statement that changes the value of j to 7. In this case, it makes no difference whether we say j++ (postincrement) or ++j (preincrement), since we're not doing anything with the returned value from the assignment operation. Only the side effect matters. In "don't care" cases like this, it is more common to write j++.

Likewise for the decrementing operators, the postfix and prefix −. The statements,

```
p−;
```

and

```
−p;
```

are also complete statements that produce identical side effects, in this case leaving the value of p reduced by 1.

That's a Big If

Many other statement forms change the path that will be followed through a program. This "decision making" power of programs is easy to overestimate: It does a poor job, for example, of handling completely unforeseen situations, as when a medical diagnosis program was given a description of a rusty car and diagnosed measles. But the power of programmed *branching* and *looping* accounts for much of computers' value in our lives.

We've seen the simplest *flow control* statement, the if, in an earlier example:

```
if (turnBulbOn) return "XXX";
else return "--";
```

An if statement follows its opening keyword with a parenthesized expression that returns a boolean value, followed by a statement or a block of statements, optionally followed by the keyword else and another statement or block of statements.

Around the Block

What is a *block*? A block is what we're creating when we use those { } symbols, which may have seemed like arbitrary decorations in some of our earlier sample programs. (They are also used to delimit a literal array, but you won't have any trouble figuring out which is meant.)

A block can be used anywhere that Java normally expects a single statement. For example, we might have a simple if...else statement that looks like:

```
if (earnings >= 0)
    System.out.println ("Earnings were $" + earnings);
else
    System.out.println ("Losses were $" + -earnings);
```

But we might want to do something more involved, like changing the color of the output as well. We can do this by using blocks, as in:

```
if (earnings >= 0)
  { textColor = black; // assuming this does something
    System.out.println ("Earnings were $" + earnings);
  }
else
  { textColor = red;
    System.out.println ("Losses were $" + -earnings);
                        // a "unary -" ^ operator

  }
```

Programmers often get in trouble when they try to deal with combinations of conditions, using nested if and if...else statements. Java, and other languages that also use this kind of statement, is rigidly logical: Remember, Java does not define DWIM(), and Java doesn't care how a program is laid out on the page. What you mean doesn't matter. The compiler only sees what you type.

In the case of nested if statements, the rule is simple. *Unless* separated by block delimiters (the braces that we encountered above), an else always goes with the most recent, previous if.

For example, you might write a piece of code like this:

```
if (monthsExperience < 12)
  if (salesVolume > salesQuota)
      System.out.println("Great rookie year!");
else
  if (salesVolume < salesQuota)
      System.out.println("Your job is on the line");
```

The intent is clear from the way this code is indented. This fragment is meant to give extra encouragement to a new employee with better-than-expected performance, and to give an under-quota warning only to a more experienced employee.

But that's not what's going to happen. Indentation doesn't change a thing as far as the compiler is concerned. What the compiler sees is logically the same as:

```
if (monthsExperience < 12)
  if (salesVolume > salesQuota)
      System.out.println("Great rookie year!");
  else
    if (salesVolume < salesQuota)
        System.out.println("Your job is on the line");
```

This code will praise or warn a rookie, while completely ignoring anyone who's been with the company for a year or more.

This problem can be solved by using blocks:

```
if (monthsExperience < 12)
  { if (salesVolume > salesQuota)
        System.out.println("Great rookie year!");
  }
else
  { if (salesVolume < salesQuota)
        System.out.println("Your job is on the line");
  }
```

In this case, the second block isn't actually needed, but it aids the readability of the code. Why make the human reader think, for even a moment, about the rules of the language when two little braces create a clearly parallel construction?

The Big Switch

Nesting if...else statements is clumsy and verbose when there are many possible cases. For better readability, you can use a switch statement, as in a railroad switch that lets a train follow any of several tracks.

A switch follows its opening keyword with some parenthesized expression that evaluates to an integer. This is followed by a block of statements that are each labeled with the keyword case, followed by an integer value and a colon (:).

Those label values must be *constants*, not variables. The code that makes the switch statement choose a branch is "locked down" during compilation, not computed on the fly.

This means that the label for each case must be either a literal value, like 3 or 'G', or a static final value. A static variable belongs to a class, rather than being copied in each instance of that class, and if it is altered by any instance, it is altered for all; a static final value cannot be altered, and therefore serves as a fixed constant for all "descendant" code. (Java reserves the word const, used to declare a constant in C++, but does not use it in the current version of the language.)

For example, in Chapter 14, we'll see a switch used to control the sending of data packets across the Internet or to another process on the same machine. To make the intent of the code clear, we'll give names to the values that are used as labels in that switch, making them static final values so that the compiler will accept them as constants.

In abbreviated form, this will look something like,

```
class Sender
  { static final int SEND_ON_NEW_LINE = '\n';
    public static void main(String args[])
      { // set up communication link
        switch (nextByte)
          { case SEND_ON_NEW_LINE: //handle this special case
            // otherwise, do the normal thing
          }
      }
  }
```

The switch looks for a label whose constant integer value matches that of the opening test expression, and starts executing at the first matching label that it finds.

If no label matches, the switch does nothing at all, and the program just goes on with the next statement after the end of the block of labeled statements.

For example, we can simulate a user making a numbered choice from a menu, with a program handling that choice, like this:

```
class MakeChoice
  { public static void main(String args[])
      { System.out.println(choiceOf(2)); }
    public static String choiceOf(int theChoice)
      { switch(theChoice)
          { case 1: return oneReply();
            case 2: return twoReply();
          }
        return ""; // to keep the compiler happy
      }
    public static String oneReply()
```

```
         { return "One"; }
      public static String twoReply()
         { return "Two"; }
   }
```

This is not a very reliable piece of code: If the user accidentally enters a 3, then the program will ignore the choice entirely and go on to the next statement.

This is why we had to include that statement,

```
    return "";
```

Without it, the compiler would not be able to guarantee that the method `choiceOf` will return a `String`, as its declaration promises to do.

You can make your code more robust with a `default` case, like this:

```
    { switch(theChoice)
         { case 1:   return oneReply();
           case 2:   return twoReply();
           default: return "Try again";
         }
      // return ""; // This is no longer needed
    }
```

There can only be one `default` case, but it need not be the last one listed.

I Shall Return

We have seen several examples, like the one just above, where a piece of code said `return` with some following expression. Exactly what does this mean?

Look again at our `bulbDisplay` example:

```
    public static String bulbDisplay(boolean turnBulbOn)
      { if (turnBulbOn) return "XXX";
        else return "---";
      }
```

The first line of this method promises that it will `return` an instance of `String`. There is a simple `if` statement that looks at the `boolean` value that was given to `bulbDisplay`, and depending on that value chooses to return either one string or another.

That's what `return` does: It tells a piece of a program to stop work and to return whatever was promised to the place where that piece of the program was invoked.

 A `default` case is commonly used to do something called throwing an exception, which we'll talk about in Chapter 11. In the meantime, just note that `throw` is another type of statement that makes us leave the method we're in.

Free Fall

In our `switch` example above, each `case` invoked a `return`. Will we always do this? No.

Consider this example, assuming that we have previously declared the `static final` values `FRESH=1`, `COLD=2`, and `FROZEN=3`. (It is a convention to name `static final` values in capitals as a reminder of their unalterable nature.)

```
switch ( foodState )
  { case FROZEN: moveFromFreezerToFridgeDayBefore();
    case COLD:   removeFromFridgeHourBefore();
    case FRESH:  cookAndEat();
    default:     goOutToEat();
  }
```

If `frozenFood` matches—that is, if `( foodState==3)==true`—then execution will start within the `switch` with the method for getting the food out of the freezer.

After this is done, the program will *fall through* to the method for taking the food out of the refrigerator, following this with the method for fixing dinner.

If the food was cold, but not frozen, then the first method call will be skipped, but the rest of the process will still be carried out. If the food was fresh, only the third case clause will be applied.

But this `switch` has a bug. Do you see it?

As written, this fragment sends us out to eat every time, not just when our `foodState` fails to match an expected value. We need something, other than a `return`, to tell Java we're done with a case and that we *don't* want to fall through to the next one.

That needed statement is called a `break`, and the end of our fragment above should look instead like:

```
case freshFood: cookAndEat();
                break;
default:        goOutToEat();
```

It's a common error to forget a needed `break` and to write a `switch` that falls through when that was not intended. Most programmers consider it good style to use a comment when a fall-through behavior is actually desired, something like:

```
switch ( foodState )
 { case FROZEN: moveFromFreezerToFridgeDayBefore();
             // FALL THROUGH
   case COLD:  removeFromFridgeHourBefore();
             // FALL THROUGH
   case FRESH: cookAndEat();
               break;
   default:    goOutToEat();
 }
```

There is one situation, however, where it's both concise and clear to omit any fall-through comment. This is when there are several `case`s that all need identical handling, as in:

```
switch (someKindOfSmallNumber)
 { case 2: case 3:
   case 5: case 7: return primeNumberResponse();
   case 4: case 9: return perfectSquareResponse();
   case 8:         return perfectCubeResponse();
   default:        return boringNumberResponse();
 }
```

Does the last statement in the block within a `switch` need to have an explicit `break`, `return`, or `throw`? No.

Should you write one anyway? Yes.

Why? Because you or someone else might add a `case` at the end of the block, weeks or months after the program first went into use. You might forget to add the now-needed `break` to what was formerly the final `case`. You would then have a fall-through situation that you didn't mean to create.

This can easily happen if the handlers for your cases become more involved than the simple examples used here. The end of the old final `case` may not be on your source code screen when you finish writing the new one.

If the old final `case` was rarely used, then it might be a long time before you discovered this error in the modified program.

Be warned: At least one Java reference book says that a `break` can be used to exit any block. But three Java compilers tested by the author refused to accept a `break` from anything but a loop or a `switch`, and said so—specifically—in their error messages when a piece of Java code tried to use `break` anywhere else.

This just serves as a fresh proof of something that's been said before about other programming languages: Ultimately, the definition of a programming language is what the compiler will accept.

While Away the Hours

The sample programs that we've looked at so far only run when they're told to run. But Java is meant to be used, not only in computers with interactive users but also in automatic devices.

It's common for such a device to run, unattended, for hours or days, twiddling its bits while it waits for something to happen. Think of a thermostat, waiting for the temperature to drop so it can have its moment of glory by turning on the furnace...and waiting for the temperature to rise, so it can feel useful again by turning it off.

The control structures that we need for situations like this are the `while` and the `do...while`. Each is a type of loop, but they differ in when we decide we're going around again.

A `while` statement checks a `boolean` value (usually produced by some kind of test expression, based on values that are altered inside the loop). If the `boolean` is `true`, the statement or block of statements after the test expression are executed. This process repeats until the `boolean` is found to be `false`.

For example,

```
while (foodOn(thisDish) > canHandle(ourDishWasher))
 { scrape(thisDish);
  }
putInDishwasher(thisDish);
```

This example didn't really need a block, but we used one as a reminder that a body with more than one statement will need those braces around it.

Sometimes, we know that we need to do something at least once, but we don't know how many additional repetitions will be needed.

For example,

```
do
    { aPlate = getPlate();
      set( aPlate );
      placesSet++
      someSilver = getSilver();
      set( someSilver );
      }
while (peopleEating > placesSet);
```

Please Continue

What if we're part way through the body of a loop, such as a `while` or a `do…while`, and we decide that the rest of the body doesn't apply this time? We don't want to `break` out of the loop, we just want to go straight to the test to find out if we need to go around again.

This is a common problem that some languages solve with an arbitrary jump instruction, often called a *go to*. But the go to statement makes it easy to write code whose structure becomes quite hard to understand, and most modern languages omit this statement by choice.

Just to make its intentions crystal clear, Java reserves the keyword `goto` (no space) even though it's not assigned any function. Java doesn't use it, and neither can you.

Instead, modern programming languages provide statement types that can transfer control, not just anywhere, but *only* to a boundary of a block or loop or other definite structure. Within a `while` loop, we can do this with a `continue`.

For example,

```
do
    { aPlate = getPlate();
      set( aPlate );
      placesSet++
      if (fingerFood(theMenu)) continue;
      someSilver = getSilver();
      set( someSilver );
      }
while (peopleEating > placesSet);
```

And What's This, "For"?

What if we're in a set of nested loops, and we want to jump out of more than one level? We could write cumbersome code that sets up some kind of signal at the level we want to leave, and check that signal at each enclosing level until we get back out to where we wanted to go.

We'll do better work in less time if we use a much simpler Java facility, the labeled `continue`.

For example,

```
setFlowers: // the label ends with a colon
    do { aVase = getVase();
        set( aVase, nearestTable() );
        do { aFlower = chooseFlower();
            arrange( aFlower, aVase );
            if ( shortOfFlowers() | shortOfTime() )
              continue setFlowers;    // skip…
          }
        while !fullEnough( aVase );
      }
    while (!allFlowered( allTables ));// …to the while
                        // that matches the labeled do
```

If we don't even want to make the `while` test at the end of the loop, we can leave the loop entirely with a `break` or a labeled `break`. In fact, we can use a `break` or a labeled `break` to leave any nested combination of loop and/or `switch` statements in a clearly structured way.

And What's This "For"?

The last flow-control statement that we'll look at here is the first one that we used in a sample program: the `for` statement.

When you first see this, it looks pretty cryptic. It appears so often, though, that you'll quickly start to understand such statements at a glance.

A `for` statement has four possible parts.

▶ Part 1: One or more statements, separated (if more than one) by commas, performed before the first pass through the loop. Usually, this part contains a single statement that sets up a condition that we'll test in Part 2 to see if the loop has finished its job.

▶ Part 2: An expression that returns a `boolean` `true` or `false` result. This expression will be checked before each pass through the loop, including the first pass. If the expression's value is `false`, the program goes on to whatever comes after the `for`.

▶ Part 3: Statement(s) to execute at the end of the first pass through the loop, and at the end of every additional pass. Usually, this part is evaluated for its side effects, changing something that's involved in the test of Part 2. It's common for this part to move us, in some way, closer to the condition that makes Part 2 return a `false` to end the loop.

▶ Part 4: A body statement (or block of statements) that gets executed every time we go through the loop.

For example, as we've seen before,

```
for (int i = 0; i < 3; i++)
  System.out.println(i);
```

prints

```
0
1
2
```

This `for` has all four parts:
Part 1: `int i = 0;` declares and initializes i.
Part 2: `i < 3;` returns `false` when we're done.
Part 3: `i++` increments i after each pass.
Part 4: `System.out.println(i);` does something useful during each pass.
All four parts are optional. For example, it's legal Java to write

```
int i = 0;
for (; i < 3; i++)
  System.out.println(i);
```

with exactly the same effect, though less clarity. The first semicolon inside the parentheses is like saying, "This space intentionally left blank."
You could also write

```
for (int i = 0; i++ < 3;)
  System.out.println(i);
```

In this version, it's the "update" part of the loop that's been left empty, as marked by that last semicolon after i++ < 3.

If there's no update part, then what gets us out of the loop? This time, we're using the full behavior of the postincrement ++ operator. It gives us the current value of the variable i, which we use in our end-of-loop test by comparing it against 3; it also increases the value of i by 1 before the program moves on.

Does this version of this loop do the same thing as the version before? No, because the test part of the for is performed the first time through the loop, as well as all the subsequent times. Before, we incremented our counter in the update part of the loop, which didn't get applied until the end of each pass through the body.

In this latest version of our loop, i gets increased by 1 before the first time that we go through the body of the loop, and it gets raised to 3 after it passes the loop-end test (2 < 3) but before it gets printed for the last time. So now the output is

```
1
2
3
```

Do you think you understand the difference between i++ and ++i? What does the following code do?

```
for (int i = 0; ++i < 3;)
    System.out.println(i);
```

Don't go on until you understand why this produces yet another different result.

By the way, this use of side effects in a for's test expression is not considered good programming style. We're only doing this to establish exactly how for works.

Comparing this kind of code to good programming style is like comparing what you do with a car on a test track to the way you drive through a residential neighborhood. The vehicle *can* do a lot of things that a well-behaved driver *won't* do when other people are around.

With that warning, we'll note that it's also legal to write

```
int i = 0;
for (;; i++)
  { if ( !( i < 3 ) ) break;
    System.out.println(i);
  }
```

In this case, the `boolean` test is an empty statement, which is treated as a `true`. We placed the test of when to leave the loop inside the body, and used a `break` to get us out when that test failed.

It's even legal to write

```
int i = 0;
for (;;)
  { if ( !( i < 3) ) break;
    System.out.println(i);
    i++;
  }
```

But at this point, why bother with a `for` statement at all? We could just as easily write,

```
int i = 0;
while (true)
  { if ( !( i < 3) ) break;
    System.out.println(i);
    i++;
  }
```

or, still more concisely,

```
int i=0;
while(i < 3)
  {System.out.println(i++);}
```

There are two differences, though, between writing a loop as a `for` and writing it as an equivalent `while`.

First, a `while` has no means for declaring loop-control variable(s) locally to the loop, as we've seen we can do with a `for`. We may wind up with variables hanging around after their purpose has ended.

Second, if we have a `continue` inside a `while`, it skips the *entire* remaining body of that loop and goes straight to the continuation test. In a `for`, Part 3 (in this case, corresponding to the `i++` above) will always be performed, even if a `continue` statement is executed in Part 4. It pays to understand these differences.

Don't Take It "For" Granted

These details aside, though, it should be clear that the `for` statement is, in most cases, just a useful shorthand for something that we can easily create using other flow control statements like `while`. But give this statement the respect it deserves: The `for` loop is much more powerful than similar-looking things in other languages, such as the FOR...NEXT loop in BASIC.

Simple looping statements in many languages can only assign a starting value, an ending value, and a step by which to change the value until the ending value is reached. Java's `for` is much more general.

For example, `for` can work with more than one loop variable at once, and it can change each variable's value on each pass through the loop by operations other than just adding some fixed-size step:

```
for (int i=1,j=3; i*j<100; i+=1,j*=2)
   System.out.println("i is "+i+", j is "+j+".");
```

See what this does. See if you can write the same thing as two nested `for` loops, each using one of these two variables as its loop-control variable. Which style do you prefer?

Summary

In this chapter, we showed

- ▶ That the Java compiler interprets our programs by rigid rules, not by indentation and other visual cues.

- ▶ That `switch` statements, often used to make choices, can also produce cascading actions— sometimes by accident.

- ▶ That logically equivalent programs can be written in different styles, some of which are much more clear than others.

- ▶ That the Java `for` statement offers flexible but potentially confusing power.

Recap

With this chapter, we have finished laying the foundations that Java has in common with almost every other programming language.

In Chapter 4, we learned how Java represents things like numbers, words, and other kinds of information. If our programming language doesn't make these basic tasks easy, we'll spend far too much time thinking about bits, instead of thinking about the facts and fantasies that our program needs to know and manipulate.

In Chapter 5, we learned about the operators that Java provides for doing things with and to our data. If our language has a limited number of operators, we spend too much time thinking about how to make something happen, instead of thinking about what that something should be.

In Chapter 6, we learned how to tell Java what we plan to do with data, giving Java the facts it needs to detect and prevent many common errors. In Chapter 7, we learned how to tell Java to do the kinds of things that make computer-based devices so useful: Things like taking notice of many facts at once, and performing comparisons and calculations that result in different actions under different conditions.

It's possible to do useful things with a computer, without any of the help that we get from a language like Java. But it requires meticulous, error-prone construction of baby-step chains of hardware-level operations performed on eye-crossing strings of bits. And moving that program to another kind of computer means doing the whole thing over.

A modern language like Java makes us more productive, giving us the time and energy to be more creative, and leaving us free to use different types of hardware as computer vendors continue to outdo each other in offering smaller, faster, cheaper machines year after year.

Now we're ready to see, more fully, what it means to say that Java is an *object-oriented* language. We've already seen some of the things that we get from this aspect of Java's design: The ability, for example, to rely on the error-preventing behaviors of the `String` class and the array.

From here on, the strengths of Java will be exploited by using predefined classes and defining new classes of our own. We will create objects that use the facilities of their own class and the "ancestors" of that class; we will accomplish things by telling our objects to send each other messages, asking each other to get something done—without saying how to do it.

That's what makes us free to send our Java programs into the world of the Net, trusting them to find a way to do what they're supposed to do. It's what lets us use programs created by others without full knowledge of those programs' internal details.

More than anything else, it's object orientation that makes Java a creative tool—not just another geeky way of telling a computer what to do.

Chapter 8
Family Affairs: What We Get from Object Orientation

In this chapter, you'll learn how objects help us model real-world systems' structure and behavior and how Java helps us avoid the earlier programming practices that invited confusion and errors. You'll also see how classes help us represent both group and individual characteristics of objects and how an object's state can be used to control its behavior.

With this chapter, we cross a crucial dividing line. That line is the boundary between programs as a tool for manipulating a computer, and programs as a tool for modeling both real and imaginary worlds.

Before this point, we were using Java to hide the finite complexity of the machine. Like any good programming language, Java does this quite well. We've jumped right over the baby-step technique of loading binary values, one at a time, and performing primitive operations upon those values, one at a time, by learning instead to write expressions like:

```
System.out.println("The average for the week was "
                    + String.valueOf(sumOfNumbers/7));
```

It would be truly painful to program this kind of thing at the level of Java byte-codes or native hardware instructions.

Early programming tools weren't very far above that machine-code level, where every word of descriptive output required a lot of programmer effort. This led to unfriendly programs that restricted users to rigid procedures, and were all too ready to make the user start over or to return misleading results.

Therefore, even if Java did nothing more than provide this higher level of expression, it would still be a useful invention. But it wouldn't be much more useful than C or other aging languages.

Time to Look Outside

For hobbyists, of course, the sense of mastery that comes with machine-level programming is almost the point of the entire process. The retail success of products like Borland's original Turbo C can hardly be explained in any other way.

But most software is ultimately used by paying customers: that is, by the customers of someone who pays someone else (like you) to write a custom program. Those end users, in general, aren't interested in computers: They're interested in airplane reservations, multiplayer games, or the location and business hours of the nearest store with metric-size spark plugs.

After this point, therefore, we'll take for granted Java's ability to hide the details of what's happening inside the computer. We'll use that ability in Chapter 11 to do things like convert values from one type to another and to divide the computer's attention between several concurrent activities; in Chapter 12, we'll use it to let programs do input and output without concern for the specific devices involved; in Chapter 13, we'll use it to access real-time data like the current date and time.

But we also want to deal with the world outside the machine. In Chapter 14, we'll want to communicate across networks as easily as we work with local files; in Chapter 15, we'll want to draw a graphical user interface that arranges its components to fit a resized window; in Chapter 16, we'll want to wrap our masterpiece in a Web page that can be seen and used from anywhere in the world. We have to learn the techniques by which we can confront, and conquer, that outside world's complexity.

How to Build a World

So far, we've been writing programs that look like a hybrid of English-language instructions and mathematical expressions. We've become proficient in using Java's versatile but tiny variety of simple data types (like `boolean`, `int`, and `double`) and its simplest predefined classes (like `String`).

We've used names for our variables and our methods that were tied to the purposes of our programs, but this is like choosing the piece that you'll use when you're playing a game of Monopoly: the game is the same, whether you're moving the Ship or the Thimble. There are only so many ideas that you can represent with a `byte`, a `float`, or a `long`.

From now on, we won't limit ourselves to the generic "game board" of data types and operations that are predefined by Java. Instead, we'll design a board and write a set of rules that match the problem we want to solve.

We'll define *classes* that describe the kinds of things that live in the space of our problem. We'll create objects that *instantiate* those class definitions. Those objects will vary in their individual characteristics, in the way that an adult male lion differs from a cub, but they will respond to the same kinds of stimulation from the other objects around them.

When we take this approach, our programs will look less like recipes and more like screenplays. Instead of mixing a pinch of bytes with an array of strings, we'll be writing stage directions and dialogue for our own exciting plots.

The formal name for this approach is *object-oriented programming*.

Anatomy of an Object

In Chapter 3, we examined the anatomy of a program. We looked at the simplest program that can be written in Java, the one that says "Hello." Even this program required us to define a class: that is, a family of potential objects.

What is an object? It combines two things:

▶ A state of being, specific to that individual object.

▶ A set of behaviors, common to all the objects of that class.

Java has no way of talking about anything that isn't "owned" by some object or class. This makes Java different from some other languages, such as C++, that also fly the flag of object orientation.

Languages like C++ make objects available, as an aid to dealing with complexity, but they do not require all programs to work within those object-oriented rules.

The Hybrid Way Is the Hard Way

This hybrid approach demands that a C++ programmer manage abstract models of real-world or imaginary objects, while thinking at the same time about the "natural" data type sizes on a particular kind of computer hardware.

It demands that a C++ compiler enforce the limits on what one object can ask another object to do, but it forbids that compiler from assuming that any location in memory is safe from arbitrary changes made by some other part of a program.

It sounds self-contradictory. It is.

Java doesn't have this kind of identity crisis. Earlier styles of programming are literally unmentionable in Java. Every element of every Java program is subject to the discipline of object-oriented methods.

King of Bits?

Let's explore the benefits of an object-oriented approach, using our animal analogy from Chapter 3. Let's look in more depth at lions.

A given lion has individual attributes, such as its weight, age, and gender. It also has leonine behaviors, shared with other lions, like hunting and roaring.

One lion may roar more loudly or hunt more vigorously than another. It's reasonable, though, to ask any particular lion to do either of these things as well as it can.

In object terms, we say that we expect a lion object to offer *public methods*—that is, methods that can be invoked by another object—for "hunt" and "roar." We would not expect a lion to offer methods for "fly" or "talk."

If we want to represent the knowledge of lions that we have described so far, using an object-oriented language, we can do that. We can begin by defining class `Lion`, with *instance variables* `weight`, `age`, and `gender`.

Instance variables are pieces of data that can have a different value in each instance of a class, because each instance carries those values within itself.

Our class should also provide appropriate public methods, like `hunt()` and `roar()`. These are defined for the class, not for the instance of the class, but these methods still have an intimate relationship with the instance values: When we invoke a method on an instance, the method can use the values that are owned by that instance to decide what the method will do.

These decisions are made by branching operators and statements, such as the `?:` operator and the `if` and `switch` statements that we learned to use in Chapters 5 through 7.

For example, if we invoke the `roar()` method of the Lion class on a lion object whose age is just a few months, a well-designed `roar()` will take note of that age and produce an appropriate sound. Invoking that same method on a four-year-old male will yield a rather different result. We'll see how to do this later in this chapter.

Note also that methods may cause an object to do something, or they may cause something to be done to an object. The lion may roar, or the lion may be caused to die.

Why Life Was Hard before Objects

How does the object approach differ from earlier styles of programming? If we didn't have object-oriented methods and tools, we might decide to represent our population of lions as a group of three arrays of values.

(This is, we must admit, a worst-case scenario: Languages like C and Pascal define more sophisticated data structures like struct and record, respectively, but these still lack many of the protections provided by object techniques.)

We might have an array of `float`s, each representing one lion's age; another array of `int`s, each representing one lion's weight; and a third array of `boolean`s, each representing one lion's gender, using a convention such as `true` for males and `false` for females.

What we know about "lion #4," for instance, would be the combination of `lionAge[3]`, `lionWeight[3]`, and `lionGender[3]`. Our knowledge of "lion #12" would be `lionAge[11]`, `lionWeight[11]`, and `lionGender[11]`. And so on.

If we wanted to go beyond data and bring our world to life, we'd have to write some *procedures.*

We might write a procedure called `createLion` that checked to see how many lions already lived in our electronic world: That is, how many compartments in each of our three arrays had already been filled with values.

The `createLion` procedure would need to be told the age, weight, and gender of our new lion, and it would store those values in a matching set of slots in our arrays.

A `makeLionRoar` procedure would determine the age and gender of a lion and would make the appropriate noise. A `makeLionHunt` procedure would determine the hunting ability of a given lion and perform the appropriate action.

This can be done. It can even be done right. It's just a lot harder than it would be if we were using object techniques.

When Your Act Is Not Together

Without objects, programming is hard because we wind up with widely scattered knowledge. In this case, we've built ourselves three separate data structures, each of which has a role in representing any one lion.

This arrangement has to be reflected, and respected, in every procedure that deals with our lions. The `createLion` procedure, for example, has to know about all three data structures. It has to know what type of data is used by each; it has to know, and enforce, the convention that the same index number is used in each array to refer to any given lion.

For example, `createLion` has to know that `lionAge[7]`, `lionWeight[7]`, and `lionGender[7]` are all characteristics of one lion.

Suppose that another member of our programming team decides that we need a procedure to make a lion die if its weight falls below a minimum value. That minimum weight would vary with age, using a formula based on whatever research we had done. Adding this behavior to our system would make it a more faithful model of the real world, which is generally a good thing.

But suppose that our coworker forgot about the `lionGender` array, since he was only thinking about weight and age as the variables that matter in deciding if a lion dies of starvation. He might write a `lionStarves` procedure that deleted the entries for a dead lion's weight and age, but that left behind its gender as an entry in that overlooked array.

What if our `createLion` procedure looked at the `lionGender` array to see how many lions were alive? Our procedures would assume that our three arrays were consistent with each other, so any given procedure might use any of the arrays to determine how many lions were around.

We'd wind up with an interesting world: One where a lion could starve to death (and be removed from two of our arrays), but still be counted in our population of lions (determined by looking at the third).

That "ghost lion" would even have a gender: A subsequent procedure, `lionReproduces`, might wind up putting the children of this ghost into estimates of the future population.

We haven't gone very far with this example, but already we can see why programming without objects is a delicate process. When data structures aren't connected to each other, in ways that reflect the programmer's intentions, inconsistencies are easy to create and hard to detect.

It's been said that without a fully object-oriented language, "software" is a contradiction in terms. This is because your program, as soon as it reaches non-trivial size, becomes extremely difficult to change without unpredictable effects on other parts of the system. "Your software is no longer 'soft' and malleable: it's more like quick-setting cement," wrote three critics of C++ (who share this author's opinion of its flaws).

Before you've finished thinking out your approach to the problem, your early ideas will already be frozen into data structures and program fragments that interact in complex ways. You will have no sure way of finding all the interactions without an error-prone, line-by-line review.

Now, let's take an object-oriented approach to lions and see how objects not only make it safe to improve a system, they make it positively inviting.

What Do You Know?

In Chapter 3 through Chapter 7, our example programs used a minimal wrapping of a class definition around one or more methods. We've gotten used to seeing a piece of code that looks like,

```
class SomeClassName
 { public static void main(String args[])
   { // some statements;
    }
  public <data type> aMethod(<argument names>)
```

```
         { // some statements;
          }
         public <data type> anotherMethod(<argument names>)
          { // some statements;
          }
         // et cetera
     }
```

A class like this can *do* things, as described by its methods, but it doesn't *know* anything—that is, there are no attributes that can have different values in one instance versus another.

Let There Be Life

Let's move on to the next step. Let's define a lion.

```
    class Lion { }
```

This isn't a very complete definition, but it will compile. It's a start.

Do notice the Java convention that class names begin with an uppercase letter, while method names and variables begin with lowercase letters. This is a good habit to develop. We never want to get confused about the difference between a group (a class) and a member of that group (an instance).

To make this clear, let's look at the simplest program that uses our new class:

```
    class Jungle
     { public static void main(String args[])
       { Lion myLion = new Lion();
         System.out.println(myLion);
       }
     }
```

If these classes, Lion and Jungle, are both defined in file Lion.java, then we can compile the whole file with a command like `javac Lion.java`. This will produce two output files, `Lion.class` and `Jungle.class`.

When we give the command `java Jungle`, the `Lion.class` file will be loaded when it's needed. The output from running `java Jungle` will look something like:

```
    Lion@13937d8
```

We can see from this that Java knows that `myLion` is a `Lion`. As we said, it's a start.

Go to the Head of the Class

How do you decide what classes you need when you set out to solve a problem? The usual rule of thumb is "look for the nouns." Things like Customer, Molecule, and Lion make good classes.

To define a less trivial lion, let's expand on that empty definition above. Let's start by saying what we expect to know about any given lion.

```
class Lion
  { float age;
    int weight;
    boolean isMale; // This name helps us remember
                    // what's meant by "true"
  }
```

Now we can make a lion that knows these things about itself:

```
class Jungle
 { public static void main(String args[])
    { Lion myLion = new Lion();
      myLion.age = 4;
      myLion.isMale = true;
      System.out.println(myLion);
      System.out.println(myLion.age);
      System.out.println(myLion.weight); // Oh?
      System.out.println(myLion.isMale);
    }
  }
```

This gives the output,

```
Lion@429c84
4
0
true
```

Note that we did *not* specify the value of myLion.weight, but we did *not* get an error message complaining about an unintialized variable. Having told Java nothing about how to make a lion, we got what's called a *default no-arg constructor*.

This is a method whose name is the name of its class: This makes it conspicuous because, unlike most method names, it starts with a capital letter.

With a constructor, we use a new operator called `new`. Applying this operator to a constructor method call returns, in this case, an instance of `Lion` with default values for all of its instance variables. These values will be zero for numbers and `false` for `boolean`s.

We'll do much more with constructors in Chapter 10.

Method Acting

This kind of Lion knows things about itself, but it doesn't know how to do anything. The class defines instance variables, but no methods.

How do you decide what methods you need? The usual rule of thumb is "look for the verbs." Activities like invoicing a Customer, ionizing a Molecule, and making a Lion roar make good methods.

In Chapter 9, we'll also learn that methods help us hide internal details of an object. This is a more sophisticated level of object-oriented programming.

For now, let's just teach our lion some verbs.

```
class Lion
  { float age;
    int weight;
    boolean isMale;
    public void hunt()
      { System.out.println("I'm hunting.");
       }
    public void roar()
      { System.out.println("Roar!");
       }
   }
```

Our class now defines both instance variables and methods. Each instance has its own local storage compartment for each instance variable; methods are defined just once, in the class, which each instance consults when a method name is called.

For example,

```
class Jungle
  { public static void main(String args[])
     { Lion myLion = new Lion();
       myLion.roar();
       myLion.hunt();
```

```
        }
      }
```

Into the Void

Do note that both of the methods that we added above are `void`. This means that neither one returns a value. Each merely makes something happen.

In some languages, this is the difference between a *function* (which returns a value) and a *procedure* (which does not). A procedure is only useful for its side effects, such as modifying a piece of data or controlling some outside device.

Object, Know Thyself

A `Lion` can do things now, but we promised you more: We said that we would have lions that knew how to act their age. We can do this with richer methods, like:

```
void hunt()
  { if ( age < 1 )
```

A Catered Function?

In some situations, it's considered good style to write programs that never rely on side effects. This style is called *functional programming*.

Functional programming makes it easier, for example, to write a program for a computer that has many parallel processing units using a single pool of memory. Side effects, which might occur at unpredictable times, might cause one process to interfere with values being used by another, making such computers quite difficult to use.

On the other hand, a method can produce a side effect and return a value as well. This is considered good programming style, especially if there's any doubt about the method's ability to finish its task.

For example, a method that updates a remote database could be designed to return `true` if the operation succeeded and return `false` if some error occurred, such as the database not being accessible at that time. Java's error handling facilities go far beyond this crude approach, but it's a useful example of combining functional and procedural techniques in a single action.

```
        System.out.println("I'm chasing mice.");
      else if ( isMale && ( age > 4 ) )
        System.out.println("I'm waiting for the party.");
          else
            System.out.println("I'm hunting.");
      }


    void roar()
      { if ( age < 1 )
          System.out.println("Meow.");
        else if ( isMale && ( age > 4 ) )
          System.out.println("ROAR!!!");
            else
              System.out.println("Snarl!");
      }
```

These are pretty suggestible lions. Tell one to hunt(), and it hunts in its own accustomed manner. Tell it to roar(), and it makes whatever noise it can.

For example, if we compile and run

```
class Jungle
  { public static void main(String args[])
    { Lion youngLion = new Lion();
      youngLion.age  = 2;
      Lion oldLion   = new Lion();
      oldLion.age    = 6;
      oldLion.isMale = true;
      youngLion.roar();
      oldLion.hunt();
    }
  }
```

we get the output,

```
Snarl!
I'm waiting for the party.
```

This is not a very realistic model. If a real lion were asleep, for example, it wouldn't do either of these things. If a lion is hunting, roaring is a bad idea—it scares away the prey.

Perhaps our lion should know its current state of activity and should respond to our instructions in a way that depends on that state.

Let's put some convenient labels on some `static final` values. This will let us use a `switch` statement, with good readability, to control what happens as our Lion behaviors get more complex. We'll let each `Lion` keep track of its current state with the `int` variable `whatAmIDoing`.

```
class Lion
 {static final int isSleeping = 0;
  static final int isEating  = 1;
  static final int isHunting  = 2;
  static final int isFighting = 3;
  float age;
  int weight;
  boolean isMale;
  int whatAmIDoing;

// Now our methods can become more interesting.

  void suggestHunt()
   {switch(whatAmIDoing)
     {case isSleeping: System.out.println("Zzzz");
                       break;
      case isEating:   System.out.println("Chomp");
                       break;
      case isHunting : System.out.println("Sssh!");
                       break;
      default:         goHunting();
      }
    }

  void goHunting()
   {whatAmIDoing = isHunting; // update the state
    if ( age < 1 )
      System.out.println("I'm chasing mice.");
    else if ( isMale && ( age > 4 ) )
      System.out.println("I'm waiting for the party.");
        else
```

```
            System.out.println("I'm hunting.");
        }
    }
```

Why did we break the matter of hunting into two methods, instead of just putting the body of our original hunt() into the default clause of our switch?

We did this because it keeps our ideas neatly packaged. This organization makes two things clear to the person reading this program. First, that suggesting a hunt won't always make it happen; second, that one lion's role in a hunt will differ from another lion's role.

If we wrote a *monolithic* ("one stone") method for hunt(), a reader would have to go through the whole thing to see these separate ideas. *Modular* methods, with appropriate names, make these ideas obvious at a glance.

Let Sleeping Lions Lie

We can see how this works by compiling our expanded Lion.java, with class Jungle defined as below, and running java Jungle one more time:

```
class Jungle
 { public static void main(String args[])
    { Lion youngLion = new Lion();
      youngLion.age  = 0.8f; //override default double
      youngLion.whatAmIDoing = Lion.isFighting;
      Lion oldLion   = new Lion();
      oldLion.age    = 6;
      oldLion.isMale = true;
      oldLion.whatAmIDoing = Lion.isSleeping;
      youngLion.suggestHunt();
      oldLion.suggestHunt();
    }
 }
```

This gives us,

```
I'm chasing mice.
Zzzz
```

Summary

In this chapter, we showed

- ▶ That objects are an intuitive way of keeping data and behaviors consistent.

- ▶ That a class defines a family of potential objects.

- ▶ That methods (the behaviors of a class) should be kept small and focused so that their function and intent are obvious.

- ▶ That methods, though shared by an entire class, can use the state of an individual object to control the method's actions when the method is invoked on that object.

Chapter 9
Enriching an Object Model

In this chapter, you'll learn how a class can hide internal details of objects and how objects can contain other objects to create intuitive structures. You'll see that classes can define more than one way of building a new object from different starting information. We'll also cover how classes can collect common ideas into a parent class. Abstract classes can force descendants to provide certain behaviors, so we'll also show you how descendant classes can modify inherited behaviors.

In Chapter 8, we assumed that we would always have complete knowledge about each of our lions. We assumed that attributes like age and weight can be determined at will. Real-world objects may not be so forthcoming.

Methods to Our Madness

Instead of referring to these attributes directly, by using the names of their instance variables, we can wrap those variables inside *access methods*. Remember, we promised to show you a second reason for defining methods. This is it.

When we ask an object to tell us about itself by invoking methods on that object, rather than just inspecting its instance variables, we get a number of benefits. For one thing, we get to change our mind about what information an object should keep on hand.

We'll explore these aspects of object-oriented programming with a new example, set in a world with fewer messy details than the world of lions. This chapter is set in the clean, crisp world of geometric objects.

Pillars of Rectitude

Let's look at a class that defines a family of rectangles, using a system of x- and y-coordinates. We'll use x to represent horizontal position, with a value that increases as we move to the right; y will be vertical position, with a value that increases as we move upward.

Don't take that last convention for granted: In many systems for doing computer graphics (including Java's Abstract Window Toolkit in Chapter 15), the (0,0) position is at the top left—not the bottom left—of the graphics coordinate system. We'll put (0,0) at the bottom left for purposes of this example.

Our class will be confined to rectangles that are either horizontal or vertical, with no inclined sides. This means that we can define a rectangle in any of several simple ways.

We can specify

▶ Locations of the top-left and bottom-right corners

▶ Locations of the other pair of diagonally opposite corners

▶ Location of any one corner, plus rectangle length and width

▶ x values of left and right sides, y values of top and bottom

From any of these minimal descriptions, we can derive all other attributes of the figure: the locations of all four corners; the dimensions of the figure; the area, perimeter, location of center, and so on.

It would be wasteful to try to keep all of this information on hand all the time. If width, for example, were to be an instance variable, then we would need to update its value whenever we changed something else (like the position of any corner).

That would force us to do a subtraction whenever we stretched or shrank a side, even if we never asked for the value of the width between one such change and another. So it seems obvious that some attributes should be calculated on demand (using a method), not looked up (in an instance variable).

These Foils Have All a Length

This discussion should sound familiar. Remember the distinction between `helloString.length()` and `helloArray.length`, back in Chapter 6? Why is an array's length an instance value, always on hand, while a string's length is only computed when something wants to know?

We weren't in the room when these decisions were made, and some consider the difference quite arbitrary. We can rationalize these choices, if we wish, by observing that the number of slots in an array is usually tied to the structure of a problem: If we have an array representing daily observations for a week, it's going to have seven slots. All the time.

The length of the string that's referenced by a given variable is much more likely to change. For example, it's common to see a fragment of code like:

```
userName = userName.trim();
```

which has the effect of taking the original userName string, removing any white-space characters at either end, and assigning the result to userName (leaving the original untrimmed string to be garbage collected). This means that userName will now, most likely, have a different length from what it had before.

This is a plausible argument for measuring the length of the character string that's tied to any String-type variable at the time that this length is needed.

In the case of our proposed Rectangle class, we have many redundant attributes, and we could represent some as instance variables while calculating the rest using methods. Our class might start to take shape (pun intended!) like this:

```
class Rectangle
 { int upLeftX;
   int upLeftY;
   int lowRightX;
   int lowRightY;

   int lowLeftX() { return upLeftX;   }
   int lowLeftY() { return lowRightY;}
   int upRightX() { return lowRightX;}
   int upRightY() { return upLeftY;   }

   int width()    { return  lowRightX - upLeftX;      }
   int height()   { return  upLeftY   - lowRightY;  }
   int area()     { return  width()   * height();     }
   int perimeter(){ return (width()   + height())*2; }
   int centerX()  { return  upLeftX   + width()  /2; }
   int centerY()  { return  lowRightY + height() /2; }
 }
```

and we can try this out with:

```
class MakeRectangle
  { public static void main(String args[])
    { Rectangle aRectangle = new Rectangle();
      aRectangle.upLeftX   = 10;
      aRectangle.upLeftY   = 85;
      aRectangle.lowRightX = 40;
      aRectangle.lowRightY = 15;
      System.out.println(aRectangle.lowRightX);
      System.out.println(aRectangle.lowLeftY());
      System.out.println(aRectangle.perimeter());
    }
  }
```

That's None of Your Business

There's a serious flaw, however, in this definition of our class. If we want to know the x-value at the left end of a rectangle called myRectangle, we can ask for either

```
myRectangle.upLeftX
```

or

```
myRectangle.lowLeftX()
```

In the second case, we use parentheses because we're invoking a method. The empty parentheses say, in effect, "This is a method, but it doesn't need any input." In the first case, we don't use parentheses because `upLeftX` is just a variable's name.

This is not good abstraction. All we want to know is the x-coordinate at the left end of our rectangle. But we can't ask for that. (We would say that `Rectangle`'s methods are *semantically incomplete*.) We can ask for the x-coordinate of either left-hand corner, but we have to know that `Rectangle` only keeps one of these values on hand. (We would say that `Rectangle` does not provide good *encapsulation*.)

In fact, we might later decide that for some particular purpose (such as simulating the movements of objects in space), we'd rather describe an object in terms of the location of its center combined with its half-width and the half-height around that point. We would then want to redefine our `Rectangle` class like this:

```
class Rectangle
  { int cX; // center's x
```

```
int cY; // center's y
int hW; // half-width
int hH; // half-height

int centerX()  { return cX;              }
int centerY()  { return cY;              }

int leftX()    { return cX - hW;       }
int rightX()   { return cX + hW;       }
int bottomY()  { return cY - hH;       }
int topY()     { return cY + hH;       }

int lowLeftX() { return leftX();       }
int lowLeftY() { return bottomY();     }
int upLeftX()  { return leftX();       }
int upLeftY()  { return topY();        }
int upRightX() { return rightX();      }
int upRightY() { return topY();        }
int lowRightX(){ return rightX();      }
int lowRightY(){ return bottomY();     }

int width()    { return  hW * 2;        }
int height()   { return  hH * 2;        }
int area()     { return  hW * hH  * 4;}
int perimeter(){ return (hW + hH) * 4;}
}
```

Unfortunately, this revised definition breaks any old code that refers to something like myRectangle.upLeftX, since there's no longer an instance variable of that name.

That's bad. That's not what we're supposed to get from object-oriented programming.

From this experience, we should learn that instance variables should generally be for internal use only. A class should provide access methods for anything that we'll want to ask.

We can enforce this principle by using access modifiers to prevent direct external operations on the instance variables, as we will now see.

The Value of Privacy—or, the Privacy of Values

We can keep anything outside our class from operating directly on our instance variables. This enforces the use of the methods of a class as the only way of interacting with an object of that class. It's done by declaring the instance variables to be private, as in:

```
class Rectangle
 { private int cX =  0; //set default values
   private int cY =  0;
   private int hW = 10;
   private int hH = 10;
 //methods go here as before
 }
```

But now we've created a new problem. If the instance variables are private, they can't be changed from outside the class. Nor have we yet defined any methods that can change those values from inside.

If you wanted to make aRectangle move two units to the right, and the instance variables were not private, you could say something like:

```
aRectangle.cX = aRectangle.cX + 2;
```

But if we ever decide to change the internal representation of Rectangle yet again, this will no longer work.

It would be better if we could just say something like:

```
aRectangle.moveRight(2);
```

and have the desired change take place, with no need to know what variable was being altered. The variable cX can be private, as we'd prefer.

We can add this ability to our class with a method like:

```
int moveRight(int howFar){return (cX += howFar);}
```

Notice that we wrapped a return() around the assignment. This means that an expression like aRectangle.moveRight(2) will itself have the x value of the new center position of aRectangle.

We'd be able to write, for example,

```
class MakeRectangle
  { public static void main(String args[])
     { Rectangle aRectangle = new Rectangle();
       // gives us default values from class
       System.out.println("Right edge at x="
                              + aRectangle.rightX());
       System.out.println("Moving center to x="
                              + aRectangle.moveRight(2));
       System.out.println("Right edge at x="
                              + aRectangle.rightX());

     }
  }
```

producing the output,

```
Right edge at x=10
Moving center to x=2
Right edge at x=12
```

What if we want to move a rectangle to an absolute location? We might write a method like

```
void moveTo(int cX, int cY)
  { cX = cX;
    cY = cY;
  }
```

But this has an obvious problem! Within this method, the names cX and cY refer to local variables of the method, not to the instance variables of the same names. We say that the instance variables have been *shadowed*.

It would be perverse of Java to make us invent deliberately different names for things that are conceptually the same. The designers of the language anticipated this problem, however, and reserved the keyword this to eliminate the confusion.

Our moveTo method will do just what we want if it's rewritten,

```
void moveTo(int cX, int cY)
  { this.cX = cX;
    this.cY = cY;
  }
```

We can test this with:

```
class MakeRectangle
  { public static void main(String args[])
    { Rectangle aRectangle = new Rectangle();
      System.out.println("Right edge at x="
                             + aRectangle.rightX());
      System.out.println("Moving center to (5,6)");
      aRectangle.moveTo(5,6);
      System.out.println("Right edge at x="
                             + aRectangle.rightX());
    }
  }
```

Note that we declared moveTo as void, meaning that it returns no value. This isn't the style we've been using. We've been defining our methods so that they return a result that confirms their success. But it seems arbitrary to return the new cX, the new cY, or some invented data structure like an array of the two values.

What we've identified here is the need for a new level of abstraction. We need to take the idea of a point in our xy-coordinate space, and make it a class—instead of representing it by two separate integer values, in a manner that may seem a lot like our bad-old-days example of the wrong way to represent lions.

Let's define

```
class XYPoint
  { int x;
    int y;

    XYPoint(int x, int y)
      { this.x = x;
        this.y = y;
      }
  }
```

where the special method XYPoint(), with the same name as its class, is a constructor method as we've discussed before. Instead of accepting the default no-arg constructor, we're defining our own that takes as its arguments the x and y coordinates of our new point.

This means that we can say something like:

```
XYPoint newPoint = new XYPoint(32, 17);
```

to get a new XYPoint instance, named newPoint, with those supplied values of x and y.

We'll talk more about constructors at the end of this chapter.

With points in our xy space being abstracted using this new class, Rectangle looks like:

```
class Rectangle
  { private XYPoint c = new XYPoint(0,0);
    private int    hW = 10;
    private int    hH = 10;

    XYPoint center()  { return c;          }
    int centerX()     { return c.x;        }
    int centerY()     { return c.y;        }

    int leftX()       { return c.x - hW; }
    int rightX()      { return c.x + hW; }
    int bottomY()     { return c.y - hH; }
    int topY()        { return c.y + hH; }

    XYPoint lowLeft()
      { return new XYPoint(leftX(),bottomY()); }
    int lowLeftX()  { return leftX();          }
    int lowLeftY()  { return bottomY();        }
    XYPoint upLeft()
      { return new XYPoint(leftX(),topY());    }
    int upLeftX()  { return leftX();           }
    int upLeftY()  { return topY();            }
    XYPoint upRight()
      { return new XYPoint(rightX(),topY());   }
    int upRightX() { return rightX();          }
    int upRightY() { return topY();            }
    XYPoint lowRight()
      { return new XYPoint(rightX(),bottomY());}
    int lowRightX() { return rightX();         }
    int lowRightY() { return bottomY();        }

    int width()       { return 2 * hW;       }
    int height()      { return 2 * hH;
```

```
int area()      { return 4 * hW * hH;   }
int perimeter() { return 4 * (hW + hH); }

int moveRight(int howFar)
  { return (c.x += howFar);                    }
void moveTo(int cX, int cY)
  { c.x = cX;
    c.y = cY;                                  }
XYPoint moveTo(XYPoint c)
  { return (this.c = c);                       }
}
```

We've added methods that work with our new XYPoint abstraction, but we've also retained the old methods that reflect the earlier representation. Old classes that don't know about XYPoints won't be broken by the changes that we've made; new classes may find it more convenient to retrieve a rectangle's corner as an XYPoint, with a single method invocation, than as separate x and y values requiring two separate method calls.

Note, in particular, that we now have *two* methods named moveTo(): One that takes two int values as its arguments, and returns nothing, while the other takes an XYPoint as its argument and returns the new center location as an object of that type.

Java will figure out, based on the types of the values supplied when that method name is called, which method should be used, as in this example:

```
class MakeRectangle
  { public static void main(String args[])
   { Rectangle aRectangle = new Rectangle();
    System.out.println("Right edge at x="
                               + aRectangle.rightX());
    System.out.println("Moving center to (5,6)");
    aRectangle.moveTo(5,6);
    System.out.println("Right edge at x="
                               + aRectangle.rightX());
    System.out.println("Moving center to "
            + aRectangle.moveTo(new XYPoint(11,19))
            + " at x=" + aRectangle.centerX()
            + ", y="   + aRectangle.centerY());
    System.out.println("Right edge at x="
```

```
                                    + aRectangle.rightX());
    }
  }
```

returning the output

```
Right edge at x=10
Moving center to (5,6)
Right edge at x=15
Moving center to XYPoint@42d3bc at x=11, y=19
Right edge at x=21
```

Methods like `moveRight()` and `moveTo()` don't do much computation: They just provide encapsulation by hiding internal details from outside programs or pieces of programs. A method can do a lot more.

Can Java Do Math?

For example, suppose we wanted to change the area of a rectangle by a given factor, such as doubling it, without altering the proportions.

To do this, we need to multiply both the width and the height by the square root of that desired factor. For example, to double the area we would multiply the width and the height each by roughly 1.414.

Taking a square root is a common operation: For example, it gets used in calculating the distance between two points whose locations are described by x- and y-coordinates. If point 1 is at (x1,y1) and point 2 is at (x2,y2), then the distance between those points is the square root of $(x2 - x1)^2 + (y2 - y1)^2$.

Some languages, such as BASIC, make square roots, powers, and other math functions built-in facilities. Java, as you may have guessed, provides them in a predefined class, just as it provides character strings through a class rather than making them a burden on the core language.

The difference is that class `String` is used to create (to instantiate) string objects, as well as defining a useful vocabulary of methods that can be used with those objects. Class `Math` is a *degenerate* class: It defines `public static` methods (like the `main()` method of our `SayHello` class), but it does not spawn objects. Many methods of the `Math` class are defined for several familiar numeric types: `int`, `long`, `float`, and `double`.

The `Math` class includes a method, `sqrt()`, that returns the square root of its argument. (The methods defined in `Math` are discussed at length in Chapter 11.)

This function is only defined, however, for floating-point values. We've defined our rectangles in terms of integer-valued coordinates.

But that doesn't have to be a problem. We can let Java "promote" our integers to floating-point values, as it will do automatically. We can then add 0.5 to the result and truncate it back to an integer, which has the effect of rounding to the nearest integer when we're working with positive numbers.

We'll have this method return the modified area. Let's do it like this:

```
int multArea(double byWhat)
  { double factor = Math.sqrt(byWhat);
    hW = (int)((hW*factor)+0.5);
    hH = (int)((hH*factor)+0.5);
    return area();
  }
```

We can see what this does with this test:

```
class MakeRectangle
  { public static void main(String args[])
   { Rectangle aRectangle = new Rectangle();
     System.out.println("Area = " + aRectangle.area());
     System.out.println("Right edge at x="
                                  + aRectangle.rightX());
     System.out.println("New area = "
                                  + aRectangle.multArea(2));
     System.out.println("Right edge at x="
                                  + aRectangle.rightX());
   }
  }
```

which returns the output,

```
Area = 400
Right edge at x=10
New area = 784
Right edge at x=14
```

Note that since we're working in a coordinate space that only uses integer values, like that of a computer graphics environment, we couldn't get an exact doubling of the area. The returned value told us what we actually got. Checking returned values like this is an important technique for writing reliable programs.

I Happened to Be in the Area

Suppose that after we'd been using our Rectangle class for some time, we found that we were using it most often for mechanical engineering problems that depended on the area of a rectangle, rather than its width and height. Suppose that we decided to make our instance variables the center location, the area, and the height/width ratio of the rectangle, instead of remembering the center location and the separate width and height values.

Our modified class might look like:

```
class Rectangle
  { private XYPoint c = new XYPoint(0,0);
    private int area = 400; // match previous default
    private float heightToWidth = 1.0f;

    XYPoint center(){ return c;                      }
    int centerX()   { return c.x;                    }
    int centerY()   { return c.y;                    }

    int leftX()     { return c.x - width() /2;  }
    int rightX()    { return c.x + width() /2;  }
    int bottomY()   { return c.y - height()/2;  }
    int topY()      { return c.y + height()/2;  }

    XYPoint lowLeft()
      { return new XYPoint(leftX(),bottomY());  }
    int lowLeftX()  { return leftX();           }
    int lowLeftY()  { return bottomY();         }
    XYPoint upLeft()
      { return new XYPoint(leftX(),topY());     }
    int upLeftX()   { return leftX();           }
    int upLeftY()   { return topY();            }
    XYPoint upRight()
      { return new XYPoint(rightX(),topY());    }
    int upRightX()  { return rightX();          }
    int upRightY()  { return topY();            }
    XYPoint lowRight()
      { return new XYPoint(rightX(),bottomY()); }
    int lowRightX(){ return rightX();           }
```

```
int lowRightY(){ return bottomY();              }

int width()
{ return (int)Math.sqrt(area/heightToWidth+0.5); }
int height()
{ return (int)Math.sqrt(area*heightToWidth+0.5); }
int area()      { return area;                    }
int perimeter(){ return 2*(width() + height());  }

int moveRight(int howFar)
  { return (c.x += howFar);           }
XYPoint moveTo(XYPoint c)
  { return (this.c = c);              }
void moveTo(int cX, int cY)
  { c.x = cX;
    c.y = cY;                         }
int multArea(double byWhat)
  { return (int)(area *= byWhat); }
}
```

As far as the outside world is concerned, `Rectangle` hasn't changed at all. It responds to exactly the same list of methods that it handled before, returning results of the same type and producing the same kinds of side effects.

With our new representation, we're treating the area of a rectangle as one of its real properties, and computing the width and height that come closest to giving that area; before, we treated width and height as real, and their product as the actual area of the rectangle.

Either of these philosophies might be more appropriate, depending on the situation. That's a decision to be made at the time you design your class.

But if you think again later, and decide to change the internal representation, you won't break any other code. You'll just get results more consistent with your goals for your program.

For example, compiling and executing the same `MakeRectangle` class that we last defined above now returns the output,

```
Area = 400
Right edge at x=10
New area = 800
Right edge at x=14
```

Each Rectangle now keeps different values on hand for its own internal purposes, and uses formulas to compute some things on demand that it used to remember all the time. If we ask about area often, we'll do fewer multiplications than we did before, when area had to be computed on demand. If we ask about length and width often, we'll do many more square roots than we did before, when these values were simply instance variables.

If our problem makes it convenient, though, to think of a rectangle as an area at a location, instead of as a width and height around a location, then this modified class will serve our needs well.

Let's Do Something Constructive

We've seen that it's possible to represent a rectangle in any of several different ways. Wouldn't it be nice if we could take advantage of this fact when we want to define a new one?

For example, if we know that we want a rectangle that stretches across a certain horizontal space and occupies a certain vertical space, it would be nice if we could ask for that—instead of being forced to figure out the combination of area and `heightToWidth` ratio that would produce this result.

We've already seen classes that defined a constructor (a method whose name is the same as that of its class), able to accept parameter values to create an instance of a class with desired properties. We've also seen that we can define more than one method with a given name, as long as each version takes different numbers and/or types of argument so Java can figure out which one we want by looking at the information we provide. Can we combine these ideas?

Yes, we can do that. We can define more than one constructor for any given class, and let Java figure out which one to use by looking at the number and types of arguments: that is, at the *signature* of the method.

Let's define a useful variety of constructors for `Rectangle`.

We've already said that we'd like to define a new rectangle by giving its left, right, top, and bottom values. This implies that we need a constructor that accepts four integer arguments.

```
Rectangle(int left, int right, int top, int bottom)
    { int width = right - left;
      int height = top - bottom;

      c.x         = left  + width /2;
```

```
c.y           = bottom + height/2;
area          = height * width;
heightToWidth = (float)height/(float)width);
}
```

Once we do this, we no longer have the default no-arg constructor at our command: If we still want to have a constructor that takes no arguments, we'll now need to define our own. It's a small price to pay, and we'll shortly see how we can make this all quite straightforward.

We said that we wanted to be able to describe a new rectangle in several different ways. For example, we'd also like to have the option of defining a new rectangle by providing the center point, the area, and the heightToWidth directly. After all, if this trio weren't a convenient way to describe a rectangle, we would not have used these three things as our instance variables.

We therefore need another constructor,

```
Rectangle(XYPoint center,int area,float heightToWidth)
    { c                 = center;
      this.area         = area;
      this.heightToWidth = heightToWidth;
    }
```

where our use of this is familiar from our earlier discussion of the constructor for XYPoint.

It would also be nice if we could define a rectangle by giving the locations of any two diagonally opposite corners. If we had not defined class XYPoint as an abstraction for a set of x and y values, we'd be in trouble, because this constructor would need four integer values (x and y for the first corner, and x and y for the second corner) as its arguments. A method named XYPoint() with this signature (four ints as its parameters) would have the same signature as our existing constructor that takes the left, right, top, and bottom coordinate values. No dice.

It wouldn't matter if we defined that constructor with different names for those parameters—for example, as:

```
Rectangle(int corner1X, int corner1Y,
          int corner2X, int corner2Y)
    {...}
```

because the *names* that we give to a method's parameters don't affect the method's *signature*. Only the number, the types, and the sequence of the parameters are important.

Java would not be able to tell that this constructor is different from the one that makes a rectangle by knowing the locations of its left, right, top, and bottom edges.

But we do have the `XYPoint` abstraction available, and our two-corners constructor can therefore look like:

```
Rectangle(XYPoint corner1, XYPoint corner2)
 { int width  = Math.abs(corner2.x - corner1.x);
   int height = Math.abs(corner2.y - corner1.y);
          // Using absolute values lets us give any two
          //  diagonally opposite corners in either
          //  possible order, without ever getting
          //  negative values of instance variables area
          //  or heightToWidth
   c     = new XYPoint((corner1.x + corner2.x)/2,
                        (corner1.y + corner2.y)/2);
   area = height * width;
   heightToWidth = (float)height/(float)width;
 }
```

But wait a moment. The last three statements in this constructor look very much like those in the constructor above—the one that takes the instance variables as its arguments. It would be good style to avoid repetition in our code by making the two-corners constructor set up the needed parameters and call one of our already-defined constructors with the appropriate components of those corner values.

One way to do this would be,

```
Rectangle(XYPoint corner1, XYPoint corner2)
    { this(Math.min(corner1.x, corner2.x),
           Math.max(corner1.x, corner2.x),
           Math.max(corner1.y, corner2.y),
           Math.min(corner1.y, corner2.y));
    }
```

If we don't care about preserving our freedom to call this constructor with any pair of corners in either possible order, this method can be made less verbose by eliminating the min() and max() methods that we've wrapped around our x and y components.

Circle the Wagons

Perhaps a little bell went off in your head when we said, earlier in this chapter, "Think of a rectangle as an area at a location." Perhaps you thought, "Any shape is an area at a location. A rectangle is just a special case."

When you hear that magic phrase, "is a," you're hearing an invitation to one of the most important ideas in object-oriented programming: the idea of *inheritance.*

Inheritance is a hierarchical relationship between classes. When one class is defined as a subclass of another, the subclass automatically has the use of all of the non-private instance variables and methods that are defined for the parent class (the superclass). The subclass can then define additional instance variables and/or methods that apply only to the subclass. This is called *inheritance and specialization.*

A rectangle "is a" shape. A circle "is a" shape. How might we specify a class Shape, with subclasses Rectangle and Circle?

```
class Shape
  { protected XYPoint c = new XYPoint(0,0);
    protected int  area = 400; // defaults as before

    XYPoint center()  { return c;     }
    int centerX()     { return c.x;   }
    int centerY()     { return c.y;   }
    int area()        { return area;  }

    int moveRight(int howFar)
      { return (c.x += howFar);        }
    XYPoint moveTo(XYPoint c)
      { return (this.c = c);           }
    void moveTo(int cX, int cY)
      { c.x = cX;
        c.y = cY;                      }
    int multArea(double byWhat)
      { return (int)(area *= byWhat); }
  }

class Rectangle extends Shape
  { protected float hwRatio = 1.0f; // height to width
```

```
    int leftX()  { return c.x - width() /2; }
    int rightX() { return c.x + width() /2; }
    int bottomY(){ return c.y - height()/2; }
    int topY()   { return c.y + height()/2; }


    XYPoint lowLeft()
       { return new XYPoint(leftX(),bottomY());  }
    int lowLeftX()  { return leftX();            }
    int lowLeftY()  { return bottomY();          }
    XYPoint upLeft()
       { return new XYPoint(leftX(),topY());     }
    int upLeftX()   { return leftX();            }
    int upLeftY()   { return topY();             }
    XYPoint upRight()
       { return new XYPoint(rightX(),topY());    }
    int upRightX()  { return rightX();           }
    int upRightY()  { return topY();             }
    XYPoint lowRight()
       { return new XYPoint(rightX(),bottomY()); }
    int lowRightX() { return rightX();           }
    int lowRightY() { return bottomY();          }


    int width() {return (int)Math.sqrt(area/hwRatio);}
    int height(){return (int)Math.sqrt(area*hwRatio);}
    int perimeter(){ return 2 * (width()+height());  }
   }

class Circle extends Shape
   { int radius(){return (int)Math.sqrt(area/Math.PI);}
     int circ(){return 2*(int)Math.sqrt(area*Math.PI);}
     int diameter()     { return  2  * radius(); }
     int leftX()        { return c.x - radius(); }
     int rightX()       { return c.x + radius(); }
     int bottomY()      { return c.y - radius(); }
     int topY()         { return c.y + radius(); }
   }
```

You'll note that the instance variables of Shape and Rectangle are protected, rather than private. This is a weaker form of access restriction: It makes variables available within a class, *or* within any subclass of that class.

Be warned: By exposing the internals of a class to derived classes, protected variables reduce our future freedom to change implementation in the parent class. It's a trade-off that you'll make based on whether you are defining classes to be subclassed and specialized by other teams, or building a toolkit to be used in a more closely held manner.

In this case, despite our having left the door open (so to speak) by using protected, the programmer using these classes may still feel that we've been less hospitable than we might have been. We've defined the obvious methods for Rectangle and Circle—for example, width() and height() in the first case, diameter() in the second—but one of our goals is to let a program treat a Shape as merely a Shape, when the particular kind of shape is not important.

If another part of a program just wants to know how much horizontal space is needed to hold a Shape, that program should not have to figure out that the shape is a Circle so that it knows to ask for the diameter. It should be able to ask for the width of the shape, regardless.

We could be cooperative and include in Circle the methods:

```
int width()    { return diameter(); }
int height()   { return diameter(); }
int perimeter(){ return circ();     }
```

This would give our Shape subclasses a common vocabulary for common ideas. We could even write a style guide that says, "Every subclass of Shape must provide the methods width(), height(), and perimeter()."

But wouldn't it be better if the Java language gave us a way to make this a mandate, instead of just a recommendation? Well, it does.

Just Read the Abstract

When we have a class like Shape, it's pretty clear that we'll never have an actual instance of that class. How would you draw a shape, knowing nothing but its area and location? How would you determine if it collided with other shapes, when any dimension could be arbitrarily long if the others are short in proportion?

Shape is what we call an *abstract* class. It only exists as a way of reducing complexity, by placing things that are common to a family of classes in one place.

An abstract class can include concrete variables and methods when every sub-class could reasonably do something in a common way. An abstract class defines abstract methods—methods with no body—when every subclass has to decide for itself how something should be done, and doesn't have the option of deciding not to bother.

If a class includes one or more abstract methods, the class itself is abstract. If a class is a subclass of an abstract class, it must either provide a concrete version (an *implementation*) of every abstract method, or the subclass itself must also be declared as abstract.

To force every subclass of Shape to support `width()`, `height()`, and `perimeter()`, we can rewrite Shape as:

```
abstract class Shape
  { protected XYPoint c = new XYPoint(0,0);
    protected int  area = 400; // defaults as before

    XYPoint center()   { return c;    }
    int centerX()      { return c.x;  }
    int centerY()      { return c.y;  }
    int area()         { return area; }

    int moveRight(int howFar)
      { return (c.x += howFar);        }
    XYPoint moveTo(XYPoint c)
      { return (this.c = c);           }
    void moveTo(int cX, int cY)
      { c.x = cX;
        c.y = cY;                      }
    int multArea(double byWhat)
      { return (int)(area *= byWhat); }
    abstract int width();
    abstract int height();
    abstract int perimeter();
  }
```

We implemented the methods `center()`, `centerX()`, `centerY()`, `area()`, `moveRight()`, `moveTo()`, and `multArea()` concretely, because every subclass can use the same implementation. We defined `width()`, `height()`, and `perimeter()`

abstractly, because the implementation of these methods will depend on the geometry of the subclass.

Refusing Your Inheritance

What if we have the opposite situation? What if a parent class has already defined a concrete method, but a subclass has a special-case situation that lets it do the job better if it defines the method differently?

This is not a problem. Unless a class defines something using the keyword final, a subclass can override anything that it inherits. The subclass does this simply by providing a new definition.

For example, a Square "is a" Rectangle. All squares are rectangles, though not all rectangles are squares. We might find it convenient to define

```
class Square extends Rectangle
  { static final float hwRatio = 1.0f; //for all Squares
    int side()      { return (int)Math.sqrt(area);}
    int width()     { return side();              }
    int height()    { return side();              }
    int perimeter() { return 4 * side();          }
  }
```

This is completely okay. We have decided to *override* Rectangle's notion of hwRatio, and its implementations of width(), height(), and perimeter(), with definitions that are appropriate for the special case of a square.

Anything that we did not override is simply inherited from Rectangle, or from its parent Shape.

What is the meaning of the modifiers static final in Square's declaration of the variable hwRatio? The modifier final, as we said before, prevents any subclass from overriding this. Any subclass of Square will be a Rectangle, and will therefore know the meaning of hwRatio. But for any Square or subclass of Square, that value must be 1.

Since that value is 1 for every instance of Square, it would be silly to make every instance keep its own copy of that value. The modifier static says that the value of hwRatio is remembered, for all squares, by the class Square. It is not an instance variable, but a class variable.

Test the success of our inheritance experiment with these examples:

```
class MakeCircle
```

```
{public static void main(String args[])
  {Circle aCircle = new Circle();
   System.out.println("Area = " + aCircle.area());
   aCircle.multArea(2);
   System.out.println("New area = " + aCircle.area());
   System.out.println("Height = " + aCircle.height());
   System.out.println("Radius = " + aCircle.radius());
   }
 }


class MakeSquare
 {public static void main(String args[])
   {Square aSquare = new Square();
    System.out.println("Area = " + aSquare.area());
    aSquare.multArea(2);
    System.out.println("New area = " + aSquare.area());
    System.out.println("Height = " + aSquare.height());
    System.out.println("Side = " + aSquare.side());
    }
  }
```

Inheritance is a hugely important idea, and one of the biggest single benefits that comes with an object-oriented approach. Like other good things, however, it's best enjoyed in moderation.

Java strikes a balance that many language designers admire, as we'll explore in the next chapter.

Summary

In this chapter, we showed

▶ That thinking in terms of objects, from the beginning of a project, makes it easier to refine a program later on.

▶ That good design makes it irrelevant whether a fact is stored all the time, or computed on demand.

▶ That constructors can rely on different signatures of supplied data types to construct an instance of a class from different descriptions.

▶ That constructors can invoke each other to clarify intent and reduce duplication of code.

▶ That we can anticipate the needs of other parts of a program that use a given class and ensure consistent behavior with abstract classes.

▶ That a class can inherit structures and behaviors from a parent class and modify those inherited features to match special-case situations.

Using Methods to
Answer Questions

Using Packages to
Organize Classes

Access Control in
Depth

Interfaces for
Combinations of Behaviors

Chapter 10
Back to the Real World: Advanced Object Techniques

In this chapter, you'll learn how methods can give a class many ways of answering a question, based on different states of any one object's knowledge. You'l also learn how packages make it easy to reuse existing classes, subject to access controls that correspond to different degrees of trust between the writers of different classes, and how interfaces make a class of objects match several reusable descriptions.

In Chapter 9, we used an artificial world of geometric shapes in a coordinate plane to illustrate some important ideas about object-oriented programming. Now, let's return to the role of object methods in confronting real-world complexity. Our lions have had enough time to rest: let's put them back to work.

As we opened Chapter 9, we noted that we might not always have the complete knowledge of our objects that we assumed throughout Chapter 8. Our lions might not feel like stepping on a scale to let us determine their weight. This was our motivation for looking at methods, rather than instance variables, as the means for asking an object to tell us about itself: A technique that we explored from many perspectives in the preceding chapter.

By invoking a method, rather than looking up a value, we give our object a chance to think about the question. We open the door to more intelligent processing, letting objects decide whether a given value should always be known, or whether it can be deferred until something asks for it.

We saw, in class `Rectangle`, that an access method can trivially return the value of an instance variable. In class `Lion`, we can likewise define method `weight()` to return, trivially, the weight if it is known.

We can also anticipate the chance that we won't know a given lion's weight. We can write a `weight()` method that looks to see if a nonzero value is stored in the `weight` instance variable.

Our method can return that value if it's found, and return an *estimated* weight otherwise. This gives us a more robust class that tolerates incomplete information.

For example, if we're observing a group of lions over some period of time, we'll know the age of each lion in the group (having tracked them by distinctive markings, radio tags, or other features).

If we don't know the `weight` of a given lion (as indicated by a zero value of the instance variable), we can estimate based on `gender` and `age`. The code might look like,

```
int weight()
 {return
  (int)((weight != 0)? weight
                        : isMale? ((age > 3)? 375
                                              : age * 125)
                      : ((age > 3)? 275
                                    : age * 92));

 }
```

In this example, the ternary ?: operator proves both concise and clear.

In Ages Past

Our `Lion` class has become more capable than the empty shell, class `Lion { }`, that we defined in Chapter 8. Our lions now know how to hunt and roar, and they can estimate their weight if the actual value is not known. But we're far from finished with this example.

For one thing, we're relying a lot on that instance variable, `age`. We use it to decide how a lion roars, how it takes part in a hunt, and how much it weighs if an estimate has to be made.

But the age of a lion is constantly changing. When, and how, do we keep that value up to date?

Based on what we've done so far, you won't be surprised if we say that determining age is better done by invoking a method than by looking up an instance variable.

The good news is that it's trivial to modify the other methods that currently need this value. For example,

```
int weight()
 {int age = age();
  return
  (int)((weight != 0)? weight
```

```
                    : isMale? ((age > 3)? 375
                                        : age * 125)
                  : ((age > 3)? 275
                                 : age * 92));

        }
```

All we have to do in method `weight()` is define a local variable that's initialized by a call to this new method.

But now we have to decide what method `age()` is going to do. Until we define method `age()`, a Lion class definition containing method `weight()` above won't compile.

Let's think afresh about what's the best thing for a lion to know about itself. Think about your own identity, as determined by all those cards you carry: Do they show your age, or do they show your birthdate?

The answer is obvious. When you need to prove your age, you do it by providing your birthdate and letting the other party derive your age from other known data. We'll do this with Lion as well.

When we create a new lion, we'll store its birthdate as an instance value. This is a perfect use of instance variables: The birthdate has a definite value for any one lion, and it's something that can't be computed—it has to be known.

It's a Date

But we have to decide how to represent a date. Do we use a convenient format like YYYYMMDD, for example, 19960315 to represent March 15, 1996?

This representation has the advantage of being easy to encode if we're modeling a real-world population of lions. Never underestimate the importance of making it easy for users to provide accurate data: It's a waste to build a piece of software that's capable of sophisticated analysis, only to cripple it with faulty information due to an error-prone user interface.

The YYYYMMDD format is not very convenient, though, for determining age or other time intervals. We would have to develop our own algorithms for subtracting dates to determine the number of intervening days.

Maybe we don't need to reinvent that wheel. Dates are a pretty common type of data: Spreadsheets, databases, and other popular packaged products often provide them as a predefined type, with built-in options for formatting and calculation. Is Java equally thoughtful?

Yes, Java does know about dates. But they aren't built into the language: Remember, Java is supposed to be compact enough so that it can be used in low-cost appliance-type devices, and some of these have no conceivable need to represent date-based data. As with character strings, therefore, Java addresses this common but not universal need with a predefined class.

It's a Package Deal

One of Java's standard packages, `java.util`, defines the class `java.util.Date`. We can `import` this package into a program with the line,

```
import java.util.*;
```

This looks a lot like a line in our Chapter 4 example, class `WeeklyAverage`, which contained the line:

```
import java.io.*;
```

When this line appeared in Chapter 4, we merely said that this line allowed us to use pre-written input methods. But on the second appearance of this `import` incantation, you're entitled to more of an explanation.

For starters, if you've been paying attention, you're wondering why we had to import `java.io.*` or `java.util.*` to get their predefined classes (`DataInputStream` and `Date`, respectively), while the predefined class `String` just seems to come from nowhere. What's going on?

Things are more consistent than they seem. Class `String` also lives in a package, specifically in a package called `java.lang`. But `java.lang` gets special treatment: it is imported automatically by all Java programs.

Given the variety of applications that Java's designers had in mind, it's obvious why the language is defined in terms of a compact core plus a number of standard packages. Can we play, too? Can we define new packages, and is there any benefit to doing this? Yes, we can. Yes, there are good reasons to do so.

Let's Not Have Any Conflicts

How do we say that a new class should be treated as part of a certain `package`? We do this with a package declaration, which must be the first line of a source code file.

If we decided to create a package called shapes, for example, to consolidate classes such as our earlier Shape and its subclasses like Rectangle, then the Shape.java source file would begin

```
package shapes;
class Shape
  { protected XYPoint c = new XYPoint(0,0);
    protected int  area = 400; // defaults as before

    …
  }
```

If another program now includes the line:

```
import shapes.*;
```

then that program can declare new rectangles as easily as it declares new strings.

Without this import statement, a program could still declare rectangles, but it would have to use the *qualified name* shapes.Rectangle instead of merely Rectangle. Imagine if every use of String, in all of our examples so far, had to be replaced by java.lang.String. It's clear that importing a package enhances the readability of our code.

There are additional reasons to combine related classes into a package. Suppose, for example, that we had one class of rectangles that were geometric objects in a plane, and another class of rectangles that were defined on the surface of a sphere.

We might use the latter for a task such as planning the movements of ships and aircraft on the surface of the Earth. On the surface of a sphere, a rectangle (defined by edges of constant longitude or latitude) would have somewhat complex formulas for calculating area, perimeter, and other attributes. But we would still want to use simple, intuitive names for the associated methods.

If one Rectangle class is defined in package planeShapes, and another is defined in package sphereShapes, then we don't need to worry about devising different names for similar ideas. We can import planeShapes.* and work with its Rectangle class, invoking methods like area(), or we can import sphereShapes.* and work with its Rectangle class that might well have some identically named methods. The use of package names will keep this straight.

We can even use both classes in a single program, by referring to them with their qualified names planeShapes.Rectangle and sphereShapes.Rectangle.

However, we could not import both of these Rectangle classes: it would not be possible to say, for example,

```
import planeShapes.*;
import sphereShapes.*;
```

But we could say, hypothetically,

```
import planeShapes.Rectangle;
import sphereShapes.Circle;
```

if this happened to meet our needs.

Stars in Our Eyes

It's easy for experienced users of the DOS, Windows, or Unix operating systems to misinterpret the asterisk (*) that appears in statements like:

```
import planeShapes.*;
```

That * looks a lot like the file name wildcard symbol. You might think that a statement like:

```
import java.*;
```

would import packages `java.io`, `java.util`, `java.net`, and all the other packages whose names fit the pattern `java.<something>`.

That's not how it works. Any single import statement imports at most a single package. Saying

```
import planeShapes.*;
```

is equivalent to saying, "Import all *classes* in package `planeShapes`." We can be more restrictive, as when we said above:

```
import planeShapes.Rectangle;
```

This imported only a single class from that package. But we *cannot* be more general and import more than one package with one `import` statement.

A Pyramid on Its Point

If we're counting on package names to distinguish one kind of rectangle from another, we'd better remember that Java programs often live on a worldwide network. How do we give a package a name that absolutely, positively will not be duplicated by some other Great Mind that thinks just like our own?

Actually, this problem has already been solved, and one of the major principles of object-oriented programming is, "Never invent what you can steal." If you're on the Internet, then you already have a unique name close at hand—that is, your own Internet domain name.

To name a Java package, take the hierarchy of Internet domains and stand it on its head. If your domain is *mycompany.com*, then you might name a package `com.mycompany.planeShapes`.

Yes, names can be nested: we can have `com.mycompany.geometry.shapes .plane` and `com.mycompany.geometry.shapes.sphere`, for example. It's purely a matter of personal preference whether you name two different packages `planeShapes` and `sphereShapes`, or `shapes.sphere` and `shapes.plane`.

There is no special relationship between two packages merely because they have some common ancestor in a multi-part name. We cannot `import shapes.*` unless `shapes` is the name of a package, so that the children of shapes are classes rather than nested-name packages.

A package name hierarchy is a clue to the user, *not* a context for the Java compiler.

The Four Ps of Privilege

Now that we understand packages, we can talk about Java's multi-layered control of access to the member variables and methods of a class.

Here is the easy part. *All* variables *and* methods of *any* class are available to the methods of that class, *no matter what* access modifiers are used on the class or its variables or its methods.

Here is the almost-as-easy part. A class is either `public` (indicated by a declaration like `public class MyClass`), or it is enclosed within its package (the default level of protection). This protection level of the class affects the meaning of the protections specified for its member variables and methods, as described and as shown by examples below.

The rest of this subject is a matter of understanding the following access modifiers, whose meanings we will describe and then demonstrate with examples for both public and packaged classes.

▶ Public: Such a member of a class is visible within its class, and to any other class in the same package. It is also visible to any other class in any other package, if and only if the defining class is `public`.

▶ Protected: Such a member of a class is visible within its class, and to any other class in the same package. It is also visible to any subclass in any other package, if and only if the defining class is `public`. (Though it may seem strange, an access modifier of `protected` is *less* restrictive than no access modifier at all, since `protected` access is open to other package's subclasses of a `public` class.)

▶ No modifier: This provides package access. Such a member of a class is visible within its class, and to any other class in the same package only.

▶ Private protected: Such a member of a class is visible within its class, and to any other subclass in the same package. It is also visible to any subclass in any other package, if and only if the defining class is `public`. Adding `private` to `protected` eliminates access by non-subclasses in the same package. But `private protected` is *less* restrictive than `private`. This compound level of access protection will not be supported in Java 1.1.

▶ Private: Such a member of a class is visible within its class, but not to any other class (including subclasses) in any package (including the same package).

To demonstrate the above, let's define the package `parentpackage` containing the `public` class `ParentClass`, a subclass of `ParentClass` called `ChildClass`, and a class not related to `ParentClass` called `PackageClass`:

```
package parentpackage;

public class ParentClass
  { public            int publicV;
    protected         int protV;
                      int packageV;
    private protected int ppV;
    private           int privateV;
  }
```

```
class ChildClass extends ParentClass
 { int publicVM() {return publicV; }
   int protVM()   {return protV;   }
   int packVM()   {return packageV;}
   int ppVM()     {return ppV;     }
// int privateVM(){return privateV;}  // won't compile
   }


class PackageClass
 { ParentClass uncle = new ParentClass();
   int publicVM() {return uncle.publicV; }
   int protVM()   {return uncle.protV;   }
   int packVM()   {return uncle.packageV;}
// int ppVM()     {return uncle.ppV;     } // likewise
// int privateVM(){return uncle.privateV;} // likewise
   }
```

In another package, the anonymous package, we define the class FosterClass that is, like ChildClass, a subclass of ParentClass—even if it has been placed in a foster home, so to speak.

```
class FosterClass extends parentpackage.ParentClass
 { int publicVM() {return publicV; }
   int protVM()   {return protV;   }
// int packVM()   {return packageV;} // won't compile
   int ppVM()     {return ppV;     }
// int privateVM(){return privateV;}    // likewise
   }
```

And we also define an unrelated class, with neither a subclass relationship nor a common package:

```
import parentpackage.*;

class StrangerClass
 { ParentClass uncle = new ParentClass();
   int publicVM() {return uncle.publicV; }
// int protVM()   {return uncle.protV;   } // likewise
// int ppVM()     {return uncle.ppV;     } // likewise
```

```
// int privateVM(){return uncle.privateV;} // likewise
// int packVM()   {return uncle.packageV;} // likewise
  }
```

If we do *not* declare `ParentClass` to be `public`, things get much simpler. Without this word in the class `ParentClass` declaration, `FosterClass` and `StrangerClass` can no longer access `ParentClass` in any way, since it is now a non-`public` class in another package. This makes them both pretty futile. The privileges of `ChildClass` and `PackageClass`, which share the same package with `ParentClass`, are not affected by this change.

Reading between the Lions

We took that "package tour" to explain where we were getting our predefined class, Date, that we want to use to represent the birth date of any given instance of class Lion. It certainly was the scenic route, but we took in some vital landmarks along the way.

Now, let's take all the things we've learned about objects and fold them into this example. This gives us something like:

```
import java.util.Date;

class Lion
 {static final int isSleeping = 0;
  static final int isEating  = 1;
  static final int isHunting  = 2;
  static final int isFighting = 3;

  private Date birthDate;
  private int weight;
  private boolean isMale;

  int whatAmIDoing;

  Lion(boolean isMale)
   {birthDate   = new Date();
    weight      = 0; // triggers estimate
    this.isMale = isMale;
```

```
    }

Lion(Date birthDate, int weight, boolean isMale)
 {this.birthDate = birthDate; // if we know,
  this.weight    = weight;    // we can say so
  this.isMale    = isMale;
  }

int weight()
 {float age = age();
  return
   (int)((weight != 0)? weight
                      : isMale? ((age > 3)? 375
                                          : age*125)
                             : ((age > 3)? 275
                                         : age*92));
  }

float age()
 {return (float)((new Date().getTime()
               - birthDate.getTime()) //milliseconds
            / (1000 * 3600 * 24 * 365.25));
                          //milliseconds per year
  }
      // Date()returns the computer's current time
      //  in milliseconds since January 1, 1970
      //  as a Date object (from the Date class
      //  imported above).

void roar()
 {float age = age();
  switch(whatAmIDoing)
    {case isSleeping: System.out.println("Zzzz");
                    break;
     case isHunting:  System.out.println("Shhh!");
                    break;
     default: if ( age < 1 )
```

```
                    System.out.println("Meow.");
                else if ( isMale && ( age > 4 ) )
                        System.out.println("ROAR!!!");
                    else
                        System.out.println("Snarl!");
        }
    }


void suggestHunt()
  {switch(whatAmIDoing)
    {case isSleeping: System.out.println("Zzzz");
                      break;
     case isEating:   System.out.println("Chomp");
                      break;
     case isHunting : System.out.println("Shhh!");
                      break;
     default:         goHunting();
     }
  }


void goHunting()
 {whatAmIDoing = isHunting; // update the state
  float age = age();
  if ( age < 1 )
    System.out.println("I'm chasing mice.");
  else if ( isMale && ( age > 4 ) )
    System.out.println("I'm waiting for the party.");
      else
        System.out.println("I'm hunting.");
  }
}
```

My, How It's Grown

From an empty class,

```
class Lion { }
```

at the beginning of Chapter 8, we've come a long way. Our class now has static variables that hold common information used by all instances; instance variables that hold local information unique to each object of the class; and a variety of constructors that create new instances based on different initial information.

The methods of our class provide useful responses under varying conditions, hiding internals from the user of this class: Hiding, for example, the difference between known and estimated values, making this model tolerant of incomplete information.

Our class also interacts with its environment, for example, by using the date/time clock of the host computer to turn an unchanging instance value (birthDate) into a dynamic piece of data (a particular lion's age).

When You're Having More Than One

We saw in Chapter 9 that it's useful to declare that one class "is a" special case of another class, and to use inheritance to escape the labor and avoid the possible errors involved in saying things all over again.

The next logical question ought to be, "What if something shares behaviors with more than one other class? Can we inherit from all of them?"

For example, class Bird might reasonably be a subclass of both Animal and FlyingThing. Class Airplane might be a subclass of both PoweredMachine and FlyingThing.

Will Java allow this? No.

Java prohibits this *multiple inheritance*, because it creates ambiguity if two different parent classes have a common parent themselves: A situation known as *diamond inheritance*, because of the diamond-shaped diagram that results when trying to draw a picture of the resulting relationship. In Java, class Airplane can be a direct subclass of only one other class. Of course, that unique parent class can itself be a subclass of something else—and so on.

But even though we can't inherit method implementations from more than one superclass, Java does give us a way to define and name sets of method names: We can ensure that a newly defined class will respond to all of the methods named in any number of these sets.

Such a set of method names, including the types of arguments (the method signatures) that each of those methods requires, is formally called an *interface*.

A class can only have an *extends* relationship with one other class. (If no such class is named, a new class automatically becomes a subclass of class Object.) But a class can have an *implements* relationship with any number of interfaces.

We can have, for example,

```
class Animal {...}

class PoweredMachine {...}

class Bird extends Animal implements Flyable {...}

class Airplane extends PoweredMachine implements Flyable
 {...}

interface Flyable
 { float wingspanFeet();
   float topSpeedMPH();
   float reflectsRadar(int   distanceMeters,
                       int   powerWatts,
                       float antennaGainDB);
 }
```

We can see that an interface looks much like a pure abstract class, defining only abstract methods. We can even use the abstract keyword in the method definitions within an interface, but it's optional and has no added effect.

Note that we have followed a Java convention of naming an interface using an adjective, rather than a noun. An interface defines a capability, and this naming convention helps us focus on what that capability is supposed to be.

We'll see a practical application of interfaces in the next chapter, which begins the third and final major section of the book.

That final section will look at the standard packages that combine with the core language to make up the Java programming environment. We now have the vocabulary and the concepts at our command to describe these classes, and the capabilities that they provide to make Java such a powerful invention.

Summary

In this chapter, we showed

▶ That methods can hide the difference between known and estimated characteristics of a modeled object.

▶ That packages provide a convenient way of referring to predefined classes and methods.

▶ That the * notation, used for referring to all of the classes in a package, *can't* refer to a group of packages with a common family name.

▶ That access modifiers affect the sharing of variables and methods between classes, depending on whether a master class is or isn't public; whether a client class is or isn't in the same package; and whether the client class is or isn't a subclass.

▶ That interfaces give Java a kind of multiple inheritance, offering multiple sets of behaviors without creating the possibility of conflicting implementations.

Creating Objects
That Share
Resources

Handling Abnormal
Situations

Enhancing Simple Types
with Classes and Methods

Chapter 11
Conversational Java: Package java.lang

In this chapter, you'll learn how class `Thread` lets us create objects that can each hold some piece of a program, taking turns with the use of shared resources like the central processor, and subject to priority-based scheduling with the ability to take different actions based on each other's state. We'll show you how class `Throwable` serves as the base for class `Exception`, which wraps information about abnormal situations into a package that can be examined and acted on by handler code to enhance reliability and fault diagnosis in complex programs. You'll also see how class `String`, class `Math`, and the simple-type wrapper classes provide both `Object`-type packaging and collections of powerful analysis and conversion functions for our data.

The acid test of knowing a language is not just knowing its words and grammar, analogous to the Java that we've learned through Chapter 10. To be fluent in a language, one must also be able to use and appreciate its idioms and figures of speech.

Imagine, for example, using a commonplace phrase like, "That's a home run," or "That's his strong suit," only to be met by a blank stare. Imagine how tedious conversations would become if every such reference had to be spelled out in detail, with the rules of baseball and card games (not to mention the complete works of Shakespeare) being always kept on hand as necessary backup.

That's what it's like to write programs using nothing but the core facilities of an object-oriented language. It's possible, but why do it? Why not anticipate everyday needs, and create the language with its own equivalents of proverbs, nursery rhymes, and folk tales? All of these would then become the building blocks of conversations that are both more interesting, and less verbose, than they would be without such facilities.

Six packages of predefined classes, called the Java Application Programming Interface, or Java API, serve this purpose for conversational Java.

One standard package is so vital that it is imported, automatically, into every Java program. That package is `java.lang`, whose name suggests its importance to the entire feel of the language. Its facilities are essential to any Java conversation that goes beyond the level of baby talk.

The package `java.lang` gives us the figures of speech, in the form of public methods of its classes, that we need to fulfill several of Java's most important goals. In terms that might be used to describe an over-the-counter drug, they make Java programs fast, safe, and effective.

Fast

Class `Thread` gives you a way to partition your programs into different activities that can take turns using the computer's resources. For example, if one activity can't proceed until the user takes some action, another activity can continue while the first activity is waiting for that user response.

This avoids making a user wait for some operation to complete, when the user would prefer to work on some other part of a task—and thereby makes a well-written multithread program seem to be running more quickly than a single-threaded program on a computer with equal hardware speed.

Safe

Class `Throwable` is the superclass of all classes that represent errors and exceptions. An executing method that encounters some abnormal condition can "throw an exception"—that is, it can create and send forth a sort of message in a bottle, describing the problem, in the hope that something will read the message and be able to do something helpful.

That exception object may be "caught" within the method that creates it, triggering an exception handler: That is, a set of instructions that the programmer has provided to correct (or at least contain) the problem. If a method lacks an appropriate handler, or if the local handler can't do the whole job, then the exception (or a modified exception, bearing different information) can be automatically passed along (or deliberately re-thrown) to whatever invoked the method that first encountered the problem.

An exception won't always be handled in a useful way, but even an uncaught exception will at least emerge as an identifiable "cause of death" for a program that couldn't handle the pressure.

Class `SecurityManager` is one of the things that makes the Java programming language uniquely suited to network environments, where users want the convenience of running useful programs that come from uncontrolled sources. `SecurityManager` gives programs ways to describe and enforce programs' privileges and limitations.

Effective

Class `String` is something of an old friend by now, but there are aspects of its behavior that we have not yet discussed. We'll look into class `String`'s facilities for comparing two string objects, in particular, the importance of understanding what it means for two strings to be equal.

Class `Math` is a purely static class. We don't create objects of this class: Rather, the class is a collection of static values and static methods that make mathematical operations more convenient, more consistent, and more accurate.

Finally, we'll look at the *wrapper* classes. These are the classes:

▶ `Character`

▶ `Boolean`

▶ `Number`

Class `Number` has the additional subclasses:

▶ `Integer`

▶ `Long`

▶ `Float`

▶ `Double`

These classes are called wrappers because they wrap the convenience of object disciplines around the efficiency of Java's simple types. These classes store information about the limits on what these simple types can represent, and they provide useful methods for converting and classifying values.

Hanging by a Thread

It's easy to write a program that puts its nose to the grindstone and doesn't look up until it's finished. Such structures are so common that they even have a nickname, the "tight loop."

Printing a document, recalculating a spreadsheet, or sorting a database are all examples of common tasks that can run as quickly as possible when they're programmed in this style. Users generally prefer, however, the flexibility that comes from placing a time-consuming task "in the background," so that a word processor (for example) can edit one document while printing another—even if this means that the printing process itself takes somewhat longer as a result. The point is, the user is getting something done during that time—or at least retaining the option of canceling the operation—instead of being forced to choose between letting the operation finish, or doing something drastic like turning off the computer.

It's easy to think of programs that might wrap a tight loop—or even an infinite loop, which never reaches an end state—around some useful side effect.

For example, somewhere on your computer screen there is probably a display of the current time. It might be a fancy analog clock, with graphical hands, or it might be a discreet little digital readout in a corner of some other program's window.

That onscreen readout is driven by a program, with no physical connection to the hardware clock that's buried somewhere inside your computer. Some piece of software is deciding, thousands of times every second, whether to use the computer's processor chip to compile a program, or print a document, or check the hardware clock and redraw a section of your display.

That decision-making activity is called multitasking.

Sixteen Tons of Number Nine Code

There are two kinds of multitasking. When the word is used without any qualifying adjectives, it refers to switching the computer's attention between more than one concurrent process.

A *process*, when the word is used in this sense, is a heavy thing, burdened by the weight of the protection that it carries to make it secure from disruption by other processes. The state and behavior of a process are independent of any other task's state and behavior. The data structures, and even the memory addresses, that get used by one process are separate from those that are used by any other.

This makes ordinary multitasking robust, but relatively slow, since the computer's operating system has to do a time-consuming *context switch* to shift its attention from one process to another.

It takes time to move the values that are sitting in the processor's internal storage compartments out to the computer's memory. It takes more time to retrieve from memory the values that were stored in the processor when the returning process last had control. All that memory, of course, is itself a costly resource.

Cooperate or Capitulate

Once you decide to do multitasking at all, you still have to choose between two ways of doing it. Your choice is between cooperative and preemptive.

Cooperative multitasking relies on each process to detect when it can readily yield control. When a program is waiting for user input, that's an ideal time to give the computer a chance to bring some other process into play.

The problem with the cooperative approach is that a single "selfish" process can starve all of the other active processes. When users get their applications software from many different providers, the odds are good that at least one piece of software will maximize its own performance at the expense of other tasks.

Most users soon find this annoying, and the market has therefore driven computer operating systems in the direction of preemptive multitasking.

With preemptive multitasking, every process is always subject to higher-level control. Something above the process can force that process into the background, and give the computer's attention to another process.

A preemptive system can assign different priorities to different activities, and force low-priority activities to yield when a higher-priority task requires immediate action.

If you want to have a spreadsheet, a word processor, and an Internet browser all open on your screen at the same time, and shift your own attention from one to another every minute or so, cooperative multitasking is an adequate solution. It's easier to write application programs for a cooperative environment than it is for a preemptive platform, since a cooperatively multitasking application doesn't have to allow for the chance that the computer might get yanked away from an operation that's not quite done. Each application's developer decides when to offer another process a turn.

If you want to supervise more critical activities, such as real-time control of a factory floor or high-speed communications with other computers, you may need the more consistent performance that becomes possible with a preemptive design. Preemptively tasked programs, however, require more discipline to write.

On the Lighter Side

Multithreading, compared to process-based multitasking, is less resource-intensive while providing superior performance—but it requires even more discipline from the developer than ordinary preemptive multitasking.

A thread is a lightweight process. Threads can be used to build a program out of objects that can take turns using the computer's resources, without the rugged individualism of separate processes.

Threads are defined by either a single programmer or a cooperating team, and are therefore able to respect each other's needs and vulnerabilities. They can be given concurrent access to resources, such as data structures and regions of memory, that have to be rigidly partitioned by separate processes.

This trusting relationship between the threads of an application reduces the cost, in terms of time and memory and other resources, of transferring control from one thread to another, compared to the more drastic context switching that takes place when the heavyweight process is the unit of control.

Java supports multiple threads at the level of the language, rather than requiring the programmer to obtain and learn special libraries of multithread routines—which in most cases merely serves to package the specific multithreading features of an underlying operating system—and to master, most likely, a different library for each platform.

This makes it likely that Java programs will actually use the power of threads to create a pleasant end-user experience. Using threads in Java only requires writing the program once, as opposed to mastering and exploiting a different approach to multithread design for each separate operating system on which a program might be deployed.

This is important, because proponents of other languages often assert that Java is inherently slow as a result of the conveniences that it offers to the programmer. The question in rebuttal should be, "Slow at what?"

A Java program that uses multithread design may well appear to the user to be faster than a single-threaded program that does the same things, even if the Java program is actually performing the same low-level operations more slowly. The difference will be that the Java program is attending more promptly to the user's requests, instead of waiting for other tasks to conclude before it responds to the user.

Where to Wear Your Threads

Multithreading meets the needs of a new generation of software: That is, of programs that require the appearance of paying attention to more than one task at a time, so that the user will never feel ignored.

In the context of Java, and its role on the Internet, the classic example is in the operation of a graphical browser for the World Wide Web. Suppose that you have clicked on a button on a Web page that offers to show you a detailed picture of a remote moon of Jupiter. The picture starts to appear, and your browser shows you an estimate of the time that will be needed to show the whole image.

You realize that the Net is heavily loaded, and that it will be over half an hour before the image completes. You don't want to wait.

If the program fragment that handled image retrieval were a tight loop, within the single massive process that ran the browser program, you'd have no attractive choice. You'd either have to wait for the image to appear, or use the brute force approach of shutting down the browser and starting it over to get a new connection.

This is not the kind of friendly, spontaneous interaction that users expect from modern software.

If the image retrieval task is handled by a thread, and user interaction is handled by another thread, then the user continues to have the ear of the computer and can ask the browser to abort the operation. That's more like it.

Enough talk. Let's see how these things work.

Different Colors of Thread

The following code defines two classes that extend class Thread. It defines a third class that creates and launches one instance of each of these newly defined subclasses. Don't worry about the statements that look like:

```
try { <something> }
```

and

```
catch ( <something> ) { <something> }
```

These statements will be explained later in this chapter, when we talk about class Throwable.

Our first thread example looks like,

```
import java.io.*; // input facilities for Listener

class Counter extends Thread
 { int i = 0;
   public void run()
     { while (i < 20)
        { System.out.println(i++);
           // print value and increase i for next pass
          try { sleep(1000); } // milliseconds
          catch (InterruptedException e) {}
```

```
          }'
      System.out.println("I'm finished counting.");
      }
  }


class Listener extends Thread
 { DataInputStream userInput
                      = new DataInputStream(System.in);
   String input = "";
   public void run()
    { while ( !input.equals("Quit") )
              // .equals, not ==
      { try { input = userInput.readLine(); }
        catch (IOException e){}
        System.out.println("You typed " + input);
       }
      // leave loop if input is "Quit"
     System.out.println("I'm finished listening.");
     }
  }


class HearYou
 { public static void main(String args[])
   { Thread counter  = new Counter();
     counter.setPriority(Thread.MAX_PRIORITY);
     Thread listener = new Listener();
     listener.setPriority(Thread.NORM_PRIORITY);
      // we'll talk about priorities in a moment
     counter.start();
     listener.start();
     while(counter.isAlive() || listener.isAlive())
       { System.out.println("Something's still alive");
         try{Thread.sleep(3000);}
         catch(InterruptedException e){}
       }
     System.out.println("No more. Goodbye.");
    }
  }
```

When you enter this file, compile it, and execute the class HearYou, your machine will behave as follows.

1 It will begin to display numbers, 0 through 19, at intervals of roughly one second.

This is the effect of calling the method, sleep(1000), in the run() method of class Counter, within the loop that begins

```
while (i < 20)
```

This loop prints the value of its counter variable each time the counter object (a thread) wakes up from its self-imposed 1000-millisecond nap, and gets another chance to take control.

2 It will echo back any letters or numbers that you type at the keyboard, inserting the numeric output in the middle of what you type if counter happens to get control while listener is waiting for you to finish entering a line.

This is the effect of defining an instance of DataInputStream as an instance variable in class Listener, and invoking the readLine() method on that stream. Your console session, supported by your computer's operating system, lets you type in characters (and echoes them back as they're typed) until you hit the Enter key, when the console session sends readLine() the entire line of input—but while this is going on, counter is still active and is sharing the same display.

3 When you hit the Enter key, whatever you've typed will be echoed again as a line of output, interspersed among the numbers that counter is still emitting.

This is the effect of printing out the value that was returned by the readLine() invocation.

4 When 19 appears, there will be no more numbers. The counter object, a thread, has returned from its run() method and been automatically discarded.

5 When you type the input Quit, listener will tell you that it isn't listening anymore. It doesn't matter if a number gets printed in the middle of your command while you're typing it, but the command does have to be typed with a capital Q.

The listener object, a thread, will return from its run() method and will be discarded. This may happen before or after the death of counter.

At this point, any further typing that you do will be ignored. It will not be echoed as you type, nor will it be repeated back to you when you hit Enter.

6 When both of these threads have died, the program will end.

Leave the Driving to Java

In just this simple example, we can see many important things about threads.

We see that neither of our new Thread subclasses contains any code to deal with other threads, either of the same kind or any other kind, that might be active at the same time.

When class HearYou creates two thread objects, one of class Counter and one of class Listener, the activities of those objects are scheduled by the Java environment. You don't have to worry about it.

We see that an individual instance of Thread can tell Java to leave it alone for a certain period of time. The sleep() method takes an integer argument in milliseconds, rather than some other unit like machine cycles, for portability to different machines with varying hardware speed: This is, however, no guarantee of accuracy to this level, since the computer's own clock may not be that precise, and the thread's "wakeup call" might be delayed by a higher-priority thread. We gave our counter the maximum priority to make it as accurate as possible.

Putting a thread to sleep is one way to make sure that other threads get a chance to run. It's also an efficient and portable way of putting a time delay into a program—much more so than writing a tight loop, for example, that counts to some value (which will have to be a higher value on a faster machine to provide a given delay).

You can use this technique even in programs that don't define multiple threads. Even the simplest Java program runs in a thread, though you normally don't need to think about it.

You can always drop a time delay into a program with a set of statements like:

```
try { Thread.sleep(secondsDelay*1000); }
        // you define secondsDelay
catch(InterruptedException e) {}
        // we're not worried about interruptions
```

For example,

```
class TimeDelay
 { public static void main(String args[])"Hello...");
      System.out.println("Hello...");
```

```
      try { Thread.sleep(5000); }
      catch(InterruptedException e) {}
      System.out.println("...and Goodbye");
    }
  }
```

Continuing with our `HearYou` example, we see that each of our `Thread` sub-classes provides a method named `run()` that seems to do the work. Each of our `Thread` objects was launched, however, by invoking the method `start()`, which neither of our subclasses defined.

You might infer that the method `start()` was inherited from class `Thread`: you would be correct. Invoking `start()` calls an object's `run()` in the new thread, while the call to `start()` returns in the thread that made that call.

This lets the class that called `start()` get back to work, while the `run()` method executes (perhaps for quite some time) in the context of the newly created thread.

Watch Your Priorities

We mentioned above the value of being able to set different priorities for different threads. Let's see how this works.

```
class Counter extends Thread
  { int i = 0;
    public void run()
      { while (i < 1000)
        { if( (i++ % 10) == 0 )
          { System.out.println(getName()
                               + " "
                               + i/10);
          }
          try{sleep((int)(Math.random()*10));}
          catch(Exception e){}
        }
      }
  }

class ThreadPriorities
  { public static void main(String args[])
    { Thread one  = new Counter(); // one thread...
```

```
one.setName("T1");
one.setPriority(Thread.NORM_PRIORITY - 2);
Thread two  = new Counter(); // another...
two.setName("        T2");
two.setPriority(Thread.NORM_PRIORITY + 2);
one.start();                    // they're off!
two.start();
while(one.isAlive() || two.isAlive())
{ try{Thread.sleep(5000);}
  catch(InterruptedException e){}
  }
 }
}
```

Enter this, compile it, and run `ThreadPriorities`. You'll see that thread T2, with the higher priority, gets more time to run and finishes counting sooner.

This example has introduced several more aspects of the `Thread` API. It illustrates the `setName()` method that assigns a thread a descriptive name, which we can retrieve with `getName()` to clarify what's happening in our program. It also shows the method `setPriority()`, which takes a single integer argument that becomes the new priority level of this thread.

Typically, applications will call `setPriority()` with an argument that is based on one of the built-in values (static variables of `Thread`) `MAX_PRIORITY`, `MIN_PRIORITY`, or `NORM_PRIORITY`. These correspond to numeric values of 10, 1, and 5, respectively, as defined in class `Thread`.

A thread that runs all the time, but which can yield to any time-critical event, might be assigned `MIN_PRIORITY`; a user interaction thread might be assigned `NORM_PRIORITY` or a higher value.

Don't expect some neat mathematical relationship between the ratios of priority values and the sharing of processing time. Threads of equal priority, for example, that don't explicitly call the `yield()` method, may or may not ever yield control to each other, depending on which implementation of the Java virtual machine is being used.

The rule is that Java's scheduler should choose the highest-priority thread that's in a runnable condition. There is preemption of lower-priority threads by higher-priority threads, but there is not necessarily a fair division of time among threads of equal priority.

The Windows 95 implementation of thread scheduling is one of the best behaved. Our examples use techniques like random-duration sleeping to ensure that examples will behave well on other platforms, such as Solaris, where simpler code did not illustrate the intended points during tests prior to publication of this book.

Priorities are useful, but programmers should understand their limits before assuming that they will see "reasonable" behavior, or even consistent behavior among different Java platforms.

Born to Run

What if we've already defined a class hierarchy that meets the needs of our problem, and we have a class that is *not* a subclass of Thread—but we still want to give an instance of this class its own Thread context, for concurrent execution with other threads?

It sounds as if we want to be able to inherit from Thread, as well as inheriting from the class that we originally chose for other reasons. That would be multiple inheritance, which Java does not allow.

But let's step back for a moment. What we want to do is create a thread and hand it an object that will execute under that thread's control. When we start that thread, it's going to call the run() method of that object.

So the only thing we need to ensure is that our object has a run() method. We don't care what that method does. The method just has to have that magic name.

This sounds like the definitive example of what we can do with an interface. We need to make sure that no matter what else an object can do, it can also be run. We could call that interface, ummm, let's see…

Runnable!

The Runnable interface is surprisingly easy to use, as we can show with a trivial modification of the HearYou example above.

```
import java.io.*;

class Counter implements Runnable // instead of
                               // "extends Thread"
  { int i = 0;
    public void run(){ /* stuff */ }}

class Listener implements Runnable  // ditto
  { DataInputStream userInput
```

```
                              = new DataInputStream(System.in);
        String input    = "";
        public void run(){ /* stuff */ }}

    class HearYou
     { public static void main(String args[])
       { Thread counter  = new Thread(new Counter());
         Thread listener = new Thread(new Listener());

       // Create each Thread with the constructor that
       //  takes a Runnable object, and returns
       //  a Thread that executes that object's run()

         listener.start();
         counter.start();
       }
     }
```

Sorry if this seems too simple. But interfaces are like that.

You Can Count on Me

One could write an entire book on advanced applications of threads. Such books exist, some of them more than half the size of this one.

We won't go that far, but we won't leave the subject of threads without first showing a more interesting application.

In our opening example, we declared our two Thread objects with the default constructors,

```
        Thread counter  = new Counter();
        Thread listener = new Listener();
```

This created two new threads whose only knowledge of the world was locked up in their class definitions. Any Counter counted to a fixed value, any Listener responded to a predetermined Quit command, and none of the instances of these classes knew or cared about any others. It was only in a calling method, such as main() in either class HearYou or class ThreadPriorities, that we had expressions like

```
        while(counter.isAlive() || listener.isAlive())
```

In a real-world program, it might be useful for threads to have some awareness of each other. This example expands on the previous example to show some ways that threads can reflect runtime input and can take notice of each other's activities.

```
import java.io.*;

class Counter extends Thread
  { int i = 0;
    int maxCount;     // a new instance variable
    Thread watched;   // and another
    Counter(int maxCount)
        // constructor takes the maximum value
        //  for the counter as a parameter
      { this.maxCount = maxCount; }

    public void start(Thread another)
      { watched = another; // remember what to watch
        super.start();     // before calling Thread's
                           // "normal" start()

      }

    public void run()
      { while( watched.isAlive() && (i < maxCount) )
          // Runs as long as the watched thread is
          //  either running, or able to run, and maximum
          //  counter value has not been reached
          { System.out.println(i++);
            try { sleep(1000); }
            catch (InterruptedException e){}
          }
        System.out.println(getName()+" stopped at "+i);
      }

  }

class Listener extends Thread
  { DataInputStream userInput
                    = new DataInputStream(System.in);
    String input = "";
    String quitCommand; // a new instance variable
```

```java
    Listener(String quitCommand)
      // Constructor takes the command for
      //  quitting this Listener as a parameter
    { this.quitCommand = quitCommand; }

    public void run()
     { while ( !input.equals(quitCommand) )
        { try { input = userInput.readLine(); }
          catch(IOException e){}
          System.out.println("You typed " + input);
        }
      System.out.println(getName() + " has stopped.");
     }
   }


class HearYou
 { public static void main(String args[])
      // Run this with a command such as
      //    "java HearYou 8 X"

    { int maxCount
            = Integer.valueOf(args[0]).intValue();
      // That was a use of a wrapper class

      String quitCommand = args[1]; // args are Strings

      Counter counter = new Counter(maxCount);
      Listener listener = new Listener(quitCommand);
      // Here we used our parameter-based constructors

      counter.setPriority(Thread.MAX_PRIORITY);
      listener.setPriority(Thread.NORM_PRIORITY);
      // Make sure Solaris pays attention

      listener.start();
      counter.start(listener); // watch listener
      // launch our new Thread-subclass objects
```

```
        while(counter.isAlive() || listener.isAlive())
          { System.out.println("Type "
                                + quitCommand
                                + " to quit.");
             try{Thread.sleep(5000);}
             catch(InterruptedException e){}
          }
        }
      }
```

A session of this program might look like,

```
C:\HowToJava>java HearYou 5 X
0
Type X to quit.
Hello
You typed Hello
1
2
3
X
You typed X
Thread-2 has stopped.
Thread-1 stopped at 4

C:\HowToJava>
```

Watch Out for Tangles

In the example above, we're controlling a loop, in part, with the result that we get by calling

```
watched.isAlive()
```

This would waste a huge fraction of the processor's attention if the loop body didn't include a call to sleep(). Practical applications of multithreading rely on more efficient mechanisms to communicate with each other. They also use Java facilities that prevent undesired interactions between several threads that share a common resource.

These facilities are surprisingly simple. A method can be declared with the prefix keyword `synchronized`, as in:

```
synchronized <return type> <method name>()
```

When one thread enters such a method, no other thread can invoke that method until the first thread leaves. If that `synchronized` method manipulates one or more private data structures, for example, then we can be sure that we won't have two threads making changes at the same time.

For example, a warehouse application might have a private data structure that represents the current inventory. It might have a method that seeks to place an order, first checking that the inventory is adequate, then reducing that inventory by the amount of the order.

If more than one thread were active, they might happen to check the inventory at almost the same time, each finding an adequate level before either one has recorded its withdrawal from that stock.

The first thread to continue with its actual withdrawal would get what it expected, but the second might try to take more than what remained.

A `synchronized` method, combining both the inventory check and the inventory reduction, would prevent this.

An entire object can also be locked by a `synchronized` statement. For example, if you wanted to do some time-consuming operations on an array, and you wanted to be sure that no other thread would be changing anything inside that array until you were done, you could write

```
synchronized(arrayName) {<do things to arrayName>}
```

No other thread can lock this array while it is locked by any other thread.

But what if we don't just want to keep other threads out of a method until our thread is finished? What if we want to have another thread wait until we're done with something, and then have that other thread take over?

Within a `synchronized` method, we can do this by using the methods `wait()` and `notify()`. For the first time since Chapter 6, we're going to draw a line and say, "We won't get into this."

The reason we're stopping here is that threads interacting through `wait()` and `notify()` can wind up in what's called a *deadlock* state, with two or more threads each waiting for the other—and waiting, quite possibly, forever. Java does not detect deadlocks, let alone prevent them.

These advanced facilities for multi-way interaction between threads and data structures are ready for you to explore whenever you're ready to deal with their implications. Appendix C, which lists useful Java resources, includes books that deal with threads in depth.

Exceptional Courtesy

You've been very patient. Ever since Chapter 4, we've been making occasional mysterious invocations of

```
throws IOException
```

or

```
try {sleep(1000);}
catch (InterruptedException e) {}
```

Why does a program have to `try` something? Doesn't a program just go ahead and do things? What happens if it gets caught?

It's time to explain this powerful, but very simple, mechanism that does so much to aid the readability and reliability of our programs.

An `Exception` is an object, an instance of a subclass of `Throwable`, that contains useful information about some abnormal condition that some method has encountered.

When a method attempts to perform some action, and it finds itself in a state that makes it throw an exception, a piece of code called an *exception handler* will get a chance to examine the `Exception` object and decide how best to proceed.

The essential ideas are as follows.

A method can announce, in effect, "I know that this might not work," by wrapping a piece of its code in a "try" block such as:

```
try {sleep(1000);}
```

In the case of the `sleep()` method of class `Thread`, we do this because a sleeping thread will throw the exception `InterruptedException` if another thread interrupts it (using a method that we have not examined). Because the method `sleep()` is *able* to throw this exception, Java will not compile a program that calls this method unless that program declares its intentions for handling that exception.

Here are some examples of what works, and what does not:

```
class Test
 { void catchAny()
    { try{ Thread.sleep(1000); }
      catch (Exception e){}
      // catches any imaginable exception
    }
   void catchIEOnly()
    { try{ Thread.sleep(1000); }
      catch (InterruptedException e){}
      // catches the only exception sleep() can throw
    }
   void throwIt() throws Exception
      // "It's not my problem"
    { Thread.sleep(1000);
    }
   void vagrant() // This won't compile
    { Thread.sleep(1000);
    }
 }
```

Following a `try` block, a program can have one or more `catch` clauses. Each of these clauses specifies a class of exception, and provides a block of code that should be executed if that class of exception (which includes any subclasses of that class) is caught.

Exceptions, being objects, belong to Java's hierarchy of classes: for example, the class `InterruptedIOException` specializes the class `IOException`.

The `catch` clauses will be tested, in the order in which they appear, until one of them matches the exception that was thrown—either exactly, or by virtue of a superclass relationship.

Consider a situation in which this hierarchy affects our code. An instance of `InterruptedIOException` is thrown, logically enough, when an input/output operation is interrupted. That `InterruptedIOException` object will contain an instance variable, `bytesTransferred`, that holds the number of bytes successfully transferred before the interruption took place.

The program may then use this information to decide what it should do next. By comparing the number of bytes transferred to the known or estimated size of the total task, the program can apply a variety of possible strategies for trying again, trying another transfer route, postponing the operation, or asking the user to select an option.

An input/output operation might also throw the more general `IOException`. Such an exception will *not* be caught by a `catch` clause that specifies `InterruptedIOException`, since the latter clause might very well expect to do something based on a caught exception's value of `bytesTransferred`. We can't assume that the general-case `IOException` will define this value.

But a clause that catches `IOException` *will* also catch the more specific `InterruptedIOException`. For this reason, `catch` clauses must appear within a method in order from the most specific to the most general.

Come Back with Your Shield, or on It

Java will not compile a method that can throw an exception unless that exception is either handled within the same method, or covered (individually or as part of a superclass) by a `throws` in the method declaration.

We've used both of these approaches. We've sometimes chosen to ignore exceptions with a local, general handler that does nothing, as in:

```
try {input=userInput.readLine();}
catch (Exception e) {}
```

or we've passed the buck with a declaration like:

```
class WeeklyAverage
 {public static void main(String args[])
                  throws IOException...
```

Here are some less perfunctory examples:

```
class Catcher
{public static void main(String args[])
 {try
  {int divideThis= Integer.valueOf(args[0]).intValue();
   int divideBy  = Integer.valueOf(args[1]).intValue();
   System.out.println(divideThis / divideBy);
   }
  catch (ArrayIndexOutOfBoundsException e)
  {System.out.println("Too few arguments: " +e);}
  catch (ArithmeticException e)
  {System.out.println("Div. by zero? " +e);}
  }
 }
```

If this example is run with no parameters, it will throw an exception with the first attempt to access `args[0]`, since there is no such value. The exception will be caught and a descriptive message printed.

If it's run with one parameter, the same thing will happen when it tries to access `args[1]`.

If it's run with two or more parameters, but the second one is zero, it will throw, catch, and report an exception when it tries to divide by zero. We could also have done something like return a default value of 1, if this were a method that was being called to return a value instead of just printing a result.

If it's run with two or more parameters, the second one nonzero, it performs the integer division and prints the result.

The Second Time Around

Note that an exception handler doesn't necessarily have to do the whole job. It can do something, then re-throw the original exception or some newly created exception, as in the following:

```java
class Catcher
 { public static void main(String args[])
    { try
       { thrower(Integer.valueOf(args[0]).intValue(),
                 Integer.valueOf(args[1]).intValue());
       }
     catch (ArrayIndexOutOfBoundsException e)
       { System.out.println("Too few arguments: " +e);
       }
     catch (ArithmeticException e)
       { System.out.println("Rethrown exception " +e);
       }
    }

  static void thrower(int divideThis, int divideBy)
    { try { System.out.println(divideThis/divideBy);
         }
     catch (ArithmeticException e)
       { System.out.println("Caught in thrower");
         throw e;
       }
    }
 }
```

Clean Up before You Leave

Following a `try` block, and after any `catch` clauses that might be used, a program can have a `finally` clause. For example,

```
static void thrower(int divideThis, int divideBy)
  { try { int quotient = divideThis / divideBy; }
    catch (ArithmeticException e)
      { System.out.println("Caught in thrower");
        throw e; }
    finally { System.out.println("Bye..."); }
  }
```

Any code in a `finally` clause is going to be executed *before control leaves that region* of the program. If the `try` block completes without exceptions, the `catch` clause(s) will be ignored, but the `finally` clause will be used.

If an exception keeps the `try` block from completing, the first relevant `catch` clause (if any) will take effect, followed by the code in the `finally` clause. If a `catch` clause is applied and throws an exception in turn, as in our example above, the `finally` clause is still going to be applied *before* the calling method gets its turn to examine the re-thrown exception.

After executing the code in the `finally` clause, the program continues normally if there were no uncaught exceptions. Otherwise, it returns to the calling method, as in our example above.

For Exceptional Cases Only

It's poor style to use exception handling for conditions that are not abnormal. For example, it might be part of some business application to divide one number by another, unless the second number is zero, in which case the program should use some standard value instead of computing the ratio.

In this case, it would *not* be appropriate to do the division, then use exception handling to trap and deal with the case of division by zero. If a zero value were abnormal, we wouldn't have a business rule for what to do when we saw one. Exception handling takes much longer than performing an ordinary conditional test.

In such cases, it is better style to use an operator like `?:` to detect and deal with this condition, as in:

```
ratioValue = ( x != 0 ? y/x : standardValue );
```

Degrees of Difficulty

The class Exception is one subclass of Throwable, whose other subclass is Error.

Unlike exceptions, errors are so unusual that no application is expected to anticipate them or tolerate them. Errors include problems that indicate an error by the compiler, or fatal situations such as a shortage of memory that doesn't get fixed by garbage collection.

The good news, such as it is, is that Java will report the cause of death rather than committing suicide without leaving a note.

We Want You to Feel Secure

Security is one of the buzzwords that's most often invoked in praise of Java. The praise is not misplaced.

Being unable to operate directly on arbitrary pointers to memory, the Java language cannot be used to write programs that invade each other or their host operating system.

Being compiled to bytecodes, rather than native machine codes, Java programs can be verified by a hardware-independent process before they run: This guards against the use of a rogue compiler that tries to go around the semantic protections of the Java language.

Being protected by a well-defined mechanism of exceptions and errors, a Java program that encounters abnormal conditions will fail in a predictable way that does not threaten the operation of other programs. It is still possible to write programs that fail to release resources, for example, by omitting finally clauses in exception-handling code, but Java's garbage collection dramatically reduces the likelihood of accidental errors of this kind.

Malicious programs that seize resources such as memory, or that impede other programs by occupying more than their share of the processor's time, can still be written in Java: It is up to the next layer of protection, the operating system, to guard against attacks of this type.

Under New Management

But there are other aspects to security that become especially important in a networked environment, where access to resources such as files has important implications.

A Java program might scan our hard disk, for example, in search of strings of digits that look like credit card account numbers, and mail what it finds to some remote address. Through the magic of threads, this could all be happening while the program is doing something else quite innocent and useful.

At the time that it starts, a Java virtual machine is unrestricted: Java programs can operate on files or make network connections at will. These privileges can be modified, however, by installing an instance of the class `SecurityManager` that's defined in package `java.lang`.

This can only be done once in a session, and the installed `SecurityManager` cannot be replaced or modified.

`SecurityManager` is actually an abstract class, meaning that it cannot be instantiated. A program must define a subclass and create an instance of that.

The base class is `abstract` because it is declared to be, not because it has abstract methods with no implementation. The reason for making it abstract is that this class, unmodified, forbids everything.

If you were able to call

```
System.setSecurityManager( new SecurityManager() );
```

in a program, you would no longer be able to use any file or any network connection; you would be barred from stopping any thread, or even from changing its priority or its name.

If you want to create a Java environment with specialized permissions, you do this by defining a subclass of `SecurityManager` and overriding its default ("deny everything") methods with more appropriate behaviors. For example, you might allow read-only access to files whose names begin with a certain pattern.

The programs you write for your own use don't need these facilities, while the programs that you use in your Web browser will run under the protection of a `SecurityManager` provided by that environment. For further details, therefore, please consult the API documentation on the CD-ROM that comes with this book (as described in Appendix D).

More Things with Strings

If you were paying close attention during your work with our various versions of class `Listener`, you probably noticed expressions of the form:

```
while ( !input.equals("Quit") )
```

Question: Why did we use this form of comparison, rather than writing (more intuitively):

```
while ( input != "Quit")
```

The reason is that the second expression doesn't mean the same thing at all.

When we use the identity operators, == and !=, on a pair of identifiers that serve as names for character strings, we are asking if these two identifiers point to the same identical string at a single location in our computer's memory.

When we use the equals() method, we are comparing the contents of two String objects, without regard to their location. This is much more likely to be relevant in programs that process user input, analyze streams of data, and ask everyday questions about words and phrases.

The Java API defines many other useful methods on Strings. We aren't limited, for example, to comparing string contents for equality. We can also ask questions about alphabetic order, using the method compareTo(), which returns an integer whose sign indicates the case-sensitive ordering of the object compared to the object that's given as the argument to the method.

For example,

```
"a".compareTo("b")     returns a negative value
"A".compareTo("AB")    negative value
"a".compareTo("A")     positive value
"Ab".compareTo("AC")   positive value: ( (int)'b' > (int)'C' )  == true
```

If you want to compare strings in "dictionary order" (that is, without regard to case), you can compare them after applying one of the methods toUpperCase() or toLowerCase(), as in

```
"a".toUpperCase().compareTo("A")     zero
```

This is one of those little things that the careful programmer quickly adopts as a habit, eliminating "gotchas" like our class Listener and its insistence on Quit (with that exact capitalization) as its command to terminate. More robustly written, the test in Listener might be

```
while(!in.toLowerCase().equals(quitCmd.toLowerCase())
```

(Don't overlook that ! at the beginning that means "not": it's surprising how many programs stumble on something this fundamental.)

We won't use any more space here to list the methods of String. For further information, refer to the Java API.

Giving You Static on Math

Class `Math` is a platypus. It's one of those things that proves an eternal truth, that anything that's possible will someday turn out to be useful.

When we first introduced the idea of objects, would you ever have thought of using a class merely to hold a collection of static values and methods? No instance variables, and for that matter, no instances.

But class `Math` lets us give Java programs a generous vocabulary of mathematical functions, which are defined to conform with strict standards for accuracy and consistency of computational results.

Class `Math` gives us values, accurate to Java's `double` precision, for the constants π and e. In keeping with programming convention, these constant values are rendered with capitalized names like `PI` and `E`.

Other methods defined in `Math`, and the types of arguments that each will accept and return, are shown in Table 11.1. Unless otherwise noted, a function returns a value with the same type as the types of its arguments, or with values of the type that results from promotion of the input to the lowest type for which the method is defined.

For example,

```
System.out.println(Math.pow(2,3));
```

yields the output 8, as you'd expect, but:

```
int eight = Math.pow(2,3);
```

yields

```
Incompatible type for declaration.
Explicit cast needed to convert double to int.
```

because `pow()` returns a double, no matter what it gets. The methods `abs()`, `max()`, and `min()` are more intuitive in their behavior, returning what you give them for all numeric types except `byte` and `short`; the `round()` methods perform reasonable type conversions, but the ceiling and floor methods, `ceil()` and `floor()`, do not.

The last two methods in the table, `rint(x)` and `IEEEremainder(x,y)`, implement special definitions of rounding and remainder. They seek to reduce the accumulation of errors that can result from consistently rounding up when a value is halfway between two integers. Both of these methods are based on definitions that round to the even integer, rather than rounding up.

That's a Wrap

We'll conclude this chapter with an overview of Java's wrapper classes. As we said at the beginning of the chapter, these let us enjoy the convenience and the readability that come from object methods, without giving up the efficiency that comes from doing most of our low-level operations with primitive types.

When we look at the powerful automatic data structures defined in `java.lang.util`, for example, we'll see that these are defined to hold `Objects` rather than the discrete values that we can store in something like an `int[]`. Wrapping a number in an instance of the appropriate wrapper class lets us use those more powerful data structures to work with numbers, as well as with more complex types of data.

TABLE 11.1 PUBLIC STATIC METHODS OF CLASS MATH

Function	Description	Types of Arguments
max(i,j)	larger of two values	double, float, int, long
min(i,j)	smaller of two values	double, float, int, long
abs(i)	absolute value	double, float, int, long
ceil(x)	ceiling (round up)	double
floor(x)	floor (round down)	double
round(x)	round (returning a long)	double
round(x)	round (returning an int)	float
pow(y,x)	y to power x	double
exp(x)	e power x	double
log(x)	logarithm of x to base e	double
sqrt(x)	square root	double
sin(x)	sine	double
cos(x)	cosine	double
tan(x)	tangent	double
acos(x)	arc cosine	double
asin(x)	arc sine	double
atan(x)	arc tangent	double
atan2(y,x)	angle whose tangent is y/x	double
random()	a double between 0.0 and 1.0	no argument
rint(x)	round	double
IEEEremainder(x,y)	remainder	double

A Matter of Character

When we wrap a `char` value inside a `Character` object, we can send it to places that expect an `Object` rather than a simple-type value.

In addition to this, however, the class `Character` also serves (like class `Math`) as a repository of useful utility methods.

The following statements explore the nature of `Character` objects versus that of simple `char` values, as well as the manner of using `Character`'s utility functions.

```
char cSimple1 = 'C';
char cSimple2 = 'C'
Character cObject1 = new Character(cSimple1);
Character cObject2 = new Character(cSimple1);

System.out.println('C' == 'C');            // true
System.out.println(cSimple1 == cSimple2);  // true
```

We're reminded that `char`s are unsigned 16-bit values; == compares those values.

```
System.out.println(cObject1 == cObject2);        // false
System.out.println(cObject1.equals(cObject2));   // true
```

We're reminded that `Character`s are `Object`s, and that (like a `String`) a `Character` has both an identity (a location in memory, which is what gets compared using ==) and a content (an unalterable field containing a single `char`, initialized when the `Character` is constructed, which is what gets compared using `equals()`).

```
System.out.println(cSimple1);    // C
System.out.println(cObject1);    // C
```

We see that `println()` can extract a meaningful string from either representation.

```
System.out.println(Character.isSpace('C'));     // false
System.out.println(Character.toLowerCase('C'));// c
```

We can call the static methods of class `Character` to operate on simple `char` values, in the same way that we call upon the static methods of class `Math` to operate on simple numeric values.

In the same spirit as the method `isSpace()` shown above, we also have `isUpperCase()`, `isLowerCase()`, and `isLetterOrDigit()`.

Other methods defined on this class are chiefly used for Unicode manipulations. Few operating environments provide full-strength support for doing anything useful with Unicode, so these are unlikely to enter into your programs. Consult the API for details.

Varnished Truth

You'll recall that when we introduced the `boolean` data type, we mentioned that only the lowercase words `true` and `false` were reserved by the Java language. Within class `Boolean` (with a capital *B*, not the lowercase *b* of the simple type), the identifiers `TRUE` and `FALSE` also have special meanings as predefined objects corresponding to these primitives.

The Boolean class also lets us write programs that don't make users worry about such details, with constructors that can accept either a primitive `boolean` value or a case-insensitive string. For example,

```
Boolean testPrimitive = new Boolean(true);
Boolean testString    = new Boolean("true");
Boolean testMixed     = new Boolean("tRuE");
```

Additional methods (unlikely to appear in your programs, but needed for semantic completeness) are described in the API.

By the Numbers

Class `Number` is an `abstract` class, with subclasses `Integer`, `Long`, `Float`, and `Double`. Being an `abstract` class, `Number` can define abstract methods, forcing any subclass to implement those methods unless it wants to be `abstract` as well.

The four abstract methods defined in Number are

▶ `doubleValue()`

▶ `floatValue()`

▶ `intValue()`

▶ `longValue()`

These convert the value of the object into a corresponding representation by one of the simple types.

This explains the strange incantations in some of our previous examples, like:

```
Integer.valueOf(args[0]).intValue();
```

which almost looks as if we kept throwing the word *value* at something until it gave up and told us what it was.

That expression says, in effect,

▶ Begin with the `String` contained in `args[0]`.

▶ Use the `valueOf()` method defined on class `Integer` to return an `Integer` object, representing the integer value obtained by parsing that character string.

▶ Use the `intValue()` method defined on class `Integer`, invoked on that `Integer` object, to return a simple `int` value.

Actually, this is overkill. We can get the same result by saying

```
Integer.parseInt(args[0]);
```

or

```
Integer(args[0]).intValue();
```

which are easier to read, and clearer in meaning. They're restricted, however, to working with base-10 integers.

The more verbose approach, using `valueOf()`, leaves more options open. For example, this method name is overloaded with another version that takes two arguments: a character string, and a number representing a *radix* (a base).

By advising this method that we're working with radix 2, we can translate a binary number to a base-10 value with an expression like:

```
Integer.valueOf("11111",2).intValue()
```

which returns the value 31 as an `int`. Or we can perform the reverse operation with:

```
Integer.toString(31,2)
```

which returns the value "11111" as a `String`.

The following example illustrates several approaches to using class `Integer`, and gives us a hexadecimal-to-decimal converter as well:

```
class WithInteger
{public static void main(String args[])
 {int general = Integer.valueOf(args[0]).intValue();
  int hexing  = Integer.valueOf(args[0],16).intValue();
  int decimal = Integer.parseInt(args[0]);
  int construct = new Integer(args[0]).intValue();
//int wontWork  = Integer.valueOf(args[0]);
//      because ^this returns an Integer, not an int
```

```
System.out.println("Base 10: " + general);
System.out.println("Base 16: " + hexing );
  }
 }
```

with a typical run looking like:

```
C:\HowToJava>java WithInteger 100
Base 10: 100
Base 16: 256


C:\HowToJava>
```

Similar methods are provided by the wrapper classes for the other simple numeric types, as listed in the API. New conversions are added in Java 1.1, for which compilers had yet to be released at the time this book was written. For example, Java 1.1 will provide the methods `toBinaryString()`, `toOctalString()`, and `toHexString()` for ease of displaying integer numbers in these formats.

The wrapper classes for `float` and `double` provide reference values for advanced IEEE-standard operations, of the kind discussed in Chapter 4: values like NaN (not a number) and `POSITIVE_INFINITY`. These classes also provide static methods like `isInfinite()` (returning a `boolean` result), or `doubleToLongBits()` (returning a direct translation of a `double` to the `long` that is represented internally by the same string of bits).

Here are some uses of class Double:

```
Double d = new Double(5.4);

System.out.println(d.doubleValue());          // 5.4
System.out.println(d.floatValue());           // 5.4
System.out.println(d.intValue());             // 5

System.out.println(d.longValue());            // 5
System.out.println(Double.doubleToLongBits(5.4));
                              // 4617765877924338074

System.out.println(Double.isInfinite(1.0/0.0)); // true
System.out.println(Double.isNaN(
           Double.POSITIVE_INFINITY * 0.0
                     ));               // true
```

Consult the API reference for a complete list of wrapper-class methods, and Appendix B for the latest information available on Java 1.1 as of the time that this book was completed.

Summary

In this chapter, we showed

▶ That threads (lightweight processes) can be constructed by subclassing `Thread`, or by implementing interface `Runnable`, to create programs that remain attentive to the user or to other external events while performing their tasks.

▶ That exception handling is based on wrapping a piece of our program in a try block, and catching an object that represents an abnormal situation arising within that code.

▶ That we can define several layers of exception handler, from the most specific to the most general, and that we can re-throw exceptions to deal with problems in the most effective way available.

▶ That Java's much-praised security is not an all-or-nothing choice between unrestricted applications and severely limited applets; that class `SecurityManager` can be subclassed to describe finely grained sets of permissions for every important aspect of a program's interaction with both the local machine and remote network resources.

▶ That the classes provided by `java.lang` for working with simple data types provide both instance methods (aimed at operating on object-style data) and static (class) methods (able to operate on "unwrapped" primitive variables).

Packaging Input
and Output
Operations in
Objects

Using Objects to
Control Data
Manipulation

Investigating Objects
in Running Programs

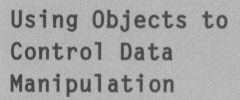

Chapter 12
Good Stuff In, Good Stuff Out: Package `java.io`

In this chapter, you'll learn how classes `InputStream` and `OutputStream` package the complexity of input and output operations into objects with useful behaviors, such as automatic conversions between various data types. You'll see how class `File` lets us treat a disk file as an object whose properties (including its contents) can be inspected and used to control what a program does with data. We'll also cover how to ask questions about an object's class, at the time that a program runs, to take advantage of specialized subclass behaviors.

If we want to connect our programs to real-world data, someone has to deal with the difference between the abstract and the ugly. The internal world of a language like Java is a realm of nearly mathematical elegance, but the outside world is a realm of crude, clashing hardware.

Consider a hard disk: Platters of metal, coated with highly refined rust, are abused by fiendish instruments of torture that rudely rearrange billions of magnetic domains.

Consider the simple cable that connects a computer to a modem: Bundles of wire, trapped within rigid arrays of connections, carry variable currents at uncertain voltages in bursts that arrive at relentless rates and on unforgiving schedules.

Somehow, though, we conceal this chaos. We rely on a combination of interface hardware, plus that hardware's built-in "firmware," interacting with a collection of device driver system software under the control of an operating system's hardware abstraction layers, coupled into Java's own virtual machine and standard class libraries, to create an elaborate facade.

The result, as seen by our programs, has the appearance of clean, neat files and other data sources and destinations, giving and receiving orderly *streams* (as we'll call them) of data. It's one of the unsung miracles of computing.

Making Good Connections

On any given computer, input and output can follow widely varying rules that govern timing and other signal characteristics. These differences are hidden by the many layers of abstraction that we barely began to describe above.

For example, a hard disk controller makes a hard disk's platters look like numbered cylinders and sectors; an operating system makes those cylinders and sectors look like a set of named files.

But object-oriented programs, of the kind that we want to write with Java, need something even more abstract. Depending on the needs of a given problem, an object might need to interact with data in memory; with data on the disk; or with data in the outside world, as when reading a sensor or controlling another device.

We don't want to write a different version of an object for every such type of external interaction. Rather, we would prefer to have a family of connector classes that can make all input and output interactions follow similar rules.

The standard package `java.io` defines classes that can represent and control such interactions. They do this, in most cases, by instantiating specialized subclasses of the general-purpose `InputStream` and `OutputStream`. This package also provides useful mechanisms for dealing with file names and file systems, wrapped in class `File`.

We've Got a File on You

Let's write a simple program that can take a file name as a parameter, and print that file to the standard output device. *Print* is a misnomer, since that standard output is usually the console window and not your hard-copy printer. But it's still referred to as printing, and the stream `System.out` that we've used in almost every example in this book is an instance of class `PrintStream`.

If we don't provide a file name to this program (that is, if we run it with no parameters), then the program should read a file from the keyboard. In this case, to end the program normally, you will need to know how your operating system marks an end-of-file in keyboard input.

Under DOS or Windows, for example, the key chord Ctrl-Z has this role. Alternatively, you can abort the program by whatever method your system provides, such as the key chord Ctrl-C (DOS/Windows, Unix) or Command-period (Macintosh) or by clicking on the Close button of the console window (most graphical environments).

Here is the code:

```
import java.io.*;

class UseStreams
  { public static void main(String args[])
       throws IOException
    { InputStream incoming
       = (args.length==0) // the () aren't needed,
           ? System.in //   but add clarity
           : new FileInputStream(args[0]);
      PrintStream outgoing = System.out;
      int nextByteOfFile;
      while ((nextByteOfFile=incoming.read()) != -1)
        { outgoing.write(nextByteOfFile); }
    }
  }
```

Let's take this example apart, and see why and how it works.

Matters of High Import

We begin by importing java.io.*, giving us access to the classes from which we will want to instantiate stream-type objects. This package is present and importable in any standard Java installation, but it is not imported automatically (as was java.lang).

We declare throws IOException as part of the declaration of method main(). This makes the rest of our code easier to read, since it reduces the visual clutter of try{} blocks and catch(){} clauses. We'd have to provide these, anyway, whenever we called a method that can throw an instance (or an instance of a subclass) of IOException.

For example, method read() throws an IOException if it fails to return an appropriate value (as we'll define below). In a real-world program, you'd have to decide if there were any useful actions that could be taken to deal with such an exception, and if so wrap a try{} block around the read()—with a non-empty catch clause body to perform that action. We discussed this in Chapter 11.

We use the ternary operator to look, concisely, at the length of our args[] array, and to assign either the standard input stream (if there weren't any arguments) or a new `FileInputStream` (using the file named in the first argument) to the variable `incoming`.

Note that `incoming` is declared as an `InputStream`, not as a `FileInputStream`. That's because we want to preserve the option of assigning the predefined stream `System.in` to this variable, and `System.in` is only declared as a general-case `InputStream`. This is the kind of thing that's documented in the Java API.

Since class `FileInputStream` extends `InputStream`, an `InputStream` variable can refer to a `FileInputStream` object—but not the other way around.

For Instance?

If we're actually reading from a file, not from the keyboard, we might want to use some of the methods that are specific to class `FileInputStream`: for example, `getFD()`, which returns a file descriptor object that encapsulates the low-level connection to a file. (Class `SecurityManager`, which we examined in Chapter 11, uses a file descriptor as the argument to the methods `checkRead()` and `checkWrite()`: these methods determine if the current Java session is authorized to use a given file in each of these ways.)

If `incoming` actually does point to an instance of `FileInputStream`, we can tell Java to show us that object's file descriptor with a statement like,

```
if (incoming instanceof FileInputStream)
        System.out.println(
            ((FileInputStream)incoming).getFD()
                        );
```

This says, in effect, "If the identifier `incoming` points to a `FileInputStream`, then create a `FileInputStream` handle to that object and invoke `getFD()` on that handle."

Without the casting operation, performed by placing `(FileInputStream)` before the name `incoming`, the Java compiler will not compile this statement. That's because `incoming` (so far as the compiler knows) is still just declared as an `InputStream` and cannot be guaranteed to support `getFD()`.

In theory, the compiler could determine from the context of this statement that the Java virtual machine will never be asked to invoke `getFD()` unless `incoming` has already been found to be of the proper class. But that's not the way things are done, and more complex programs could become quite difficult to understand if programmers could rely on this kind of "declaration by implication."

Note also the use of parentheses in:

```
((FileInputStream)incoming).getFD()
```

to say, in effect, "Make a `FileInputStream` with `incoming`, *then* apply `getFD()` to that object." If we had written merely

```
(FileInputStream)incoming.getFD()
```

then we would be saying, "Apply `getFD()` to `incoming`, and cast the returned file descriptor to a `FileInputStream`."

The latter is doubly absurd: First, because an ordinary `InputStream` like the uncast `incoming` cannot be queried for its file descriptor; second, because a file descriptor (an instance of a class that extends class `Object`) cannot be cast to a `FileInputStream` (a class that extends `InputStream`).

The expression above is our first use of the helpful operator `instanceof`, which we lacked the context to explain in a meaningful way when we presented most of Java's operators in Chapter 5.

Like the operator `new`, which we deferred until Chapter 8, `instanceof` waited to make its appearance until we could show you how it gives our programs greater power.

Chewing through the Bytes

We use a concise, idiomatic technique to read from our input stream, and to compare the result to the signal value for the end of a stream. The expression

```
nextByteOfFile=incoming.read()
```

assigns an integer value, between -1 and 255 (inclusive), to the `int` variable `nextByteOfFile`, and returns that `int` as the value of the assignment expression.

Note that method `read()` is declared as an `abstract` method in class `InputStream`, meaning that any subclass of `InputStream` must *implement* a method named `read()`. This method, in any subclass of `InputStream`, must return the value of the next byte available to the stream (its unsigned value) in the lowest eight bits of a 32-bit. `int`.

Method `read()` returns an `int`, even though we're reading input from the stream one byte at a time, because the `byte` type is a signed type whose value ranges from −128 to 127. It's more natural to deal with incoming bytes from a file as unsigned values from 0 through 255.

We compare the returned `int` value against −1, which method `read()` returns when it encounters an end-of-stream condition; we use that comparison as the `boolean` test for a `while` loop.

The body of the loop then writes the incoming byte to the output stream, using `write()`, which also takes an `int` as its argument. Anything in the upper 24 bits of that 32-bit `int` will be discarded: *only* the lowest byte of the `int` will be sent to the stream.

The `while` loop evaluates its test expression, reading the next byte of input as a side effect, and the loop continues until the end of the file is reached or the end-of-stream key is typed.

If you run this class with no parameters, you won't be prompted for input, but you can start typing as soon as the Java interpreter displays its start-up messages. If you run this class with an input parameter like \autoexec.bat, you'll display your autoexec.bat file (if you're on a DOS or Windows machine) as if you had used the TYPE command from the DOS prompt.

Because we can see what a `PrintStream` is doing, it makes a good starting point for demonstrating how we can extend a class and override its methods to meet a more specialized need.

For example, we can define

```
public class UpperOut extends PrintStream
  { UpperOut (PrintStream out)
      { super(out); // use PrintStream's constructor
      }
    public void write(int w)
      { super.write(Character.toUpperCase((char)w));
        // and invoke PrintStream's write() on a
        //  modified argument
      }
  }
```

This gives us a new kind of `PrintStream` whose `write()` method converts all output to uppercase. If we modify class `UseStreams` to say,

```
UpperOut outgoing = new UpperOut(System.out);
```

then we will see this changed behavior when we execute `UseStreams` with either file or keyboard input.

We could also put the conversion into the `while` loop of `UseStreams` itself, but with the separate class `UpperOut` we can offer this pre-packaged behavior for use by other classes. If we later decide that we'd prefer mixed-case output, changing the definition of `UpperOut` will take care of every such case. That's the leverage that object methods can provide.

Other useful methods defined on `InputStream` include:

▶ `available()` Returns the number of bytes that can be read from this stream without *blocking*. Blocking is the name for what happens when a `read()` method is waiting for a stream to provide its next byte.

When invoked on a file, `available()` usually returns the remaining number of bytes in the file; when invoked on `System.in`, `available()` might return zero if there's nothing currently waiting to be read, but on Windows 95 it throws an `IOException`.

We can see how this method might be used, with the case of non-file input being trapped, by replacing our `while` loop in `UseStreams` with this version:

```
while((nextByteOfFile=incoming.read()) != -1)
        { outgoing.write(nextByteOfFile);
          if (nextByteOfFile == '\n') // a new-line
           try{System.out.println(incoming.available()
                              + " bytes remaining.");}
           catch(IOException e){}
             // another way to deal with non-file input
        }
```

▶ `skip()` This method takes a `long` as its argument, skips over that many bytes of input or to the end of the input stream (whichever comes first), and returns a `long` equal to the actual number of bytes that were skipped.

▶ `close()` This method closes the stream, releasing any resources that were being used to read it.

These methods have varying implementations, depending on the specific subclass of `InputStream` whose implementation we're using. In several cases, the base class `InputStream` defines a method that does nothing.

BE WARNED!

As you might suspect, there is a class `FileOutputStream` that's used in much the same manner as `FileInputStream`. If you call the `FileOutputStream` constructor with a `String` parameter, you'll create the file with that string as its name as a side effect of returning the writable stream.

If you try to construct a `FileOutputStream` with the name of a file that already exists, and that file is a read-only file, an exception will be thrown.

But, if you construct a `FileOutputStream` to an existing, writable file, you *destroy* the contents of the file and start building it again from scratch: you do not open the existing file for appending of new data.

Since Java's class `File` has a `delete()` method that could be used to "zero" a file on purpose, we can safely say that this behavior of the `FileOutputStream` constructor is a bug. Opening a `FileOutputStream` should append to an existing file, not destroy it, and some future version of Java may fix this flaw.

It's All in the Files

This brings us to the next higher level of abstraction, class `File`. We earlier opened a `FileInputStream` using only the primitive `String` of the file's name, using the expression:

```
new FileInputStream(args[0]);
```

We can give ourselves more control over the process by saying something like:

```
File infile = new File(args[0]);
InputStream incoming = new FileInputStream(infile);
```

Why take this extra step? Because now we have a `File` object, `infile`, and we can apply the methods that class `File` provides.

These methods include

▶ `exists()` returns a `boolean` value

▶ `canRead()` returns a `boolean` value

▶ `canWrite()` returns a `boolean` value

▶ `delete()` returns `true` if the file was successfully deleted

▶ `length()` returns a `long` value

These methods appear in statements such as:

```
System.out.println(infile.length());
```

Data on Demand

Ordinary input streams, or even `FileInputStreams`, supply input a byte at a time. What if we want to read binary data that comes in chunks bigger than a byte? Do we have to read those bytes, and shift and add binary values, until we've built the needed `int` or `double` or other simple type?

Heaven forbid.

This is such a common need that `java.io` defines the class `DataInputStream`, which we used in our example classes `WeeklyAverage` and `Listener` for the convenience of its `readLine()` method. That method returns a character string without making us build it up byte by byte: Neither `InputStream` nor `FileInputStream` defines such a method.

`DataInputStream` is at least as useful, though, for its ability to read numbers in the form of their binary representations, directly as strings of bits. When we construct a `DataInputStream`, using an `InputStream` as our argument, we get to apply the following methods (among others) to the result:

- ▶ `readShort()` reads two bytes and assembles them into a `short` with value (byte1<<8) + byte2.

- ▶ `readInt()` reads four bytes, returning
  `int (byte1<<24)+(byte2<<16)+(byte3<<8)+byte4`.

- ▶ `readLong()` reads eight bytes, returning a `long`.

- ▶ `readFloat()` reads 32 bits, as with `readInt()`, then applies `intBitsToFloat()` and returns the `float`.

- ▶ `readDouble()` is similar to `readFloat()`, but using a `long` and `longBitsToDouble()`.

There's More

If you're planning to write an operating system, a Web browser, or other utility software that needs intimate access to files or file systems, you'll want to explore the API of `java.io` in greater depth.

You'll want to look at class `PushBackInputStream`, for example, which lets your program put back the character that's just been read so it can be read again. This is convenient if you need to read a stream until you see a byte that meets some condition, then change to some other activity that has to be able to "see" that same byte for more specialized processing.

But many of the advanced facilities of streams are embedded within methods such as `println()`, whose versatility we have seen throughout the examples in this book.

With object-oriented methods, it's common for such things to be so well encapsulated by higher-level classes and methods that we never appreciate how much these lower-level tools are doing to make our lives easy. We'll see more facilities of this kind in our next chapter, which looks at the classes in package `java.util`.

Then we'll be ready for the final three chapters on networking, graphical user interface construction, and the creation of Web-based applets. It's been a long road, but we're very close to achieving those goals that have done so much to guide Java's design and propel its rapid acceptance.

Summary

In this chapter, we showed

- ▶ That we can use a general-purpose variable (such as one that's declared as an `InputStream`) to refer to an instance of a more specialized class (such as a `FileInputStream`).

- ▶ That we can use the operator `instanceof` to see if an object supports more specialized methods than its declaration suggests, and that we can cast an object back down to its specialized subclass so that those methods can be invoked on the result.

- ▶ That we can extend a class (such as `PrintStream`) and specialize the resulting subclass to have useful behaviors (such as character case conversion) that are then defined (and can later be redefined) in one place for any program that needs this behavior.

- ▶ That there can be dangerous quirks in an API, such as the poorly chosen behavior of wiping out an existing file if it is opened for output from a `FileOutputStream`.

- ▶ That a higher-level abstraction, such as class `File`, lets us first find out if a file is present by a given name—using method `exists()`—so that our programs can tread lightly through such minefields.

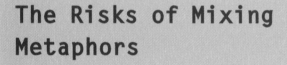

Chapter 13
Department of Water and Power: Package `java.util`

In this chapter, you'll learn how the data structure classes from package `java.util` automate data management tasks that would be cumbersome to perform with ordinary arrays. We'll look at how the classes derived from `Dictionary` provide powerful lookup functions that can minimize data update effort and maximize retrieval speed; and how the `Enumeration` interface automates delivery of successive values from an object that collects or produces data. You'll see that class `Date` offers useful flexibility in working with dates and times, but shows a surprising lack of consistency between different Java implementations, and that class `Random` offers random-value generation more flexible than that of the `random()` method in class `java.lang.Math`.

In Chapter 10, we wanted to represent the birth dates of lions. We could have used facilities of the Java core language, like classes, to devise a kind of object that stored date/time values; we could have given that class of objects a set of methods that retrieved and stored the computer's own clock setting, along with methods for assembling a date from details like the year, the month, and the day.

Instead, we borrowed code from package `java.util`, importing class `java.util.Date` to provide these services.

What's in the Package

The rest of package `java.util` is in that same spirit. Its classes aren't needed to shape the basic personality of the Java language, as were the classes in `java.lang`. They'll come in handy, though, in smoothing our way through small but tricky tasks on our path toward some larger project.

Data Structures

Several of these utility classes define types of data structure, and provide methods for using them to store, retrieve, and manage information. When you have more ways to package data, you're more likely to use a structure that fits the problem, instead of force-fitting your concept of the problem into a type of structure that's poorly suited to the problem—but happens to be on hand.

We saw this problem arise, for example, in Chapter 8, when we pretended that we only knew about arrays: We produced a correct but unwieldy design for our jungle full of lions.

Objects, in general, are a better approach, and the powerful classes in `java.util` may inspire you to devise elegant solutions to many other problems. We'll discuss the classes `Vector`, `Stack`, `Hashtable`, and `Properties`.

A Java vector isn't a combination of a magnitude plus a direction, which is one common definition of *vector*. Rather, class `Vector` describes an array that stretches and shrinks as needed, automatically making room for more elements whenever it gets full.

`Stack` is a subclass of `Vector` that provides a "last in, first out" mechanism. This has many applications in calculation and process management. The predefined `Stack` class turns out to have some surprising conceptual flaws, however, that violate basic disciplines of object-oriented design: the programmer must provide that missing discipline when using this class.

`Hashtable` is a subclass of `Dictionary`. As that ancestry suggests, a `Hashtable` is a data structure that makes it easy to look up a value: It lets us store values in pairs, with one member of each pair being the key for retrieving the other. `Hashtable` has built-in mechanisms for rapid retrieval without a time-consuming search, even when our collection of key/value pairs becomes quite large.

`Properties` is a subclass of `Hashtable` that lets us devise hierarchies of default values, simplifying data updates and reducing consumption of memory when many different keys retrieve the same value. We'll illustrate the power of `Properties` with an extended example.

In the course of the examples that we use to explore these data structures, you'll see some uses of streams based on what we learned in Chapter 12, and some illustrations of the deeper meanings in the hierarchy of classes. We're at a point where we can really gain leverage from the aspects of Java that we already understand.

Timing is Everything

Another noteworthy class in `java.util` is our previously used class `Date`. You might think that designing such a class is no big deal: You could devise your own, with a field that counts seconds (or even milliseconds) from some arbitrary zero point. Your class could provide `public` methods for converting that internal representation into conventional units of year, month, day, and so on.

If you're thinking this way, that's great. It means that you're starting to take an object-oriented view of the world around you. Class `Date` may inspire you to develop your skills in more depth, because its facilities are surprisingly limited—and weak in their encapsulation of internal representations. You may very well decide to devise your own approach if your needs don't fit within `Date`'s limits.

Not-Quite-Random Numbers

It's a paradox of computer applications that these highly predictable machines are often used to simulate random events. When we want to experiment with models of an uncertain world, we rely on a computer's freedom from wishful thinking and its lack of unconscious bias. These traits more than make up the difference between truly random and merely random-like behavior.

We'll look at class `Random`, which offers facilities not provided by the `random()` method that's defined in class `java.lang.Math`.

Beyond Arrays: Getting Out of the Loop

Arrays, with their numbered compartments holding separate data values, inspire a style of programming that relies on loops and nested loops. The typical control structure in these programs tends to be a `for` loop that increments some kind of counter variable, as in:

```
for (i=0; i < someArray.length; i++)
  { // do something with someArray[i];
   }
```

Looping in this predetermined way is called *iteration*, a word that comes from the Latin word for *again*. There are many situations in which arrays (with their fixed size) and iteration (with its fixed control strategy) are entirely appropriate, as we saw in our `WeeklyAverage` class—where we knew that there were seven days in a week, and that we wanted to obtain exactly one value for each day.

But there are many situations in which the array is a mediocre choice. Imagine a computerized checkbook. The number of checks written from one month to another will vary. If the array were our only data structure, the programmer would have to guess how large that array should be.

Memory will be wasted if the array is too large, but the user will find the application totally unacceptable if it ever fails to accept as many entries as the user wants to make. This is a no-win situation for the programmer, who will probably wind up with two sets of unhappy users: One set complaining that the program is a memory hog, and the other set complaining that the program lacks the capacity that they need.

A major goal of Java is the delivery of applications to a worldwide community of users. We should therefore have data structures that adapt to the situations they encounter, instead of being built on a shaky foundation of guesswork that will almost always be wasteful—and yet will still be unreliable.

We Have the Technology...

You could rise above this weakness of arrays by taking a little more trouble. You could write a set of methods that detected when an array was nearing its capacity limit. When that happened, you could make a new array of a larger size, copy the values from the original array into the new one, and assign the new array to the variable name that originally referred to the array that you've now outgrown. Think of a hermit crab, searching for a larger shell.

We still have to deal with some vital details. We'd be able to use the instance variable `length` to determine, at any time, the size of the array that we were currently using, but we'd have to find some other scheme for remembering how many values were actually being stored.

For our checkbook example, we could loop through the compartments of the array until we found a zero value, assuming that we would never write a check for $0.00. Of course, this would fail to handle voided checks.

There are other situations, moreover, in which a zero could be normal and valid data. We'd have to find something else to signal a null value, or maintain some kind of counter variable that we updated whenever we stored a value in a previously unused element of our array.

Suppose we were working our way through our checkbook when we found an out-of-order entry: For example, a check that had been put in a wallet or purse, and had accidentally gone unused until several higher-numbered checks had already been written.

We'd want to go back and insert that check in sequence: This would mean copying all of the later entries to some temporary array, putting the late arrival where it belonged, and copying the other entries back to their new positions above the late arrival.

...But Who Wants to Do It Again?

None of these chores is overwhelming. What's exhausting is the thought of devising such workarounds again, and again, and again—not to mention reading someone else's code, and trying to figure out:

(i) Exactly how they did this.

(ii) Whether it will actually work under a wide range of conditions.

This is the kind of situation that inspires the creation of a utility class like Vector.

Vector Victorious

A Java Vector could just as well be called a magic array. If you tell it to store another object, that object is automatically added at the end of the currently stored collection. You don't have to keep track of the next empty slot.

If you tell a Vector to store a new object when it doesn't have room, it automatically gets bigger to make additional space. If you want to insert an object in between other objects already stored, a Vector automatically moves each of the objects above that point to the slot with the next-higher index.

When we say *object*, we mean it. A Vector stores items of class Object, a superclass of all other classes.

This means that any Vector can store any type of Object in any of its slots—in the same way that we saw, in Chapter 12, that we could use a FileInputStream wherever we needed any kind of InputStream. But a Vector cannot store a simple type, like an int or a float, without first wrapping that simple value in an instance of an appropriate class.

For example,

```
Vector aVector = new Vector();
aVector.addElement(new Integer(3)); // This is fine
aVector.addElement(3);              // This won't compile
```

Smart data structures, like Vector, encourage smarter programs. But it's still up to the programmer to use Vector's facilities in an efficient way. Your Vector will do what you ask, not what you should have requested.

Expansion Plans

The biggest decisions you make about a Vector are its initial size and its growth strategy. These decisions appear in your constructor.

The simplest form, taking no arguments, appears in a statement like:

```
Vector thisMonthsChecks = new Vector();
```

This yields a default number of elements, not specified by the Java API, with a capacity management strategy of doubling in size whenever it runs out of room. With the Sun, Symantec, and Microsoft compilers on Windows 95, the following code:

```
import java.io.PrintStream;
import java.util.Vector;

class TestVector
  { public static void main(String args[])
      { PrintStream out=System.out; // now that we know
                                    // about streams...

      Vector testVector = new Vector();

      //...we don't need to type System.out any more!
      out.println(testVector.size());
      out.println(testVector.capacity());

      for (int i=0;i<12;i++)
        testVector.addElement(new Integer(i));

      out.println(testVector.size());
      out.println(testVector.capacity());
      }
  }
```

returns the output

```
0
10
12
20
```

We see that a new `Vector`, not otherwise specified, began with space for ten elements and grew to twenty when that space was filled. The initial size is not specified by the API, but the doubling behavior is.

This example demonstrates the following methods:

▶ `size()` returns the current number of *stored* elements.

▶ `capacity()` returns the current number of *spaces* that can be used without requiring growth.

▶ `addElement(Object addThis)` stores an element after the last current element, increasing the size of the vector by 1.

Note also that we had to wrap the value `i` in an instance of class `Integer` before we could store it in `testVector`. Remember, we said that a `Vector` stores `Object`s: `Integer` is a subclass of `Object`, but a simple `int` is not. This is a use of the wrapper classes that we introduced in Chapter 11.

We can reduce the overhead of using a `Vector`, in particular the number of time-consuming growth operations, by starting with a capacity that reflects our estimate of our needs. We do this with a constructor of the form:

```
Vector testVector = new Vector(11);
```

If we substitute this in the example above, we will get the output:

```
0
11
12
22
```

A `Vector` created in this manner still has the default behavior of doubling in size whenever it gets full. If that behavior is more aggressive than we want, we can modify this by using a constructor of the form:

```
Vector testVector = new Vector(10, 4);
```

where the first argument is the initial capacity and the second is the growth increment: Not a growth *factor*, like the default doubling behavior, but a value that is *added* to the capacity whenever growth is required.

When substituted in the example above, this results in the output:

```
0
10
12
14
```

While your program is running, you can avoid the overhead of many separate growth operations by using the method `ensureCapacity(int atLeast)`. This compares the current capacity to the specified `int` value, and enlarges the `Vector` (if needed) to meet that minimum.

Contrast the behavior of `ensureCapacity()` with that of `setSize(int exactSize)`, which will discard elements if the new size is specified to be less than the current size.

What if `setSize()` is invoked with an argument that is larger than the current size? Consider the following code:

```
Vector aVector = new Vector(10);
System.out.println(aVector.capacity());
System.out.println(aVector.size());
aVector.ensureCapacity(17);
System.out.println(aVector.capacity());
System.out.println(aVector.size());
aVector.setSize(27);
System.out.println(aVector.capacity());
System.out.println(aVector.size());
aVector.addElement("I'm at the end");
 // a string literal instantiates a String to hold it
for (int i=26; i<29; i++)
   System.out.println(aVector.elementAt(i));
```

This yields the output (with comments added to the listing),

```
10              // the initial capacity
0               // the initial size
20              // capacity "at least 17"
0               // size still 0
40              // capacity doubled to fit size of 27
27              // size is exactly 27 (0 through 26)
null            // added elements are nulls
I'm at the end  // this is what we added (index = 27)
java.lang.ArrayIndexOutOfBoundsException: 28 >= 28
```

Several things happened here. Most notably, method `setSize()` didn't just change the capacity of `aVector`: It changed the size, that is, the number of things stored in `aVector`, triggering its growth behavior (the default doubling of capacity) to make that possible.

The elements of aVector up through the specified size were filled with something called null. The next element that we added was tacked on after those nulls, which will retain their positions until they're replaced or until those positions are deleted by some other operation.

The elements farther beyond, however, can't yet be used because those positions are not yet active. When we tried to look at a position that held no value (not even a null), the access method threw an exception.

This is the first time that we've seen the reserved literal null. Like true and false, it's a name that can't be used for anything else. Unlike true or false, it has no type: null is not even an Object.

We haven't needed null before this point, because we've never created an object before it was needed. But setSize() had to put something into aVector, and null—the reference to an uncreated object—fills that role. We'll see it again in this chapter.

By using setSize() to fill out a Vector with nulls, we gain the freedom to store things at element index values that we otherwise could not use because they were previously beyond the end of the occupied portion of the Vector. This makes a Vector more like an ordinary array, with its components randomly accessible instead of being accumulated in order.

A related method, trimToSize(), takes no arguments, but discards any unused elements at the end of the vector: That is, it adjusts the vector's capacity down to its current size.

You Put Your Element In, You Get Your Element Out

We've talked about how to make Vectors and how to put things into them with addElement(). There's more.

We can insert an element at an arbitrary location with the method insertElementAt(Object insertThis, int thisIndex).

As we promised in our opening praise of these magic arrays, this method takes all of the objects stored at or above the specified index value and moves them up by one. This increases the size of the vector by 1, as with addElement(). (As with arrays, a Vector's index values begin at 0.)

Contrast the behavior of insertElementAt() with that of setElementAt(Object imposeThis, int thisIndex). This puts the Object imposeThis at the specified location, replacing whatever was there before.

We can also remove an element, letting everything above it drop down by one position, with removeElementAt(int thisIndex). This method is void: it does not return the element that it removes, it just gets rid of it.

We can see what's in a vector using `elementAt(int index)`. This retrieves the specified object without side effects—that is, without affecting the contents of the vector. We used this above. We can also use the methods `firstElement()` or `lastElement()`, whose functions reflect their names.

If you try to retrieve an element at an index that isn't in use, or insert an element at a disconnected location, your method will throw an exception (as we just saw). Your code can guard against this by testing the proposed index value against the current size of the vector.

In some cases, the `boolean` value returned by the method `isEmpty()` may be the only information that you need.

A `Vector` can also be searched. The method `contains(Object someObject)` returns a `boolean` value. The Java API documentation is surprisingly vague about the precise meaning of *contains*. Does a vector contain a string if it holds a string that meets the content test of `equals()`, or must we pass the stricter identity test of the `==` operator?

We can investigate this:

```
import java.io.PrintStream;
import java.util.Vector;

class TestContains
  { public static void main(String args[])
     { PrintStream out   = System.out;
       Vector testVector = new Vector();

       String s1 = "I'm here";
       String s2 =  "'m here";
             s2 = "I" + s2;

       out.println(s1 == s2);              // identical?
       out.println(s1.equals(s2));          // similar?

       testVector.addElement(s1);

       out.println(testVector.contains(s2)); // well?
     }
  }
```

With all of the available Java tools on hand when this book was written, this code returned

```
false
true
true
```

In other words, a Vector "contains" a character string if it includes a string that has the same contents, even if the two physical strings of characters in memory are contained by different objects. This seems like an area where the API could use some clarification.

If you want to know more about where an object sits in a Vector, you can use the methods indexOf(Object neededObject) to find the location of the first occurrence, or lastIndexOf(Object neededObject) for the last occurrence.

These methods return the signal value -1 if the specified object was not found, and return the index value otherwise. There is no ambiguity, since legitimate index values are always zero or greater.

You can remove the first occurrence of a specified object with removeElement(Object anObject). This returns a true if it found and removed an object matching anObject, false if no such object was present.

This behavior yields concise code in a task such as deleting all elements with a certain value, as in the following example:

```
import java.io.PrintStream;
import java.util.Vector;

class TestThis
{ public static void main(String args[])
  { PrintStream out    = System.out;
    Vector testVector = new Vector();

    int[] someValues  = {2,4,2,6,3,5,2,6,4,6,2,7};

    for (int i=0; i < someValues.length; i++)
     testVector.addElement(new Integer(someValues[i]));

    out.println(testVector.size());
    printVector(testVector, out);

    Integer killThis = new Integer(2);
```

```
    while(testVector.removeElement(killThis));

    // The while test has a side effect. The loop needs
    //  no other body. When there are no more 2s, the
    //  test will fail and the program will move on.

    out.println(testVector.size());
    printVector(testVector, out);
  }

  public static void printVector(Vector thisVector,
                                   PrintStream aStream)
  { String vals="";
    for (int i=0; i < thisVector.size(); i++)
     vals=vals+thisVector.elementAt(i);
    aStream.println(vals);
  }
 }
```

which returns the output,

```
12
242635264627
8
46356467
```

The vector has been conveniently purged of all objects matching the given object, and has shrunk to fit. This behavior has many applications.

Stacking the Deck

There are many situations that call for something like a `Vector`, but with the specialized behavior of letting us accumulate collections by adding things to the top—and getting them back in a last-in, first-out sequence.

When you hear the verb *specialize*, you should automatically think "subclass." The behavior that we've described is like a stack of papers on your desktop, hence the name `Stack` for this subclass of `Vector`.

Additional methods defined on class `Stack` are `push()` and `pop()` (adding and removing an object at the top of the structure), `peek()` (looking at an object without removing it), and `search()` (returning the "distance" from the top of the stack to the topmost occurrence of an object, or returning –1 if the search fails).

But there's a basic flaw, not to mince words, with this implementation of stacks.

A stack should only allow insertion and removal of items at the top of the stack, using the operations generically known as *push* and *pop* (from which class `Stack`'s methods get their names). Looking at the topmost object and putting it back can be considered a composite operation: pop, look, and push, not violating this basic discipline.

But `Stack` extends `Vector`, inheriting all of its methods, and it does nothing to prevent the use of inherited methods that operate on other locations below the top.

Resist the temptation to mix your metaphors. If you want to use a stack, because the discipline of a stack fits your problem, restrict yourself to the specialized subclass methods that fit that discipline.

To do otherwise risks confusion. For example, look at the following code:

```java
import java.io.*;
import java.util.*;


class MixMetaphors
 { public static void main(String args[])
   { PrintStream out = System.out;
     Stack testStack = new Stack();

     int[] someValues = {0,2,3,4,2,6,3,5,2,6,4,6,2,7};

     for (int i=0; i < someValues.length; i++)
      testStack.addElement(new Integer(someValues[i]));

     Integer findThis = new Integer(2);

     printVector(testStack, out);
     out.println("Index "+testStack.indexOf(findThis));
     out.println("Search "+testStack.search(findThis));

     testStack.removeElement(findThis);

     printVector(testStack, out);
     out.println("Index "+testStack.indexOf(findThis));
     out.println("Search "+testStack.search(findThis));
```

```
            int discard=((Integer)testStack.pop()).intValue();

            printVector(testStack, out);
            out.println("Index "+testStack.indexOf(findThis));
            out.println("Search "+testStack.search(findThis));
            out.println("");
        }

    public static void printVector(Vector thisVector,
                                PrintStream aStream)
      { String vals="";
        for (int i=0; i < thisVector.size(); i++)
         vals=vals+thisVector.elementAt(i);
        aStream.println(vals);
        }
    }
```

The output is below. Is this what you would expect? Remember, we're looking for the index of the "first" occurrence of 2, and searching for the distance from the top of the stack to the "topmost" occurrence of that same value.

```
02342635264627
Index 1
Search 2

0342635264627
Index 3
Search 2

034263526462
Index 3
Search 1
```

Look hard, and you'll figure out what's going on. The "top" of the stack, where methods `push()` and `pop()` do their work, is at the *end* of the vector—that is, at the *highest* current index.

An object at the beginning of the vector (the bottom of the stack) is at *index* 0. An object at the end of the vector (the top of the stack) has a *search* value of 1.

There's plenty of rope here to hang yourself. If you ask for a stack, treat it like one. If you start mixing stack operations at the top of the stack, counting positions from 1 to the left, with vector operations at arbitrary positions, counting index positions from 0 to the right, you're bound to make simple but time-consuming errors.

A Case of Forgotten Identity

Another important aspect of using vectors, including stacks, appears in the statement above

```
int discard=((Integer)testStack.pop()).intValue();
```

The method that pops a stack returns an object. It doesn't know anything about what subclass of Object the returned value might be.

In this case, even though we know that this vector contains only objects of class Integer, we cannot use the method intValue on the object returned by pop(): That is, not unless we explicitly cast it back to Integer, as we did here. We've already explored this idea while working with streams in Chapter 12.

Such casting bypasses protections that object methods normally provide. Vector and Stack are powerful, but like other power tools they can also let you make a bigger mess more quickly.

Wear those safety glasses, and measure twice (for example, by using the operator instanceof that we tried out in Chapter 12) before you cut once.

You Can Look It Up

Vectors rescue us from one of the arbitrary aspects of using arrays, namely, the need to anticipate the size of a structure at the outset of a problem. But we still wind up needing to associate each stored value with some numbered location in the data structure.

We could get around this by storing things in pairs: a label, or *key*, followed by the value that we want to associate with that key. We could use indexOf() to find the key, then look at the following index position for the associated value.

This would let us work in either direction. We could just as well search for a value, then look back one position to see what key it used.

But this approach has a serious flaw when used with more than trivial amounts of data. The time required to search through an entire vector grows in proportion to the vector's size. Users become annoyed when a program doesn't scale well to substantial applications.

For this reason, it's common to devise something called a *hash code* method that takes a piece of data, and generates a key value based on some characteristic of that data. Hash codes are a computer science subject, and there's extensive discussion in the literature of how to devise an efficient coding scheme to yield keys that are uniformly scattered over the entire range of possible key values.

Java's class Object defines method `hashCode()`, which returns an `int` (a 32-bit value, you'll recall) for the object on which it's invoked. As defined for `Object`, this method returns a value that is based on the memory address of the object, so it's guaranteed to be unique.

But that's the only good thing that you can say about this approach. Memory locations have nothing to do with the reasons that people store data.

The Java API calls upon subclasses of `Object` to override its `hashCode()` method with a method that's appropriate to the subclass. That subclass method should be defined so that instances of that subclass will produce the same key value if they pass the test of `equals()`.

For example, two strings that print to `"I'm here"` should return identical keys, regardless of whether their variable names refer to the same actual instance of `String`.

We can demonstrate this as follows:

```
import java.io.PrintStream;

class TestHashing
  { public static void main(String args[])
     { PrintStream out = System.out;

        Object o1 = new Object();
        Object o2 = new Object();

        out.println(o1 == o2);
        out.println("Un== Objects:");
        out.println(o1.hashCode());
        out.println(o2.hashCode());
        out.println(); // no arg -> a blank line

        o2 = o1;

        out.println(o1 == o2);
        out.println("== Objects:");
```

```
        out.println(o1.hashCode());
        out.println(o2.hashCode());
        out.println();

        String s1 = "I'm here";
        String s2 =  "'m here";
              s2 = "I" + s2;

        out.println(s1 == s2);
        out.println("Un== Strings:");
        out.println(s1.hashCode());
        out.println(s2.hashCode());
    }
  }
```

A typical run of this code produces output that looks like:

```
false
Un== Objects:
4369820
4376724

true
== Objects:
4369820
4369820

false
Un== Strings:
-1737162519
-1737162519
```

We say "typical" because if you run this several times, you'll see that the hash codes returned for the generic Objects o1 and o2 will vary from one run to the next.

But the first key printed will always match the third and fourth keys, because hashCode() always returns an identical value for an identical object during any single execution of an application.

The hash keys for the strings are based on their contents, and will always be the same for any run.

Move to Table the Motion

We don't actually need to understand hashing to use the `Hashtable` class that's defined in `java.util`.

 By the way, do note that for once a class name does not have an embedded capital letter. It's Hashtable, not HashTable. The latter spelling will not work.

To create a `Hashtable`, we declare and initialize an object of this type, as in:

```
Hashtable thisTable = new Hashtable();
```

To store a value with a retrieval key, we use the method `put(Object theKey, Object theValue)`:

```
thisTable.put("A name", "Peter");
thisTable.put( new Integer(39), "Peter's age");
thisTable.put( System.in, new Thread("A Thread"));
```

These examples are intentionally bizarre. You're not likely, for example, to store a number as a key, and a description of that number as the value that you look up using that key. But you can if you want to.

Any object can be a key; any object can be stored under that key.

We get our values back, logically enough, with `get(Object theKey)`:

```
System.out.println(thisTable.get(new Integer(39));
System.out.println(thisTable.get(System.in);
System.out.println(thisTable.get(new Thread("Another");
```

Wait a minute. That last key was never used to store a value. What will we get in return?

What this sample code prints from that last statement is the text string, *null.* This is the now-familiar printable representation of the `null` reference that we introduced above. We return this, rather than the -1 that's returned when we fail in a method like `indexOf()`, because -1 *could* be a value stored under a key; it could *not* be an index into a vector.

Put Some More Leaves in the Table

Like a vector, a Hashtable grows as needed. And as with a vector, you can reduce the overhead of frequent regrowing operations by starting with a tailored initial capacity, using a constructor that takes an integer number as the initial number of entries to provide.

That initial capacity is only a recommendation: The constructor method may adjust the capacity to make the table work more efficiently. You don't need to know. The method `size()` will tell you how many keys are currently stored in the table.

You can also boost performance, at the expense of memory consumption, by reducing the allowable *load factor* of the table. Load factor is the ratio of the number of entries to the capacity of the table.

As load factor gets close to 1, lookup operations become slower because too many hash codes are pointing to the same location in the table. This means that too much time gets spent resolving what are called *collisions*, where the access method has to figure out which key/value combination was actually wanted.

A table could, in principle, contain a unique location for every one of the 9 billion possible values of the 32-bit integer hash code, but that's a lot of memory.

To specify a load factor, construct your table with a third form of constructor, giving it an `int` value for the initial capacity and a `float` value for the highest allowable load factor.

When a Hashtable reaches its specified load factor, it automatically grows and redistributes its contents. If the hash code formula is a good one, this will reduce the frequency of collisions in direct proportion to the increased capacity.

Other Hashtable methods are the following:

▶ `clear()` empties the table.

▶ `containsKey (Object someKey)` returns `true` if an object is associated with `someKey`.

▶ `contains(Object someValue)` returns `true` if `someValue` is associated with any key. This is a time-consuming method, and it *doesn't* give you the key that will retrieve this value from the table.

If you want to know what key is being used to store some value, you may be able to find out by searching the string that's returned when you invoke the `toString()` method on a Hashtable. In the case above,

```
System.out.println(thisTable);
```

produces the output:

```
{39=Peter's age,
 A name=Peter,
 java.io.BufferedInputStream@1393118
  =Thread[A Thread,5,main]
}
```

Note, however, that printed representations of objects may not be very informative. For example, the stream object, `System.in`, does not bear that name as any part of that string.

Note also that the sequence in which these items appeared in the table had nothing to do with the sequence, in time, in which they were stored. Hashtables associate values with keys. If you want to control the order of appearance in the data structure, vectors and stacks let you do that.

A more polished method of looking through an entire table is to use the method `keys()`, which returns an instance of the interface called `Enumeration`. This interface requires support for the methods `hasMoreElements()`, returning a `boolean`, and `nextElement()`, returning an `Object`.

Methods that return an `Enumeration` are also defined for the elements of a `Hashtable` or a `Vector`, in each case using the method name `elements()`.

For the table above, the method `keys()` and the `Enumeration` that it returns could be used like this:

```
Enumeration theKeys = thisTable.keys();
Object theNextKey;
while ( theKeys.hasMoreElements() )
  { theNextKey = theKeys.nextElement();
    System.out.println( theNextKey );
    System.out.println( thisTable.get(theNextKey) );
  }
```

producing, in this case,

```
39
Peter's age
A name
Peter
java.io.BufferedInputStream@1393118
Thread[A Thread,5,main]
```

The interface `Enumeration` is also defined in package `java.util`, and your own classes can implement this interface. This requires you to define your own versions of the two required methods, and to provide the mechanism needed for an instance of your class to emit elements in succession on each invocation of `nextElement()`.

Your Property Is in Default

Like the relationship of Stack to Vector, there's a subclass of Hashtable that
adds behaviors useful in many applications. That subclass is called Properties,
and it's designed for key/value pairs that are both strings.

The chief feature of the Properties class is that a program can specify default
values to be used if no value is stored with a given key.

This can be done on a case-by-case basis, where the method
getProperty(String key, String defaultValue) will return defaultValue
in a case where a normal get() would return a null.

Defaults can also be defined more generally, by constructing a new
Properties table with a constructor that takes another Properties table as its
argument. That argument table then becomes a backup for the new one. If you try
to look in your new table using a key that isn't there, the default table will be
checked—and that default table can have a backup of its own, and so on.

If you have a large number of possible values that need to be stored under descriptive labels, but many of those label/value combinations are identical for many
objects, then this mechanism can save a lot of memory. You can make a tree of
Properties tables, with each level of that tree adding new details, and only overriding defaults in special cases.

For example,

```
import java.util.Properties;
import java.io.PrintStream;

class Props
{ public static void main(String args[])
  { Properties city = new Properties();
    city.put("City", "Los Angeles");
    city.put("Area Code", "213");

    Properties family = new Properties(city);
    family.put("Last Name","Doe");
    family.put("Area Code","310");
    family.put("Address","123 Wilshire");

    Properties sonAtCollege = new Properties(family);
    sonAtCollege.put("First Name","John");
    sonAtCollege.put("City", "Cambridge");
```

```
        sonAtCollege.put("Area Code","617");
        sonAtCollege.put("Address","77 Mass. Ave.");

        Properties daughterAtHome = new Properties(family);
        daughterAtHome.put("First Name","Janie");

        Properties randomAngeleno = new Properties(city);

        summarize(daughterAtHome);
        summarize(sonAtCollege);
        summarize(randomAngeleno);
      }

    public static void summarize(Properties aTable)
    {
      PrintStream out=System.out;
      out.println(aTable.getProperty("First Name")
              + " "
              + aTable.getProperty("Last Name"));
      out.println(aTable.getProperty("Address"));
      out.println(aTable.getProperty("City"));
      out.println("Area code "
              + aTable.getProperty("Area Code"));
      out.println("");
      }
    }
```

This produces the following output:

```
Janie Doe
123 Wilshire
Los Angeles
Area code 310

John Doe
77 Mass. Ave.
Cambridge
Area code 617
```

```
null null
null
Los Angeles
Area code 213
```

Look through the code and follow the trail of defaults. Janie's first name comes from her personal properties; her last name, address, and area code come from the `family` table declared as her table's defaults; her city is from the `city` table that holds the defaults for the family.

Dates and Times

Whether it's science, high finance, or real-time factory-floor control, computers need to work with values of time. Clocks pervade electronic equipment, whether we're talking about coffee makers, videocassette recorders, or cameras.

With its many intended applications, Java should abstract the complexities of years, months, days, hours, minutes, seconds, even fractions of seconds into convenient representations that we can manipulate with straightforward methods.

Well, the `Date` class comes close.

Make that, almost comes close.

To be perfectly frank, class `Date` is not a very robust piece of code. Ask it for an object that corresponds to "April" and "31," and it gives you the same thing that you would get for "May" and "1."

Some people would say that this is a reasonable design decision.

Okay, ask `Date` for the time that comes 128 seconds after midnight. Would you believe, 11:57:52 p.m. of the day before? That's what you'll get from Sun's Java setup, though Microsoft's tools let time keep moving forward.

Does this sound as if one version of the Java environment is letting a byte overflow, and wrapping around to the negative extreme value of this simple type? Does this still sound like designed behavior?

Try to do anything with any date/time after the evening news is over on Monday, January 18, 2038. You will get an exception. `Date` does not do a very good job of concealing the limits of a finite number of bits.

And forget about asking basic questions like, "How many days will pass between these two dates?" Class `Date` doesn't know. If you want to compute such things, you'd better pick up a reference book on calendar-based calculations and write your own methods in a more intelligent subclass of `Date`—in the manner that we extended class `PrintStream` in Chapter 12 when we wanted to give it additional needed behaviors.

Faster Than a Speeding Bit

It's convenient that the minimal constructor, `new Date()`, gives us the system time to the nearest millisecond—at least, to the closest approximation that the system's hardware clock allows.

This can be used, for example, in performance benchmarks. This is the author's personal favorite, known as Tak:

```java
import java.util.Date;

public class Tak
 { public static void main(String args[])
    { int result=0;
      long starttime = new Date().getTime();
      for (int i=0; i < 100; i++) result=tak(18,12,6);
      System.out.println(100.0 /        // passes
                        ((double)(new Date().getTime()
                                  -starttime)
                    / 1000.0)    // per second
                 + " passes per second");
    }

    public static int tak(int x, int y, int z)
       { if (y >= x)
            return z;
         else
            return tak(tak (x-1, y, z),
                       tak (y-1, z, x),
                       tak (z-1, x, y));
       }
 }
```

Method `tak()`, by the way, demonstrates something called *recursion*. The method `tak()` actually calls itself with a modified set of arguments. When it gets to a point where it calls itself with a second argument (y) that is not less than the first argument (x), it finally returns a value. That value is returned to the previous call to the method, and so on as the recursion "unwinds."

When called with the starting values 18, 12, and 6, `tak()` will ultimately be called 63,609 times, making 47,706 subtractions before it finally gets around to returning the value 7.

Tak is a mutant (but now dominant) strain of a benchmark by Ikuo Takeuchi. Tak was created when John McCarthy of Stanford University gathered considerable data after misremembering the original algorithm. When the code above is executed on a 90MHz Pentium system using Sun's `java` interpreter, it returns a value of 3.9 passes per second; Microsoft's `jview` yields 79.4 passes per second, a respectable figure in the neighborhood of fast C++ code.

Doing Dates

As you can tell, we're not very enthusiastic about `Date`. Feel free to use it, though—within its rather pathetic limits—by providing, and returning, the appropriate combination of parameters (as described in Table 13.1) to the methods defined in Table 13.2.

Why does parameter Second range from 0 through 60, permitting a 61-second minute? Because it's legal, though rare, for a Java virtual machine to support the

TABLE 13.1   PARAMETERS USED IN CONSTRUCTORS FOR CLASS DATE

Parameter Name	Parameter Type	Parameter Meanings and Ranges
Time	long	Milliseconds since midnight on January 1, 1970 < 2147483648000 (19 Jan 2038 03:14:07 GMT)
Year	int	Year minus 1900 < 138 (2038 A.D.)
Month	int	January = 0, December = 11
Date	int	1 through 31—*not* starting with 0
Day	int	Sunday = 0, Saturday = 6
Hour	int	0 through 23
Minute	int	0 through 59
Second	int	0 through 60

TABLE 13.2   CONSTRUCTORS FOR CLASS DATE (USING PARAMETERS FROM TABLE 13.1)

Constructor Signature	Notes on Returned Date Instance
Date()	System time to nearest millisecond
Date(year, month, date)	Time = midnight
Date(year, month, date, hours, minutes)	Exact minute
Date(year, month, date, hours, minutes, seconds)	Exact second
Date(time)	Nearest millisecond

officially defined "leap seconds" that are used to keep official time synchronized with the slowing of the Earth's rotation.

Depending on the precision that we need, we can initialize a new instance of `Date` to anything from the nearest day to the nearest millisecond. We do this with an expression of the form new Date(<parameters>), or with the no-arg constructor to read the computer's own clock.

There is another `Date` constructor that takes a character string as its argument. That character string has to be something that can be understood by `Date`'s `parse()` method, which can take apart a value like "29 Jan 1996" or even "Mon, 26 Aug 1996 21:57."

Among the methods supported by `Date` are `before()`, `equals()`, and `after()`, each taking another `Date` as its argument and returning a `boolean`; `setSeconds()`, `setMinutes()`, `setHours()`, `setDate()`, `setMonth()`, and `setYear()`, each taking an `int` as described in Table 13.1 and adjusting a component of the `Date` to match; `setTime()`, taking a `long`; and corresponding `get` methods for all of the just-listed `set` methods.

One may hope that a future version of Java will preserve the current `Date` class API, but improve the internal representations and/or tighten the specification to eliminate the inconsistent behaviors and arbitrary limits of current implementations.

Seriously Random

As we mentioned at the beginning of this chapter, it's ironic that machines designed to be as perfectly predictable as computers are frequently used to mimic random events—for example, in "Monte Carlo" methods that use brute force repetition to solve problems that don't have elegant solutions.

"Random-like" is the best that a computer can do, unless you want to hook up a serial port to a piece of decaying uranium. It is possible to build or buy such a source of truly random events, which your program could use as a foundation for modeling anything from bacterial growth to financial market movements.

It's cheaper, however, to use class `Random`. This class may seem redundant with the method `random()` in class `Math`, but it adds some useful facilities.

Writing a piece of code that generates usefully pseudo-random values, meeting all the mathematical tests for absence of underlying pattern, is a fairly advanced skill: class `Random` is a respectable piece of work.

There are two ways to get a new random-number generator. The first constructor, `Random()`, starts the sequence using a seed value that comes from the current system time. The second constructor, `Random(long thisSeed)`, uses the supplied `long` value as the seed: this makes it possible to reproduce results by using the same seed in every run. An instance of class `Random` can also be restarted with a new seed value, using the method `setSeed(long restartSeed)`.

An instance of `Random` will produce, on demand, uniformly distributed values of any of the four simple numeric types. Methods `nextInt()`, `nextLong()`, `nextFloat()`, and `nextDouble()` perform this task: `int` and `long` random values are distributed over the range of these types, while `float` and `double` random values are distributed over the range between 0.0 and 1.0.

An extremely valuable method on `Random` is `nextGaussian()`, which returns `double` values that conform to a Gaussian normal distribution with mean of 0.0 and standard deviation of 1.0. Many simulations of natural processes will benefit from this method.

Summary

In this chapter, we showed

▶ That `Vector`s provide definable strategies for growing a data structure on demand, but require attention to details such as the difference between capacity and size.

▶ That `Stack`s add useful specializations to class `Vector`, but that they also introduce opportunities for confusion.

▶ That general-purpose data structures work with `Object`s, not with the specific data types found in an array, and that casts and the `instanceof` operator must replace the usual protections afforded by object techniques.

▶ That the `keys()` and `elements()` methods, returning `Enumerations`, make it easy to step through the values stored in a `Hashtable` even if we don't know what keys were used to store them.

▶ That a multilayered approach to `Properties` tables can reduce the number of identical data values that need to be recorded.

▶ That class `Date` accepts many different descriptions of a date/time value, but that it demonstrates arbitrary behaviors when given data in other than the most common formats.

▶ That recursion is an alternative form of control that can perform a complex task with a small amount of code.

▶ That random-like simulations needing a wide range of integer-type values, or needing normally distributed values, can obtain these things from the methods of class Random.

Core Technologies
of the Internet

Uniform Resource
Locators

Examining URL
Contents

Working with IP
Addresses

Using the Internet
Protocols

Chapter 14
Building on the Standard Packages: java.net

In this chapter, you'll learn how computers on the Internet share a single system of connections, but send and retrieve data to and from specific locations on that network. We'll dissect the format of the uniform resource locator, discuss the security responsibilities of an Internet host machine, and look at local files on your system using the classes defined in package java.net—applying the same methods that give a program access to network-based resources. We'll also build classes that send and receive messages to each other, exactly as they would across the Internet—but within the physical environment of your own computer.

The Internet is a worldwide improv theater, with continuous performances of a show that gets rewritten every day. Its subplots touch on everything that the human race knows or imagines. It makes information available anywhere in the world, often for the price of a local phone call; it accelerates the fermentation of new ideas, and propels its own technical advancement, so much so that "Web time" has become an expression for developments taking place in weeks that would previously have taken months, or for progress over periods measured in months rather than years.

But this network has no central point of control, nor even a formal definition that stands still long enough to publish. This cooperative network of millions of computers is so vast, and so dynamic, that it mocks the title of "expert." No one can claim to know so much about the Internet that there is no one from whom he or she can learn still more: If there were such an expert at sundown on a Friday, that status would not last through the weekend. Every week, and certainly every month, brings with it new Net-based resources and new entrants into the market of Internet tools, technologies, and services.

At most, it is possible to have a useful mastery of the standards by which the Internet's resources become accessible to any client computer. That is the mission of package java.net: to package those vital standards into classes, so that a program can create an instance of a class that captures the essential details of what a Java program wants to give, or get, via the Net.

The classes in `java.net` let a program speak to the Internet in its native language, so that the programmer can think of the Net as simply a resource—like a desktop computer's own file system—without constant, repetitive, and error-prone attention to low-level details.

This makes the resources of the Internet available to any Java program, running on any combination of computer and operating system that supports an implementation of the Java virtual machine.

Therefore, even though this chapter is far from being the longest in this book, it is surely among the most important. The classes in `java.net`, one might well say, are the stars that turned this off-Broadway language into a box-office blockbuster.

How Far Do You Want to Go?

If you want to build an online theater, or stage an Internet opera, you're going to need knowledge that's beyond the scope of this book. Like a theater owner who needs to deal with local labor, you'll need to know how Java programs can call upon native code—that is, upon programs that work directly with the computer that's running the browser and its add-on modules, without going through the Java virtual machine.

Like an architect who has to worry about lighting, bathrooms, and emergency exits, you'll need to know how the browser interacts with the host operating system: How it gets access to the screen, keyboard, and mouse; how it shares the processor's attention with other running programs; and how it keeps a remotely loaded Java program from doing any damage while still giving it a chance to do useful work.

This book is addressed to content creators, not to their enablers; to would-be writers of skits and one-act plays, not to those who yearn to produce an online version of *Der Ring des Nibelungen*.

Our discussion of `java.net` will therefore focus on the needs of the application writer, not the needs of the system-level programmer building a general-purpose browser or server. Books that offer more advanced coverage of various Java topics are listed in Appendix C.

What's in the Package

The classes in `java.net` fall into two major groups: classes for finding places, and classes for exchanging information with resources at those places.

The first set of classes works with a 1990s notion of "place" that includes both the name of a location, and the method of gaining access to the resources that it holds. This is as much a matter of definitions and agreements as it is a matter of technology.

The second set of classes moves us toward the gray area where we are dealing, not with Java programming as such, but rather with the volatile blend of technology and politics that makes up any international communications system. Java will bring you to the Net, but it can't make the worldwide Net itself any more reliable or controllable.

Internal Intranets are another realm, where Java's power combines with centralized management to build powerful systems on non-proprietary foundations.

What Do You Want? And Where Is It?

The uniform resource locator (URL), a novel invention in 1993, has become the world's pervasive tool for naming information resources. You see URLs on billboards, television ads, business cards, and anywhere else that someone has something to sell or something to say.

The standard classes `URL`, `URLConnection`, and their supporting classes let Java programs use the many types of information that can be described by such a label.

Unlike other connections, such as those of the interstate highways, the Internet's interconnections change from one moment to the next. You can't give reusable directions that will get you from one point to another on the Net: All you can do is say where you want to go, and let the network itself determine the best currently available path to that point.

This implies a system of unique and absolute addresses to mark the ends of the trip.

That's what we get from the Internet Protocol address (a 32-bit binary number) and the Domain Name System (a mapping of human-readable names to IP addresses). The class `InetAddress` encapsulates an IP address and lets a program translate (in either direction) between raw numeric addresses and their more convenient names.

Messages in Bottles

When a single, worldwide system of physical connections is shared by millions of computers, exchanging data among constantly changing subsets of that group, there has to be a system that gets the right data to the right machines. The IP address is just one part of the overall Internet Protocol, the set of rules that's followed by cooperating computers and service providers to make this miracle routine.

Under the Internet Protocol, a message from one machine to another is broken into chunks of data called *packets*. A packet contains not only a message or piece of a message, but also information on its origin, its destination, and some extra data permitting error detection.

The Internet's many connections create an enormous number of paths between any two points. At any point on the network, a system that receives a packet can forward it to another machine that is (in some sense) closer to the packet's destination. Eventually, it gets there—most of the time.

A User Datagram Packet (UDP) stuffs your data into a digital bottle, so to speak, and drops it into the ocean of the Internet to find its own way. The vagaries of Internet routing may cause these packets to arrive out of order; some may never arrive at all.

But a connection may be so consistent that these risks can be ignored, or the penalty involved in losing a packet may be small. In either of these cases, classes `DatagramPacket` and `DatagramSocket` make it easy to use this approach. We'll demonstrate these in this chapter.

Making the Connection

If a network user needs to be sure that a message got through, a connection can be established using the Transmission Control Protocol (TCP).

TCP is an additional set of rules, on top of those that govern the low-level behavior of the individual packets on the Internet: hence the composite name, *TCP/IP*, to describe the overall rules that govern such communications. In practice, many networks use TCP/IP for everything, both local and long-range transfers of data. In fact, some Java development systems even assume that they can use it within the confines of a single computer, for example, to connect a Java debugger to an application under test.

TCP gives the sender confirmation that transmissions were received without errors. The receiver can ask the sender for another copy of any packet that doesn't pass inspection, with the receiver applying the error-detecting information that's built into each packet.

Packets also carry sequence information, so that the receiver can assemble validated packets into a message that's certain to be the same thing that was sent.

TCP is reliable, but it's not especially efficient. Maintaining a connection between remote machines consumes network resources, while monitoring the exchange creates overhead for the sender. Don't ignore the UDP alternative.

But where TCP is appropriate, or even where it's just standard, classes `Socket` and `ServerSocket` encapsulate the details of a TCP connection into convenient objects. These objects can be endpoints of the input/output streams that we learned to use in Chapter 12.

Using these abstractions, the other objects in a program don't need to care (and in fact, don't even know) if their input/output transactions are with another process in the same computer, or with another location thousands of miles away.

What Do You Want?—The URL

The format of a URL, and the types of resources that it can be used to label, is defined by evolving standards. The source for current information is itself a URL, that of the World Wide Web Consortium, whose many resources can be found by starting at **http://www.w3.org/pub/WWW/** and browsing from there.

The current standard gives the following as the general format of a URL:

```
<scheme>:<scheme-specific-part>
```

"A URL," according to the standard, "contains the name of the scheme being used (`<scheme>`) followed by a colon and then a string (the `<scheme-specific-part>`) whose interpretation depends on the scheme."

What kind of schemes are we talking about? The standard lists the following options:

▶ file—Host-specific file names

▶ ftp—File Transfer Protocol

▶ gopher—The Gopher protocol

▶ http—Hypertext Transfer Protocol

▶ mailto—Electronic mail address

▶ news—USENET news

▶ nntp—USENET news using NNTP access

> ▶ prospero—Prospero Directory Service

> ▶ telnet—Reference to interactive sessions

> ▶ wais—Wide Area Information Servers

Ask for Whatever You Want...

On the Web, HTTP (Hypertext Transfer Protocol) is so common that most people don't even include the `http://` prefix when providing a URL. But this is a vital part of the URL, since it tells the user's system how to ask the remote machine for the information of interest.

A user's Web browser takes a simple operation like clicking the mouse on an underlined URL name on the screen, and turns it into a message to the remote server that looks like:

```
GET /pub/WWW/TheProject.html HTTP/1.0
```

The server responds with the message `OK`, and sends the requested information— or perhaps it replies with a message like `UNAUTHORIZED`.

...But Don't Do Whatever You're Asked

The HTTP server has to be constructed with an eye on potential invasions by clever users. For example, on DOS and Unix machines, the "file" named `. .` is an upward path through the hierarchy of file directories.

It is up to the server to prevent a remote user from using `. .` as part of a retrieval request, in cases where this would give access to directories that were not meant to be public. HTTP itself does not prevent such things.

The complete, 60-page document that describes HTTP is on the Web, of course, at **http://ds.internic.net/rfc/rfc1945.txt**.

Your Very Own URLs

Your own local file system is itself accessible through URLs, as indicated by the `file` option in the list of schemes above.

Your Web browser probably lets you look at any local file. SunSoft Inc.'s Java WorkShop, a Java programming toolkit, is actually constructed as a browser-style environment that is populated by Java programs: The Java WorkShop environment opens local files, such as its online documentation, using the same URL syntax that it uses to retrieve remote resources.

Microsoft, IBM, and other vendors of operating systems have said that their future products will integrate many functions of the browser into the user interface shell, essentially eliminating the difference between a local file and any other URL-named resource.

The following program demonstrates the use of the classes URL and URLConnection, as well as the interaction between URLConnection and our Chapter 12 friend InputStream, to inspect a local file.

```java
import java.net.*;
import java.io.*;
class LookAtURL
 { public static void main(String args[])
                                    throws Exception
    { int eof = -1; // read() returns this at the end.
      int next;     // Need an int for values 0-255:
                    // could use a short, but read()
                    // returns an int.
// Construct an instance of URL from a name
      URL u = new URL("file:/C:/HowToJava/Test.html");
      // What do we know about this URL?
      p("Protocol: " + u.getProtocol());
      p("File:     " + u.getFile());

// Construct an instance of URLConnection from that URL
      URLConnection uc = u.openConnection();
      // What more can we learn from this object?
      p("Contents: " + uc.getContentType());

// Construct an InputStream to the URLConnection
      InputStream ui = uc.getInputStream();
      // Display the contents of the file
      p("=========");
      while ( (next = ui.read() ) != eof)
        System.out.write(next);
// write() just puts out the lowest bye of the int.
// print() would print the int's numeric value as
//  string. Try it and see what happens.
      ui.close(); // just to be tidy

}
```

```
    public static void p(Object prtThis)
// (another way of avoiding many System.out.println()s)
      { System.out.println(prtThis);
       }
    }
```

You can put any file name that you want in place of the quoted path/file name in the code above. The file that we used was a minimal HTML (Hypertext Markup Language) file named Test.html, with contents:

```
<html>
<head>
<title>
A Local File
</title>
</head>
<body>
This is a test
</body>
```

In this color-coded listing, we're using the same blue color for HTML tags that we use for Java's reserved words when we show you Java source code: Their roles are analogous.

In a Web browser, this file appears as shown in Figure 14.1.

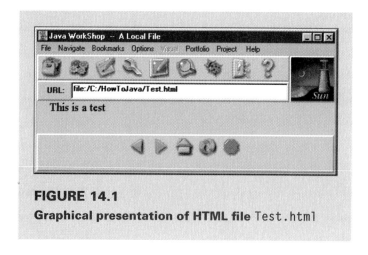

FIGURE 14.1
Graphical presentation of HTML file Test.html

The output from executing class `LookAtURL`, using the input file `Test.html` as shown, is

```
Protocol: file
File:     /C:/HowToJava/Test.html
Contents: text/html
=========
<html>
<head>
<title>
A Local File
</title>
</head>
<body>
This is a test
</body>
```

If we look at an ordinary file like `AUTOEXEC.BAT`, the `getContentType()` method will return a different description, giving us the output line:

```
Contents: content/unknown
```

A program can use the value returned by `getContentType()` to decide how a file should best be displayed.

Encapsulating a URL or a URL connection gives us the benefits that we'd expect from a well-designed class. We get access methods like `getFile()` that describe the object, and utility methods like `getInputStream()` that let us do useful things with that object.

Where Can You Get It?—The IP Address

An Internet Protocol address is a 32-bit number, conveniently written as a series of four numbers separated by periods: each of those four numbers represents a single 8-bit byte, for 32 bits in all.

Class `InetAddress`, which encapsulates an IP address, doesn't have constructors in the usual sense. Rather, it has static methods `getLocalHost()`, `getByName()`, and `getAllByName()`.

Like the static methods of class `Math`, the static methods of class `InetAddress` are invoked outside the context of any object. They are class methods, in the parlance of other object-oriented languages such as Smalltalk.

The method `getLocalHost()` returns an object that encapsulates the IP address of the local system. The method `getByName(String aNameOrAddress)` takes a name like `www.pcweek.com` and returns a matching `InetAddress` object. For example,

```
InetAddress pcWeek
            = InetAddress.getByName("www.pcweek.com");
```

This method will also accept a string like `206.66.184.204`—the same address in its numeric form.

The method `getAllByName()` takes a host name as its argument and returns an array of `InetAddress` objects, one for each host supporting that name. Some sites provide such redundant hosts in the interest of performance and/or reliability.

Once you have an `InetAddress` in hand, invoking the method `getHostName()` on that object returns its name as a string. Invoking the method `getAddress()` returns the numeric IP address as an array of four bytes, beginning with the highest byte of the address in element 0.

Doing Datagrams

If a computer's only identification on a network were its IP address, then it would have no way to accept communications using different protocols at the same time—and there would be no way for one process on a given machine to address a message uniquely to one other process on that same machine.

In addition to the IP address, therefore, Internet Protocol also defines integer-numbered *ports*. These are not hardware devices, like a parallel or serial port: they are merely numeric names.

A 32-bit field gives us 4.3 billion distinct IP addresses, fewer than we would need to give even one such address to every person now living.

Urban areas like Los Angeles are already creating new telephone area codes at a frantic pace, to accommodate compulsively connected people with a phone, a fax, a modem, a cellular phone, and a pager: As "smart homes" start to proliferate IP addresses for various intelligent appliances, this 32-bit limit may therefore become a problem sooner than anyone imagined when the IP address scheme was devised.

Some port numbers are conventionally reserved for particular types of connection: for example, port 80 for HTTP access to a given server.

A *socket* encapsulates a combination of an IP address and a port. It gives us a single object on which we can invoke, for example, methods like `send()` and `receive()` to exchange UDPs between two machines or between two processes on a single machine.

Here is a Java class, Sender, that sends UDPs. When you run it, choose a number to be the port number of that sender, and another to be the port number of the intended receiver. For example, you might invoke Sender with the command:

```
java Sender 101 301
```

Here is the code:

```
import java.net.*;

class Sender
{ static final int sendOnNewline = '\n';
  static final int end           = -1 ;
  public static void main(String args[])
                                     throws Exception
  { InetAddress iAddr = InetAddress.getLocalHost();
    int sPort = Integer.parseInt(args[0]); //send port
    int rPort = Integer.parseInt(args[1]); //recv port
    DatagramSocket sock = new DatagramSocket(sPort);
    byte[] makeLine = new byte[80]; //line in progress
         // This size limits us to 80-character lines
    int inLine      = 0 ; // # of bytes ready to send
    int nextByte;    // int for read() values (0-255)
                     // This doesn't deal with Unicode
    while ( (nextByte = System.in.read()) != end)
     { switch (nextByte)
        { default:    // it's OK to have default first
              makeLine[inLine++] = (byte)nextByte;
              if (inLine < makeLine.length)
                break;
          // else fall through to send the full line
          case sendOnNewline: // or just case '\n'
              sock.send(new DatagramPacket(makeLine,
                                    inLine,
```

```
                                                iAddr,
                                                rPort ));
                        inLine = 0; // start a new line
                        break;
                    }
                }
            }
        }
```

A sender is pretty boring without a receiver. When you run the following, do it with a command like:

```
java Receiver 301 quit
```

where the port number matches the second number you gave when you ran Sender. Here is the code:

```
import java.net.*;
class Receiver
 { public static void main(String args[])
                                    throws Exception
    { int rPort     = Integer.parseInt(args[0]);
      DatagramSocket sock  = new DatagramSocket(rPort);
      byte[] takeLine       = new byte[80];
      DatagramPacket p;
      String killCommand    = args[1];
      String receiveString = "";

      while ( ! receiveString.equals(killCommand))
       { p = new DatagramPacket(takeLine,
                            takeLine.length);
        sock.receive(p); // fills packet
        System.out.println(receiveString =
                        new String(p.getData(),
          /* a String constructor   */     0, 0,
          /*  for building chars  */  p.getLength()));
       } /*  from a byte[] array */
    }
}
```

Open two active windows on your screen: for example, MS-DOS windows if you're running Windows 95. Run `Sender` in one window, `Receiver` in another. You'll see that as you type messages in the sender's window, each line that you type is sent to the receiver's session when you hit Return. This happens until you send a message that is the same as the second argument (in the example above, `quit`) that you supplied when you ran `Receiver`. At that point, the receiver terminates.

 To terminate the Sender, send the end-of-file character, typically Ctrl-Z.

Try starting up at least one other sender, in yet another window, with a different sending port number for its own use but with the same target port—for example, with the command:

```
java Sender 201 301
```

You'll see that more than one active sender can send messages to a single active receiver, if the port numbers are properly chosen. And any sender can issue the command that shuts the receiver down (see Figure 14.2).

Sockets and Security

TCP/IP sockets, with their persistent connections between one system and another, are a controversial subject.

Suppose that you were to download a Java application, embedded in a Web page. Suppose that this application were able to establish connections with other systems anywhere else on the Net. Suppose that while it was performing the function that you had in

FIGURE 14.2

Two instances of Sender (top left, top right) sending User Datagram Packets (UDPs) to a single instance of Receiver (bottom center), and commanding the receiver to shut down.

mind, other threads were carrying out a hidden agenda employing those connections.

Your computer, without your knowledge, could become a part of a covert theft-of-service scheme or some other intrusive attack.

For this reason, current practice does not permit an application in the context of a Web browser to establish a connection with any other machine, except for the application's own "home base" Internet node.

This is not as limiting as it sounds. By connecting back to its home node, an application can put the user's computer to work in presenting and analyzing a commercial service provider's centralized data.

The application's home node can also receive requests from the application and pass them along to other Internet nodes, assuming that the home node has the privileges needed to do this.

Standards are being developed to establish levels of certification that would let a trusted application enjoy broader privileges (see Appendix B). This is one of the areas in which Java's continuing refinement is most likely to make a major difference in what your applications can do.

They Also Serve

An instance of class `Socket` is returned from any of several constructors, taking as their arguments a port number combined with either the host's name (a character string) or an `InetAddress` object for that host.

A client that wants to get something from a server simply creates a socket when it's needed, and initiates the request, using the protocol that goes with that port on the server. The client application treats the socket as it would any other input/output connection.

Of course, the application must know that protocol's vocabulary of commands, such as HTTP's `GET`. This is not part of the Java language as such.

A server's task is more complicated, because the server has to be prepared for incoming requests. A server machine creates a `ServerSocket` object that waits for such requests: When a request comes in, the `ServerSocket`'s `accept()` method creates a `Socket` on the server to handle the new connection for as long as it stays active.

Think of the `ServerSocket` instance as a telephone switchboard, except that it "builds the telephone" to handle each new incoming call. If limited resources prevent the creation of that socket right away, requests for connection will be placed in a queue until they can be handled.

A `ServerSocket` can be constructed with a default limit of 50 pending connection requests, or with a different constructor that takes a specific value for this limit as one of its arguments.

We've gone as far as Java goes in the text-based world of the console session. Even without the fancy graphics of the Web, we've found immense power to model such Internet resources as remote files and privately addressed messages from one running program to another.

But just as Java's network classes make all remote systems look the same to a program, Java's graphical classes will help us make better-looking programs that look the same to any user on any Java-capable computer. When we combine the network classes of this chapter with the Abstract Window Toolkit classes of Chapter 15, we'll have the whole package of benefits that makes Java applets—our final topic in Chapter 16—such an important creative medium.

Summary

In this chapter, we showed

- ▶ That uniform resource locators (URLs) can serve as addresses for many things besides Web pages.

- ▶ That User Datagram Packets (UDPs) and Transmission Control Protocol (TCP), both layered on top of the packet-based Internet Protocol (IP), give us different combinations of efficiency and reliability in point-to-point communications.

- ▶ That the `URL` and `URLConnection` classes let us ask questions about resources, as well as merely retrieve them.

- ▶ That the connections we make, by way of these classes, are just a starting point: applications must employ data transfer protocols, and servers must devise and enforce security policies, before an Internet-based service is complete.

- ▶ That we can establish Internet-style connections within a single machine, as well as across the Net, to explore the use of the classes that encapsulate connections and packets for network communications.

The Abstract
Window Toolkit

Portable
Methods/Native
Peers

Components, Containers,
Windows, Frames, and Panels

Handling Action Events

Using Layout Managers

Using Fonts and Colors

Drawing on a Canvas

Chapter 15
Building on the Standard Packages: java.awt

In this chapter, you'll learn how the differing graphical hardware and color/graphics conventions of various types of computer are hidden by the encapsulations of the Abstract Window Toolkit—fondly known as standard package java.awt. You'll see how the machine-independent classes and methods in this package call native peer classes, implemented for each Java platform, to make a portable Java application have a familiar look and feel to the user of any client environment. You'll explore the layers of abstraction that let Java arrange pushbuttons, drawing regions, and other elements of a graphical application as if they were all merely tiles of various size being arranged in a decorative mosaic—and see how much work it takes to make that graphical interface a functional front panel to a user-driven application.

In Chapter 14, we compared the Internet to a theater. If the networking classes in package java.net are the doors to that auditorium, then the graphical classes of package java.awt are the sets and the costumes. These classes give us the embellishments that make the difference between the simple "poetry reading" of a console application and the far more complete experience of a point-and-click user interface, using styled fonts and colors.

Do not underestimate the challenge that you take on when you decide to write a program that looks good, and puts the user in charge, as well as carrying out a complex function. The classes in java.awt, and the graphical construction tools that various development systems wrap around these classes, make it easier to get an audition—but they won't give you a better story to tell, or the directorial skills that it takes to make that story interesting.

These graphical classes are also acknowledged to be the least satisfactory long-term solutions to be found in any of the standard packages. Future versions of the Java language are likely to rise above these classes, though not actually leave them behind.

Learning the internal workings of java.awt provides a useful lesson in devising and using layers of classes and subclasses to stratify a complicated problem into smaller, more manageable problems. But graphical tools today, and a superior package of graphical classes in the near future, should temper our enthusiasm for mastering the more abstruse aspects of this package.

So Many to Choose From—Graphical "Standards"

The classes in `java.awt` let you write and compile a program once, and have it appear with a "standard" graphical user interface no matter where it runs—despite the differing conventions of Java's many deployment environments. To a Windows user, the program looks like a Windows application; to the user of a Macintosh, the program looks native to that machine.

This is done by writing programs that construct a user interface from the family of classes that descend from the abstract class `Component`. A component has a few key characteristics: It can be painted on the screen at a known position, occupying a specified region, and it can receive input events (for example, a click of a button on the mouse) from its environment.

As an abstract class, `Component` has no instances. Rather, we extend and specialize this class to create concrete subclasses. These subclasses will provide the appearance and behavior of pushbuttons, scroll bars, and other onscreen objects that are sometimes known as *widgets* or *controls*.

Below the layer that's visible to our programs, these portable classes are calling other classes known as *peers*. Peers are not portable, but come in platform-specific sets.

Peers implement specified Java interfaces: This means that the portable classes in `java.awt` can assume that certain method names and signatures will be supported by those peers. And when all is said and done, the generic Java code for drawing a pushbutton—for example—can put a native Windows or Macintosh or Motif pushbutton on the screen of a user's computer.

The Java application's code need not make any provision for the differences between the graphical standards of these environments.

Get Out Your Crayons, Let's Draw

Other classes and methods in `java.awt` let a portable Java program produce other attractive graphics—apart from user interface objects—without concern for the differing conventions and resources of different users' machines.

Such graphics output options include styled text in various colors, fonts, and sizes; geometric figures; and instances of `Image`, a class defined in `java.awt` that encapsulates various graphics file formats.

We get these artistic abilities from the methods defined on class `Graphics`. Any instance of a subclass of `Component` inherits the method `getGraphics()`. That method returns an instance of the `Graphics` class: a "sketch pad," so to speak, for use by that `Component`.

An instance of `Graphics` has to be supported by a corresponding peer, or else there's no actual mechanism for showing anything on the screen. If a given computer environment does not provide a peer for a given subclass of `Component`, then invoking `getGraphics()` on an instance of that subclass returns a `null` reference.

This means that a limited-function device, such as a hand-held personal assistant, can support a subset of the standard graphical user interface: For example, it might provide pushbuttons, but omit scroll bars, on the assumption that applications for such a device will be designed to fit the dimensions of its screen. A portable Java program can detect that it is running in such an environment by checking to see what's returned from a `getGraphics()` call, and can make programmed decisions about how to present itself based on what it finds.

In the normal case, the `getGraphics()` call returns an instance of the `Graphics` class: graphical methods (to draw strings of text, for example) are then invoked on that object. We'll see how this is done later in this chapter.

The Least We Can Do

Java achieves its graphical goals by taking the easy way out. Package `java.awt` defines portable classes that encapsulate common subset functions and behaviors: the kinds of things that any graphical environment will provide.

The alternative approach, providing the union of all capabilities of all supported environments, quickly becomes a money pit. Novell's AppWare Foundation sought to be a "bug-for-bug compatible" superset of Windows, Macintosh, and Unix, but quickly collapsed beneath the diminishing returns that came from working hardest on the quirks that users noticed least.

Opinion is even somewhat divided as to whether Java's use of native peers makes it too difficult to bring Java to a new platform, compared to the alternative approach of drawing graphical controls with a smaller (and more easily ported) set of primitive methods (such as lines and shadings).

The author inclines to the view that native peers, despite the work that they entail, are important to end-user acceptance of Java applications. The author has seen Smalltalk-based development systems, for example, that drew controls similar to the native controls, instead of actually using the native varieties: There have always been differences in appearance and behavior that got in the way of well-conditioned habits, and made the portable applications second-class solutions.

Say Hello, Nicely

A minimal graphical program displays styled text in a bordered, controllable window. This has the same practical value as our first example, class `SayHello` in Chapter 3—that is to say, it's just a foundation for building more useful programs.

Like `SayHello`, however, this minimal program will establish many vital points. Even this simple exercise in graphical programming is far more complex than passing a stream of bytes to a text-mode console window, as we've done to get our output in every other example up until now.

`SayHello` looked like this:

```
class SayHello
  { public static void main(String args[])
      { System.out.println("Hello");
      }
  }
```

We didn't bother to say so at the time, but this class (whose declaration has no `extends` clause) implicitly extended `Object`. The only behavior that we needed from this class was provided by `System.out`, an object that is always on hand. Class `SayHello` didn't need an "educated" parent class.

Our more stylish, graphical version—let's call it `SayBonjour`—needs a lot more support. It can't just dump bytes to a console: It needs a border, it needs fonts, it needs a lot of things that it can't inherit from a primitive `Object` and that the `PrintStream System.out` can't provide.

Choose Your Parents with Care

We'll therefore make `SayBonjour` a subclass, not of `Object`, but of `Frame`: a class that we'll meet more formally in a moment.

For now, suffice it to say that a frame is a portable equivalent of a window (which makes this a sensible name, don't you think?). Extending `Frame` gives our new class `SayBonjour` something to wear, in the form of a border and a title and fashionable accessories like a Close button.

In Any Event, Mind Your Manners

So that SayBonjour will be welcome wherever it goes, we'll make sure it knows how to make a graceful exit. It will have to respond to the Event, as it's called, of being told to go away, in whatever manner the local operating system may deliver this message—by a click on the Close button, for example, or by a similar choice from a default system menu.

As a child of Frame, SayBonjour is a grandchild of Window, which in turn is a child of Container, itself a child of Component. The Component class defines a general-case method called handleEvent(), which gets inherited all the way down this chain.

When an event takes place, such as the user pushing the button of the mouse, the framework of the Abstract Window Toolkit constructs an instance of class Event and gives it as an argument to method handleEvent(), invoked on the instance of Component where that event occurred.

We will override the handleEvent() method in class SayBonjour to deal with the particular case of being told to go away. The new implementation of this method will look at the id field of the Event object that it receives when it is invoked, to see if it has the int value 201—which also carries the more memorable label WINDOW_DESTROY (a public final static value of class Event). The names and int values of the AWT's defined events are listed in the API reference (see also Appendix A).

We'll pass any other types of Event upward, through the hierarchy of classes, by invoking handleEvent() on SayBonjour's superclass. From there, the call to this method will keep on climbing until it finds an implementation, which it will find in class Component, if not before.

Speak Only When Spoken To

Finally, SayBonjour should have something to say. In a graphical environment, text is more than just ASCII bytes or Unicode characters: it's something that has to be drawn.

Fortunately, java.awt encapsulates such arts and crafts inside appropriate methods, so we can ignore the messy details. One could write an entire book about fonts and their rendering on the screen: we can (and will) take this process for granted.

We don't even need to tell SayBonjour when to speak. As a well-bred child of Frame, SayBonjour will take its cue from the environment around it. The environment will determine when SayBonjour's window needs to be drawn, or redrawn—either on first creation, or when it becomes visible after having been obscured.

When this happens, a method named `paint()` will automatically be invoked on the instance of `Graphics` that's owned by this `Frame`. Later in this chapter, we'll explore some of the details of what happens when this method is called.

Say "Bonjour," Mon Ami

To summarize

▶ `SayBonjour` will extend `Frame`.

▶ It will override `handleEvent()`, which it inherits (through `Frame` and its ancestors) from `Component`, to deal with the special case of being told to go away.

▶ It will override `paint()`, which it inherits (through the same hierarchy) from `Component`, to draw (or redraw) some graphically rendered text whenever the `Frame` is updated.

Here is the code:

```
import java.awt.*;

class SayBonjour extends Frame
 { public static void main(String args[])
   { Frame sB = new SayBonjour();
     sB.resize(256,128); // width, height in pixels
     sB.show();
   }

 public void paint(Graphics sBG)
   { sBG.drawString("Bonjour!", 32, 58); // x, y of B
   }

 public boolean handleEvent(Event anEvent)
   { if (anEvent.id == Event.WINDOW_DESTROY)
       System.exit(0);
     return super.handleEvent(anEvent);
   }
 }
```

When we compile and launch this application, using commands like those shown at upper left in Figure 15.1, we get something that looks like the window at the upper right of that figure.

A more interactive application can be built by adding cases for a wider range of events to the local implementation of handleEvent(). For example,

```
public boolean handleEvent(Event anEvent)
    { switch (anEvent.id)      // a perfect use of switch
       { case Event.WINDOW_DESTROY:
            System.exit(0); // return is academic, but
            return false;  // compiler doesn't know that
         case Event.MOUSE_DOWN:            // draw when?
            Graphics sbG = getGraphics(); // draw where?
            sbG.fillOval(anEvent.x, anEvent.y, 5, 5);
            return true;              // draw what?
      // returning true means nothing else is needed
         default:
            return super.handleEvent(anEvent);
       }
    }
```

When you modify class SayBonjour to use this more capable version of handleEvent(), clicking the mouse anywhere in the window will leave a small filled circle at that point. The handleEvent() method is obtaining the current Graphics context, inspecting the x and y fields of the Event object (which were automatically filled in with the coordinates of the mouse when it was clicked), and calling

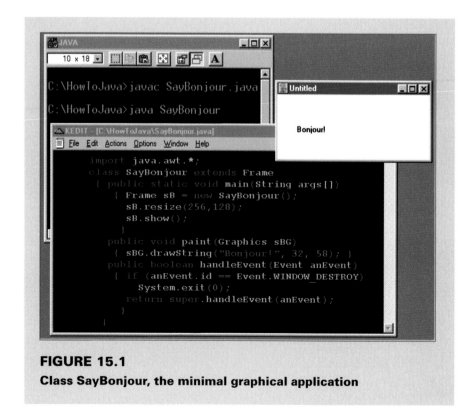

FIGURE 15.1
Class SayBonjour, the minimal graphical application

the graphical method requested. We'll look at the vocabulary of graphical methods in more detail later.

If you resize the window, however, the circles all disappear. Why? Because resizing the window calls `paint()`, and `paint()` doesn't know anything about those circles.

The `paint()` method does know about the drawn character string, which is why this reappears even if partially covered by another window and then re-exposed. Any circles that were under that other window, however, will not be restored. The AWT framework determines which piece of the window needs to be repainted, and does what's needed—but only as far as it knows.

Graphical Environments: The Big Picture

Earlier, we spoke of the common subset of appearances and behaviors that have to be provided by all graphical environments. Let's be more specific about what that common subset includes, and use this as a framework for exploring more of the facilities of package `java.awt`.

Our checklist for this common subset comes from the acronym WIMP: Windows, Icons, Menus, and a Pointing device.

Windows—Not Just Microsoft's

A graphical environment has to give each of several running applications its own area of the display, preferably letting the user control each region's size and location.

Package `java.awt` meets this need with classes `Panel` (a simple rectangular area) and `Frame` (a top-level window on the user's electronic desktop, including a title, a border, and possibly a menu bar).

A panel can be placed in a nurturing environment like a Web page, as well as inside a frame. Both `Frame` and `Panel` are called container classes, since they can contain other components of a graphical user interface.

Icons and Menus—Because Choice Is Good

A graphical environment should replace typed commands, whenever possible, by selections from choices of available actions. Those choices may be offered as:

▶ Mouse-sensitive graphical symbols (known individually as *icons*, or in groups as *palettes*).

▶ Graphical imitations of real-world devices, like pushbuttons.

▶ Menus, appearing on demand.

Applications should indicate, by graying out choices or simply by hiding them, when a choice is either irrelevant or unavailable.

Package `java.awt` delivers such choices via the classes `Button`, `Checkbox`, `CheckboxGroup` (sometimes called radio buttons, since they're like the buttons on an automobile radio—you can only choose one), `Choice`, `List`, and `Menu`. These will look and behave as the user expects, thanks to Java's use of native peers.

For example, you don't need to write the code that makes a button look as if it's being pushed (as shown in Figure 15.2). You get this behavior free.

In addition to buttons, checkboxes, and other choice-oriented components, `java.awt` also provides text-entry controls for both single- and multiline data (see Figure 15.3). Consult the Java API for the details of the user action events that are relevant to each type of component.

Leave the Layout to Java

You don't have to tell Java where a user interface component should go in its container. Polished applications will want to control such things, but Java offers simple solutions for simple situations.

Specifically, an application can simply add buttons (or other components) to a container, after putting that container under the control of a `LayoutManager`.

Strictly speaking, we should say, "Under the control of something that implements the interface `LayoutManager`," since this is the name of an interface, not a class. (Its name deviates from the convention of naming an interface with an adjective, rather than a noun.)

Classes that implement this interface can descend from `Object`, or from any other class, as long as they provide the following methods. This list gives the type of value, if any, returned by a method; the name of the method; and the argument

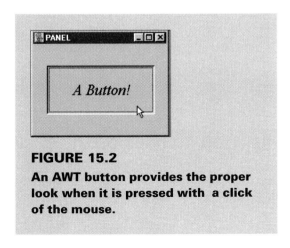

FIGURE 15.2
An AWT button provides the proper look when it is pressed with a click of the mouse.

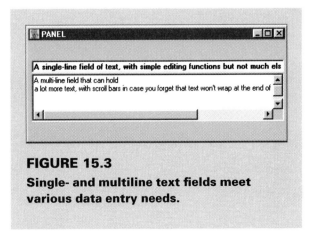

FIGURE 15.3
Single- and multiline text fields meet various data entry needs.

signature of the method, consisting of a type and a descriptive name for each argument.

▶ `void addLayoutComponent(String componentName,Component theComponent)`

▶ `void layoutContainer(Container theContainer)`

▶ `Dimension minimumLayoutSize(Container theContainer)`

▶ `Dimension preferredLayoutSize(Container theContainer)`

▶ `void removeLayoutComponent(Component theComponent)`

The class `Dimension`, which is the returned type from two of the methods above, is analogous to the class `XYPoint` that we defined as an example in Chapter 9. Just as `XYPoint` had fields for x- and y- coordinates of location, `Dimension` has fields for a `height` and a `width` (both of type `int`). The default constructor, `new Dimension()`, returns a `Dimension` with members `.height` and `.width` both equal to zero.

Any container supports the method `Component add(Component aComponent)`, and will use its associated `LayoutManager` (if it has one) to position that component on the screen.

The simplest form of `LayoutManager`, class `FlowLayout`, is a subclass of `Object`: It "flows" components into an onscreen container, in the same way that a word processor wraps text to fit within changed margins.

Here is a program that takes a number as a start-up argument and populates a frame with that number of buttons, all bearing numeric labels.

```
import java.awt.*;
class FlowButtons extends Frame
 { public static void main(String args[])
    { Frame fB = new FlowButtons(
                          Integer.parseInt(args[0]));
      fB.resize(256,128);
      fB.show();
    }

  public FlowButtons(int howManyButtons)
    { setTitle("Call this a layout?");
      setLayout(new FlowLayout());
      for (int i=1; !(i > howManyButtons); i++)
```

```
        add(new Button(Integer.toString(i)));
    }

  public boolean handleEvent(Event anEvent)
   { if (anEvent.id == Event.WINDOW_DESTROY)
       System.exit(0);
     return super.handleEvent(anEvent);
   }
 }
```

Figure 15.4 shows three instances of this program, each with the same number of buttons but in windows that have been resized to different shapes: the buttons have flowed to fit.

Keeping Our Ducks in a Row

In general, we won't want the components of a user interface to rearrange themselves like this. We'll want them to stay in formation, though perhaps they should change in size if the user stretches or shrinks the window.

We can do this with more powerful implementations of `LayoutManager`, like `GridLayout` and `GridBagLayout`. The former arranges components into a grid with a given number of rows and columns. The latter is more flexible: It maintains a rectangular alignment but does not require identically sized cells or a constant number of cells in each row.

Figure 15.5 shows a four-function calculator, based on a tutorial exercise for SunSoft Inc.'s Java WorkShop development

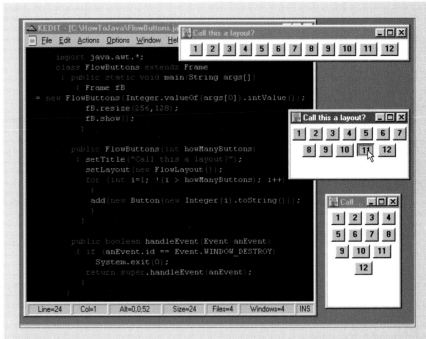

FIGURE 15.4

Class FlowButtons demonstrates FlowLayout's automatic rearrangement of components in a container (in this case, a Frame) as that container is resized.

system: This program has been modified to make the buttons change shape as the application's window is resized.

Notice also that the equal button and the calculator's display are wider than the other cells in the rectangular array: these pleasing effects are easily achieved with a `GridBagLayout`.

Now That You Know It, Forget It

It is possible to use classes like `GridBagLayout` by writing Java code. It is also possible to create Java programs by manually composing streams of Java byte-codes, but it's a poor use of your time: a compiler does the job in fractions of a second.

In the same way, anyone writing more than a trivial Java application will use a graphical interface builder.

Figure 15.6 shows the difference between defining a layout with code versus doing it with a higher-level tool such as the Visual Java module of Java WorkShop.

The layout, an early stage of the calculator that appears in Figure 15.5, can be controlled by choosing values from menus with a tool like the Attribute Editor at upper left; this task can also be done by editing code, like that shown in the window near the bottom of the screen.

The former approach takes a tiny fraction of the time to produce far superior results.

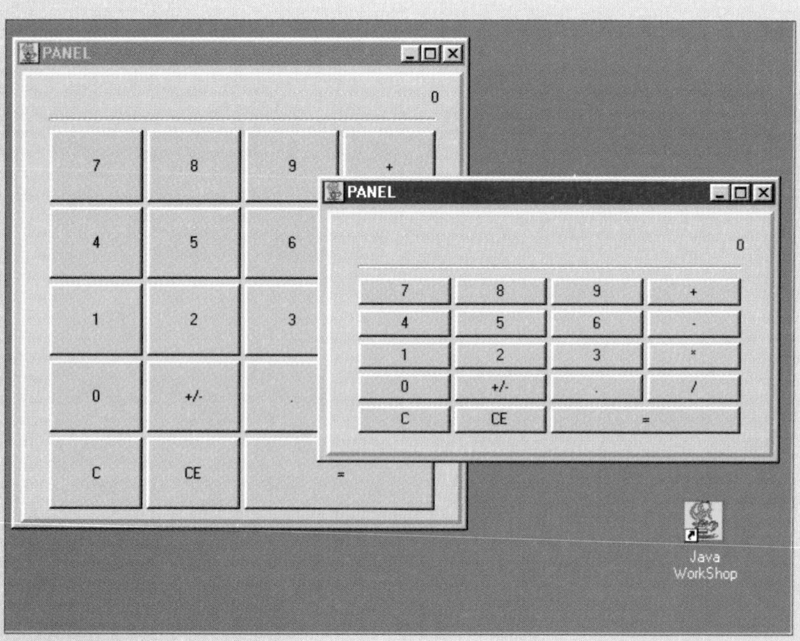

The Pointer— Because the User Is in Charge

Besides, you'll have more important things to do. Because once you have the graphical interface built, you're ready to add the real value to your application.

FIGURE 15.5
A GridBagLayout can maintain relative sizes, shapes, and positions of components even as their container is resized.

When the user clicks on that button, it's not for the aesthetic pleasure of watching it "push." The user wants something useful to happen, and you have to write the code that makes it so.

A graphical environment should let the user—not the program—dictate the sequence in which input will be provided, and the manner in which a program's various functions will be performed.

Our example programs, for instance, have often used parameters that the user supplied when starting the program, or loops that asked the user for specific input in a predetermined sequence.

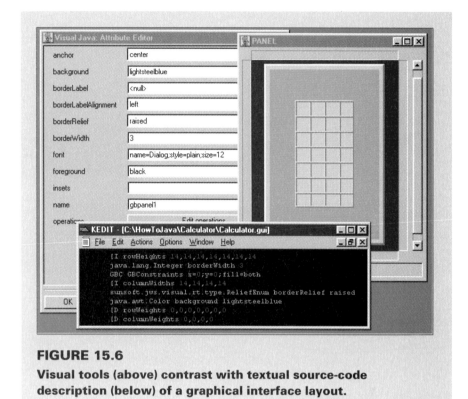

FIGURE 15.6
Visual tools (above) contrast with textual source-code description (below) of a graphical interface layout.

In a graphical environment, users expect instead a "fill in the blanks" approach that lets them enter values in any order that's convenient, then click on a button or take some other action to tell the program that it may proceed.

A program should also preserve the user's inputs, let the user change individual values at will, and repeat an operation using those modified input values. The program should never demand that all of the values be re-entered, though it should offer the option of starting over.

Graphical Programs Play in a Tougher League

With these high expectations, you'd better get used to the idea that writing a graphical-interface program means a whole lot more work—no matter how powerful the tools may be for drawing the user interface on the screen.

For example, a Java program to acquire seven numbers, and print their average, took only 28 lines of code in Chapter 4—not including comments and blanks. That's a lot less code than it takes to write just the event handling routines for the buttons of our graphical four-function calculator.

Writing those event handlers requires building a mental model (and implementing that model in Java statements) of what's called a *state machine*, with internal flag values that tell the program how to handle the same events in different situations.

For example, when you're entering numbers into a calculator, what's really happening? Think about the first number that you press: this clears the initial zero on the display and shows the selected number. The next number has to push that first digit over to the left, and update the value of the multi-digit number that you're building. And so on.

Just handling the construction of a calculator entry, one key at a time, requires a piece of code something like this (based on SunSoft's tutorial example):

```
void number(int x)
 { if (pendingDelete) // about to start a new entry
     { clearEntry();
       pendingDelete = false;  // entry in progress
     }
   if (decimalSeen)   // we're on the right of " "
     { value += (double)x * fraction;
       fraction *= 0.1;
     }
   else              // we're still pushing to the left
       value = value * 10.0 + (double)x;
 }
```

Integrated development environments allow us to inspect the interaction between a graphical interface and the underlying code, as shown for this same handler routine in Figure 15.7.

In this case, we don't even reach this point in the program until after the button that was clicked has been identified. Still more code is needed for actually doing the math, let alone updating the display to reflect the keystrokes and the results.

This example is developed at length in the on-disk tutorial that's provided with Java WorkShop, which is included on the CD-ROM that accompanies this book. We won't duplicate that material with any further discussion here.

The point to take away from this is that graphical programs aren't just more difficult to put on the screen. Their interactive, user-driven nature makes them far more complex to design and build in other respects as well.

Could Shakespeare Make a Movie?

Finally, don't underestimate the artistic burden of creating a graphical application that looks as good as users have come to expect.

Look at Figure 15.8, showing the browser-style environment that Java WorkShop uses to display and execute its various tools. Look closely at the open-end wrench icon that Java WorkShop uses to select its build manager, the module that controls the process of compiling an application's files.

Pretty, isn't it? It looks like a real live chrome-plated wrench. The realistic look of this and the environment's other icons makes Java WorkShop both visually appealing and intuitively usable.

But now, look at Figure 15.9, which shows an enlargement of that same chrome wrench icon. Look at the elaborate use of color to achieve that reflective, three-dimensional appearance. Think about applying that level of effort to literally dozens of icons, throughout the various screens that appear as an application runs.

If text-based programming is a form of poetry, graphical programming is a form of

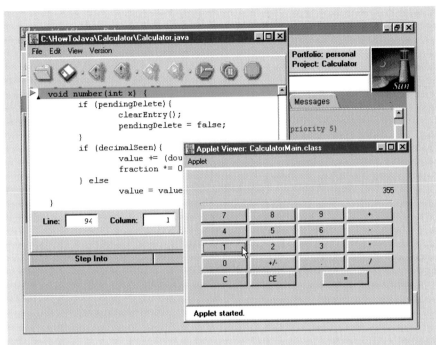

FIGURE 15.7

An integrated debugger (in this case, that of SunSoft Inc.'s Java WorkShop) allows investigation of interactions between graphical interface and underlying code.

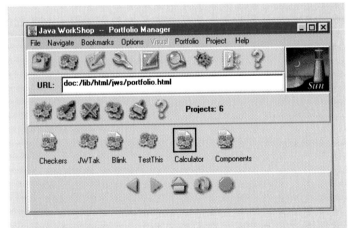

FIGURE 15.8

Java WorkShop's colorful icons aid quick identification of tools, in addition to their aesthetic appeal.

moviemaking. Talent, even brilliance in one form of creativity, says little about one's prospects in another.

In short words: This is hard.

Don't Make It Graphic Unless That Makes It Better

If Java could not do graphics, it would still be an immensely powerful language. Java's object-oriented design, and its powerful abstractions such as threads, streams, exceptions, and dictionaries, make Java a superb power tool; its portable virtual machine makes it a "cordless" tool as well, one that goes to the work instead of making the work come to it.

Likewise, the World Wide Web would be a stunning achievement even if it also lacked elaborate graphics. Text-only HTML pages, available as an option on many Web sites, load more quickly than their illustrated counterparts; text is more easily searched than graphics, and is readily turned into synthesized speech for visually impaired users or for output to users whose eyes must stay focused on something else.

Some argue that visual images are a universal language, while a text-based Web would impose American English on every other country in the world. There are, however, many counterexamples: for instance, the broken wineglass icon that is a "universal" symbol for fragile contents has been mistaken in some countries as meaning "damaged goods."

Yes, Java does graphics more easily than many other languages. No, that doesn't mean that graphics are essential to the application that you want to deliver. Let the problem, not the tool, guide the solution.

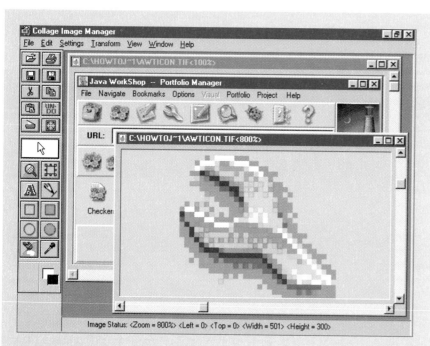

FIGURE 15.9

Achieving artistic effects, such as realistic icons, requires painstaking effort at the level of individual pixels in onscreen graphics.

Let's Get Really Graphic

We said that the second major mission of `java.awt` was simple drawing of graphical content. Drawing takes place on the rectangular region of the component whose `Graphics` object invokes the drawing method.

The color of anything that's drawn, and the font and style of drawn text, are controlled with the methods `void setColor(Color aColor)` and `void setFont(Font aFont)`, respectively. To mix several fonts and/or colors in one `Graphics` object, one works in stages: First set the font and/or color, then draw, then set the next font and/or color, and so on until done.

An instance of class `Color` encapsulates three values that can each range from 0 to 255: one for each of the red, blue, and green components of the color, providing 24-bit color or 16,277,216 possible hues.

An instance of `Color` can easily be constructed from three `float` arguments, each ranging from 0.0 to 1.0 (representing the range between minimum and maximum contribution) for red, green, and blue respectively. We use this constructor in class `CircleCanvas`, below.

For convenience, the methods `brighter()` and `darker()` can be applied to an existing instance of `Color` to return another instance of a suitably modified hue. The API leaves the details to the implementor.

An instance of class `Font` encapsulates a combination of font name, point size, and style. The style can be any of 0 (plain), 1 (bold), 2 (italic), or 3 (bold italic). In other words, style is a 2-bit attribute, combining an italic bit and a bold bit.

For example, we can modify class `SayBonjour` to use 64 point Times Roman Bold Italic (see Figure 15.10), or as close as our system can come to this, by invoking the method `setFont()` within the `paint()` method of this class:

```
public void paint(Graphics sBG)
  { sBG.setFont(new Font("TimesRoman",
                    Font.BOLD|Font.ITALIC,
                    64);
    sBG.drawString("Bonjour!", 32, 58);
  }
```

FIGURE 15.10

Class SayBonjour takes on a new look when font, font size, and font style are controlled by a setFont() call.

Render unto Caesar

To render what looks like a single line of text, but using more than one font (including any change of style or size) on that line, requires a separate `drawString()` call for each segment of that line. The program must know the length of each segment so that the next segment of text can be positioned.

This is done by constructing an instance of class `FontMetrics`, using the current `Font`—obtained, if necessary, by invoking `getFont()` on the current instance of `Graphics`—as the argument to the constructor.

We then invoke method `stringWidth(String theString)` on that `FontMetrics` object, using the `String` to be drawn as the argument of the method. The method returns the width required to render that `String` in that `Font`.

For proportionally spaced fonts, this is quite a convenience, though `java.awt` still leaves ample room for improvement in rendering mixed text.

Java's Drafting Tools

We saw `drawString()` used in `SayBonjour` at the beginning of this chapter. Other `Graphics` methods use the same coordinate system: The horizontal (x-) and vertical (y-) coordinates both begin, at zero, in the top-left corner of the rectangular area that goes with a `Graphics` object.

Drawing methods supported by class `Graphics` include the following, all of which are `void`, with all parameters being of type `int` unless otherwise noted:

▶ `draw3DRect(x, y, width, height, raised)` This draws a rectangle with either a raised or a recessed appearance, depending on whether the `boolean` argument `raised` is `true` or `false`.

▶ `drawArc(x, y, width, height, startAngle, arcAngle)` The starting angle, in degrees, is zero at three o'clock and increases counterclockwise. Negative (clockwise) angles may be specified. The arc is drawn through `arcAngle` degrees from that starting position.

▶ `drawBytes(bytes, offset, length, x, y)` This takes an array of `bytes`, a starting offset into that array, and the number of `bytes` beginning at that point, to be drawn as a `String` of text in the same manner as with `drawString()`.

▶ drawChars(chars, offset, length, x, y) This is similar to drawBytes(), but takes an array of chars instead.

▶ drawLine(x1, y1, x2, y2)

▶ drawOval(x, y, width, height)

▶ drawPolygon(xPoints, yPoints, nPoints) The first two arguments are arrays of int, the last is the int number of points to be connected by lines. For example, this version of the paint() method in class SayBonjour will enclose the drawn string in a box:

```
public void paint(Graphics sBG)
    { int[] xPoints = {10,10,110,110,10};
      int[] yPoints = {10,110,110,10,10};
      sBG.drawString("Bonjour!", 32, 58); //x,y of "B"
      sBG.drawPolygon(xPoints,yPoints,5);
    }
```

▶ drawRect(x, y, width, height) The drawRect() method produces a rectangle with square corners.

▶ drawRoundRect(x, y, width, height, arcWidth, arcHeight) This produces a rectangle with rounded corners; arcWidth and arcHeight are the horizontal and vertical diameters (not the radii) of the arcs at each corner.

▶ fill3DRect(x, y, width, height, raised) This draws a filled-in version of the 3-D rectangle outlined by draw3Drect().

▶ fillArc(x, y, width, height, startAngle, arcAngle) This draws a filled-in arc.

▶ fillOval(x, y, width, height) This draws a filled-in oval.

▶ fillPolygon(xPoints, yPoints, nPoints) This draws a filled-in polygon.

▶ fillRect(x, y, width, height) This draws a filled-in rectangle.

▶ fillRoundRect(x, y, width, height, arcWidth, arcHeight) This draws a filled-in rounded rectangle.

On a Blank Canvas

If a program draws on a container, other components in that container may get mixed up with that drawing.

It is neater to define a subclass of class `Canvas`, with a `paint()` method that does the desired drawing on the `Graphics` instance owned by that `Canvas`-type component. Instances of a `Canvas` subclass can be managed by a `LayoutManager`, just like any other kind of `Component`.

The following code populates a `Frame` with four instances of a subclass of `Canvas`, whose `paint()` method draws a filled-in circle of random color whenever that method is called.

```
import java.awt.*;
class FlowCircles extends Frame
  { public static void main(String args[])
      { Frame fC = new FlowCircles(4);
        fC.resize(384,384);
        fC.show();
      }


    public FlowCircles(int howMuchCanvas)
      { setTitle("Welcome to my Gallery");
        setLayout(new FlowLayout());
        for (int i=0; i < howMuchCanvas; i++)
          {
          Canvas newCC = new CircleCanvas();
          add(newCC);
          newCC.resize(96,96);
          }
      }


    public boolean handleEvent(Event anEvent)
      { if (anEvent.id == Event.WINDOW_DESTROY)
          System.exit(0);
        return super.handleEvent(anEvent);
      }
  }
```

```
class CircleCanvas extends Canvas
 { public void paint(Graphics ccG)
    { ccG.setColor(
       new Color(
        new Double(Math.random()).floatValue(),
        new Double(Math.random()).floatValue(),
        new Double(Math.random()).floatValue()));
      ccG.fillOval(0,0,96,96);
    }
 }
```

Figure 15.11 shows the result when three instances of this program are executed, each in a window that has been stretched to a different shape. You can resize the window of a running instance of this application and see the circles rearrange themselves and take on new colors.

But if you cover a running copy of this application with another window, then move that obscuring window so that you uncover the circles a little bit at a time, you'll see something odd. Each uncovered strip of the arrangement of circles will appear in a different color.

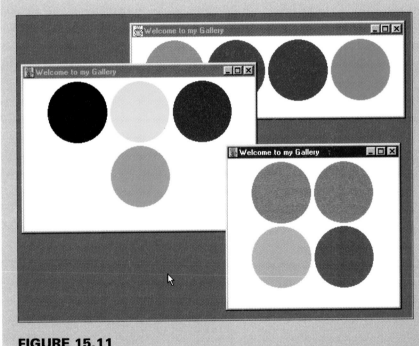

FIGURE 15.11
Canvases, like other components, can be rearranged automatically by a FlowLayout manager.

This is because the AWT framework is calculating the region of the window that actually needs to be repainted, and is only repainting that portion. If colors don't change from one drawing of a figure to the next, this is a useful time-saver. In this case, it's not what we want at all.

Make this change in the `paint()` method, and all will be well.

```
class CircleCanvas extends Canvas
     { public void paint(Graphics ccG)
        { ccG = getGraphics(); // add this line
           ccG.setColor(...      // continue as before
```

We can also prove that a `Canvas` is just a component that can be mixed at will with other `Components` in the same `Container`. For example, we can add a `Button` to our `Container` after we add each `Canvas`, by inserting a line as shown (in context) below.

```
...
add(newCC);
newCC.resize(96,96);
add(new Button(Integer.toString(i)));
...
```

This produces a result like the one in Figure 15.12.

Now we have it all: the core Java language, the input/output and networking abstractions, and the graphics. We're ready to walk on the Web side, with the aid of the final standard package: `java.applet`.

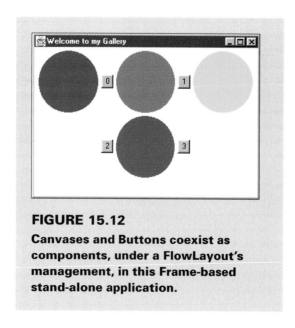

FIGURE 15.12
Canvases and Buttons coexist as components, under a FlowLayout's management, in this Frame-based stand-alone application.

Summary

In this chapter, we showed

▶ That the object hierarchy serves us well when it comes to laying out a graphical application, with the general idea of a `Component` covering both user interface elements and drawn figures.

▶ That this hierarchy covers behavior as well as appearance, with particular action events (such as mouse clicks) being handled by a particular component subclass—while others are referred up the chain to superclasses.

▶ That layout managers can automate the rearrangement of graphical elements within a resized window, or that more sophisticated layout managers can make an application preserve its arrangement while resizing the individual elements of its user interface.

▶ That fonts and colors, under a program's control, can respond to user events such as resizing a window and repainting its contents.

▶ That canvases give us a tool for partitioning a window into separate areas so that graphical operations won't interfere with each other.

▶ That the attractive appearance and user-driven nature of graphical-interface applications involve a substantial programming effort, even with the aid of interactive tools for generating the code that describes a complex layout.

Chapter 16
Building on the Standard Libraries: java.applet

In this chapter, you'll learn how a Java program becomes part of a Web page as viewed by a Java-enabled browser, whether the user is "surfing the Net" or connecting to a private corporate intranet. We'll contrast Java's approach with that of scripting languages, such as JavaScript, and see the difference between a program that runs in a browser (an *applet*) and a stand-alone application that runs in a console text-mode session or in its own graphical window on the desktop. And we'll see how the world of Java merges into that of the Internet, as applets obtain runtime instructions from Hypertext Markup Language tags.

The phrase *Java applet*, unknown before 1995, appeared in only 30 published articles during its first year in the public eye.

In the first half of 1996, however, this phrase appeared in almost ten articles per week, counting only the publications indexed by the Computer Library database. Use of this phrase in the trade and technical press more than tripled during that six-month period.

Surprisingly, Java applets even became a topic of comment in the popular and business press as well, with *Business Week* calling Java "a pop-culture icon."

After fifteen chapters, you understand Java—but what the heck is an applet?

An Idea Whose Time Has Come—Again

Applet was once a generic term for any small, single-function program (such as the Calculator applets on Windows or Macintosh computers). The term came into use along with desktop-style environments, as pioneered in popular use by Apple during the late 1980s after earlier (and overpriced) experiments by Xerox.

Prior to desktop environments, any application took over the entire machine, and applications like the Lotus 1-2-3 spreadsheet had to provide their own menu commands for system functions like formatting a floppy disk—because access to these functions would otherwise require saving work, quitting the application, and restarting the entire session after attending to that one tiny chore.

With an electronic desktop, it made sense to offer more focused tools, since more than one tool could be loaded at the same time. The user could activate any loaded tool with just a point and click of the mouse.

After the arrival of Microsoft Windows 3.0 in 1990, marketing one-upmanship and product-review feature lists gradually nudged the major commercial developers back toward overwhelming applications. Many users resent the resulting products' complexity, not to mention their voracious appetite for hard-disk storage and memory. The time was ripe for the reinvention of applets when Java happened to come along.

Now on Tour: Java and the Applets

Since then, *applet* has become so tied to *Java* that many end users think that these are equivalent terms. Applets aren't unique to Java, nor is Java limited to applets, but the technology of Java and the idea of the narrowly focused application are an ideal match.

The content provider with specialized knowledge can package that knowledge in an applet, producing a high-performance program without the labor of learning a low-level language—and without the redundant effort of producing and supporting different versions for different hardware platforms. Learning Java makes it easier for developers to offer specialized software.

The software buyer with specialized needs can avoid the high cost (in money and computer resources) of buying a feature-bloated product just to get one key capability—and can enjoy the low price (due to low costs of marketing and distribution) that comes with Web-based product delivery, without the risks that come with "untrusted" code that lacks Java applets' `SecurityManager` protections. Specialized needs make software buyers go shopping for Java-based products.

With the facilities developed in the first fifteen chapters of this book, you're already well prepared to create industrial-strength applications in any domain: Applications with the reliable mathematical behavior of FORTRAN, the concurrent tasking facilities of Ada, the convenient graphics of BASIC, the intuitive object-oriented architecture of Smalltalk, the cross-platform consistency of REXX, and the speed of C++. Java is far more than just a scripting language for animated Web sites.

But there's no reason why you shouldn't enjoy the commercial benefits (or even just the ego enhancement) that comes from putting your work on world-wide display. Entire books have been written on the subject of designing a world-class Web page, but this one final chapter will tell you how to dress your Java code to have a good time at the party.

What's in the Package

Class `Applet` is the leading member of `java.applet`, the last of the standard packages that together make up the Java API.

At this point, our fluency in Java has grown so strong that we can define Java applets using terms that were utterly foreign in Chapter 1. An applet is an *instance* (there's one new word) of a *subclass* (there's another) of `java.awt.Panel` (which is itself a subclass of `Container`, a subclass in turn of `Component` in the standard *package* `java.awt`—the Abstract Window Toolkit).

In Chapters 11 through 15, we saw the practical benefits that come from inheriting and specializing the behaviors of general-purpose classes. Class `Applet`, as we'll soon see, is one more excellent example, extending a `Component`'s ability to handle events with a `Container`'s ability to participate in nested layouts—and refining the result with `Applet`'s awareness of the browser environment around it.

The other members of this package are the interface `AppletContext`, the interface `AppletStub`, and the interface `AudioClip`. Interface `AppletContext` specifies method names and signatures by which an applet can seek information on its environment. For example, `getApplet(String anAppletName)` returns a reference to another applet on the same HTML page with the name `anAppletName`, or returns `null` if there is no such other applet.

This lets one applet determine if another particular applet is present. Applets can communicate with each other by calling each other's `public` methods (if this is allowed by security settings).

If an applet doesn't know the names of other cohabiting applets, it can call the method `getApplets()` to obtain an `Enumeration` (an interface that we explored in Chapter 13) of the other applets on the page. The inquisitive applet can then work its way through that `Enumeration` with calls to `nextElement()`, examining each of its neighbors one by one.

If an applet is running in a URL-capable browser, and not just a simple applet viewer, then it can call the method `showDocument(URL someURL)` with an instance of class `URL` (see Chapter 14) as the argument. This lets an applet use the surrounding browser as a resource retrieval engine.

That's the kind of power that makes leading software executives say that the look of today's browsers is the look of tomorrow's operating systems.

The interface `AudioClip` gives applets another capability not currently supported for stand-alone Java applications: that of playing sounds, albeit only in the 8-bit Sun .au file format. The `Applet` method `getAudioClip(URL where, String whichOne)` returns an `AudioClip` reference. At its leisure, the applet can invoke the `AudioClip` methods `play()`, `loop()`, or `stop()`. Calling `play()`

restarts the sound segment from its beginning; calling `play()` on more than one `AudioClip` at once will mix the sounds.

We've taken interface `AppletStub` for granted; so can you. The `Applet` method `setStub()` is called automatically when an applet comes into existence, returning the hooks that are used by other methods like `getParameter()` (whose use we'll see toward the end of this chapter).

Getting Embedded with Applet

If you want to embed a Java program into a page on the World Wide Web, or view it with an Internet-style browser across a private intranet, then your program must be defined as a subclass of `Applet`.

This will mean that your program—that is, your applet—supports the methods that are defined on the `Applet` class to start and stop your applet as it goes in and out of view; to reclaim computational resources when the applet is no longer needed; and to control the interaction between the applet and the environment where it's running.

An applet lacks the desktop-level supporting structures, such as a window border and a system menu, that it would need if it were to run as a separate application. Class `Applet` extends the AWT class `Panel`, not class `Frame`.

Depending on the execution environment, an applet may also lack the access to local resources (such as files) that's normally granted to a stand-alone application. This is not a technical limitation, but a policy decision. Applets often originate on "untrusted" Internet hosts, so current Web browsers generally bar an applet's access to any resources other than those at the applet's point of origin.

The rationale for this was discussed in Chapter 14; the mechanism for defining and enforcing such restrictions, class `SecurityManager`, was described in Chapter 11.

Live Globally, Run Locally

Like any Java program that's ready to run, an applet resides in one or more `.class` files. These contain the bytecode instruction streams that drive a Java virtual machine.

Those `.class` files will normally be produced by a Java compiler, but they may also come from a compiler for IBM's NetRexx or for the non-proprietary language Ada 95. Figure 16.1 shows Thomson Software Products's ObjectAda for Windows development system: This offers the option of compiling the object-oriented multithreading language Ada 95 to produce Java bytecodes, as well as the usual mode of compiling and linking for native execution under Microsoft Windows on an Intel x86 or compatible processor.

A Java applet and its Ada 95 source code appear together in this somewhat disorienting screen shot. It feels more than a little bit strange to read a piece of code that says, for example, `procedure init(...)`. It's like hearing a familiar language being spoken with a foreign accent. As with a human language, however, the meaning remains the same.

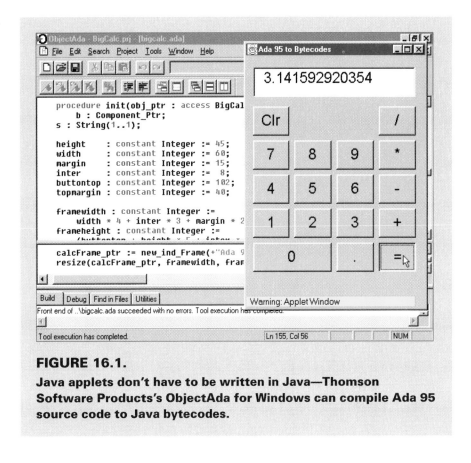

FIGURE 16.1.

Java applets don't have to be written in Java—Thomson Software Products's ObjectAda for Windows can compile Ada 95 source code to Java bytecodes.

Ada 95 and other languages are being hosted on the Java virtual machine, just as they were hosted on hardware microprocessors like the Alpha or the PowerPC when these chips debuted. When the Java virtual machine appears in hardware form as "Java chips," these languages will be able to run on the computers or other devices that use them.

But once a program is compiled into bytecodes that can pass Java's runtime validations, the source language no longer matters. It is reasonable to call such programs Java applets, regardless of their original language, because the rules of the Java platform determine what these programs can do.

Launching the Applet from the Page

When a Java-enabled browser opens an HTML-format file, or "gets" an HTML page using the HTTP protocol that we described in Chapter 14, it will detect any markup tags that show the presence of an applet.

Here is the HTML file, containing `<applet>` and `</applet>` tags surrounding the needed information, that tells a browser to load the applet defined by the locally stored file `BonAppetit.class`. This is an animated, applet-packaged version of our `SayBonjour` application from Chapter 15; you'll see the Java source code in a moment.

```
<applet
    name="BonAppetit"      // appears in status messages,
                           //  can be used by getApplet()
    code="BonAppetit.class"  // the .class file to run
    codebase="C:/HowToJava/BonAppetit"   // where it is
    width="576"
    height="256"           // how to display it on the page
    align="Top"
    alt="If you had a Java-enabled browser,
         you would see an applet here."
>      <hr>If your browser recognized the applet tag,
       you would see an applet here.<hr>
</applet>
```

The applet's source code need not be disclosed to the user. Only the compiled `.class` file needs to be accessible to the browser.

If you want to offer executable content that incorporates proprietary data or trade-secret knowledge, this format is an advantage over other methods of adding executable content to a Web page, methods such as the scripting languages JavaScript or VBScript.

If You Want to Stick to the Script

With scripting technologies, source code in the scripting language is usually embedded in the HTML page. For example,

```
<SCRIPT LANGUAGE="JavaScript">
document.write("Bonjour<HR>")
</SCRIPT>
```

This "full disclosure" may limit the commercial viability of delivering high-value services.

But don't get the impression that Java is merely some sort of compiled JavaScript. Java's compiled bytecodes do offer better protection for intellectual property, but Java also goes beyond JavaScript by providing an extensible object hierarchy, inherently safe strong type checking, multiple threads, and exception handling. JavaScript lacks all these features.

Here is the Java source code for BonAppetit:

```
import java.applet.Applet;
import java.awt.*;
public class BonAppetit extends Applet
 {public void paint(Graphics baG)
                         // bon appetit Graphics
    { for (int i=1;i<129;i++)
       { baG.setColor(Color.white);
         baG.setFont(new Font("TimesRoman",
                          Font.BOLD|Font.ITALIC,
                          i));
         baG.drawString("Bonjour!",160-i,96+i/4);
         baG.setColor(new Color(255-i*2,64-i/2,32-i/4));
         baG.drawString("Bonjour!",160-i,96+i/4);
        }
      baG.setColor(Color.white);
      baG.setFont(new Font("TimesRoman",
                       Font.BOLD|Font.ITALIC,
                       128));
      baG.drawString("Bonjour!",32,128);
     }
   }
```

As we said at the beginning of the chapter, this applet is—by definition—a class that extends class Applet.

In other respects, however, it looks quite similar to a stand-alone application like SayBonjour. In particular, it has a paint() method that will automatically be called whenever the environment detects an event (such as resizing or uncovering the applet) that may require redrawing its graphical content.

Figure 16.2 shows the design that this applet produces, though it can't show the "zoom" effect of the running program.

When stored as a compressed graphics file, this design consumes 24,093 bytes. Compare that to the more efficient representation of this same graphic by the small file of Java code that can draw it whenever desired. The

FIGURE 16.2

A still picture can't show the "zoom" effect, but this is class BonAppetit in a Java-enabled browser.

HTML page that downloads this applet is 318 bytes in size; the `.class` file of the applet is another 909 bytes, for a total of 1,227 bytes.

Even if we ignore the need for an HTML file to frame the static image, the image is almost 20 times as large as the Java version's HTML file and `.class` file combined. With fast Pentium-class PCs connected to the Internet via slow dial-up connections, and with the Internet itself being challenged to keep up with increasing activity, we can make a compelling case for Java just from its ability to shrink the number of bits that need to be moved around.

There are many situations in which it's far more economical to send instructions than to send their results: Even pictorial graphics can be radically compressed using techniques such as fractal transforms that are extravagant in their use of cheap processor cycles to reduce their need for costly bandwidth.

Having a hardware-independent Java virtual machine at the end of every Internet connection is therefore a most attractive prospect.

The Rest of the Applet API

Our applet `BonAppetit` didn't use all of the capabilities that `Applet` provides for making our applets work smoothly.

Rather than calling the `main()` method that kicks off a Java application, an applet will normally come to life with its method named `init()`. If a method by this name is present, the browser (or an equivalent applet viewer program) will invoke this method before it makes any other demands.

This makes the `init()` method a good place to allocate resources: for example, creating any threads that the applet will use.

An applet should provide specific code for releasing such resources, and should package this code in a method named `destroy()`. Think of `init()` and `destroy()` as the walls of a building: The user enters the structure to use the applet, and won't leave until beginning some other quite separate task.

If method `init()` is defined, the program that hosts the applet will wait for that method to return before it enters the applet's "room" in that imaginary building: that is, before it calls the method `start()`.

Method `start()` is the place where an applet should put any code that needs to run whenever the applet comes into view. A common example might be the code that begins cycling through a series of images to produce an animation effect.

The exit from the room, so to speak, is the method `stop()`. This is not so drastic as `destroy()`: It will be called whenever an applet's region of its Web page goes out of view, when the applet might want to stop consuming processor cycles doing things that the user won't see.

Method `stop()` is also called before any call to `destroy()`, so there is no need for `destroy()` to perform redundant operations or validations. When `destroy()` is invoked by an applet's execution environment, it can assume that it is working with an applet that is already stopped.

Wake Up and Look at the Web Page

Within the body of the applet, other methods can make inquiries about the Web page in which the applet is running. For example, `getParameter(String parameterName)` can determine if the HTML file that launched the applet contained a tag of the form:

```
<param name=parameterName value="someString">
```

If so, this call returns "`someString`" as an instance of class `String`. For example, we could launch `BonAppetit` from an HTML page that contained the tag,

```
<param name=Greeting value="guten Tag!">
```

With methods like class `Color`'s `darker()` (which we mentioned in Chapter 15) and class `Applet`'s `getParameter()`, an applet can tailor itself to the environment where it's running.

For example, we can modify `BonAppetit` to make its background a randomly chosen color, then use `Color`'s method `darker()` to choose a foreground color that will still be visible.

The greeting that we give can be extracted from the HTML file as a named parameter. The same code, launched by different HTML files, can thus yield site-specific behavior. Here is the modified code:

```java
import java.applet.Applet;
import java.awt.*;
public class BonAppetit extends Applet
  { public void paint(Graphics baG)
    { String greet  = getParameter("Greeting");";
      int    fStyle = Font.BOLD|Font.ITALIC;
      Color backG   = new Color(
            new Double(Math.random()).floatValue(),
            new Double(Math.random()).floatValue(),
```

```
                    new Double(Math.random()).floatValue());
        this.setBackground(backG);
        Color foreG  = backG.darker().darker();
        for (int i=2;i<129;i++)
         { baG.setColor(foreG);
           baG.setFont(new Font(fName,fStyle,i*2/3));
           baG.drawString(greet,160-i,96+i/4);
           baG.setColor(new Color(255-i*2,64-i/2,32-i/4));
           baG.drawString(greet,160-i,96+i/4);
          }
         baG.setColor(foreG);
         baG.drawString(greet,32,128);
      }
   }
```

Typical results, showing two different sessions launched by different HTML files holding different parameter strings, appear in Figure 16.3.

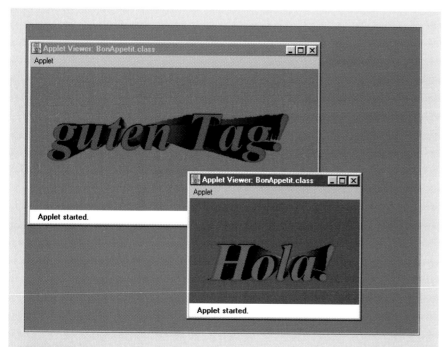

FIGURE 16.3

With different parameter values in different HTML files, the same `.class` file can deliver different behaviors in different browser sessions or in different parts of a single Web page.

We're Finally at the Beginning

At this point, we're right on the boundary line between what is Java, and what is the world in which Java was designed to function.

Further discussion of applets, for example, would be more about the formats used for audio and image content on Web pages than it would be about the ways that Java retrieves such resources. If you want to work with multimedia, these are things you need to know, but these topics have little bearing on using Java to control an orbiting telescope or to provide a natural-language interface to a database management system.

In the novel *Stand on Zanzibar*, writer John Brunner used a chapter title to make a sardonic comment on technology: "It's Supposed to be Automatic, But Actually You Have to Push This Button." He was saying that technology creates new choices, rather than making our current choices easier.

As a programmer, you live on the next higher level: You get to decide what the button will do when someone pushes it. There are very few modern artifacts that don't have at least some software between every user action and its effects. For all of the limits that may seem to come from the formal notation and strict semantic rules of a programming language, this is a discipline that creates a thousand freedoms for every such restriction.

That's your journey. You've learned enough Java to discuss the language in terms of its own facilities, and to discuss the world of the Internet in terms of how Java can manipulate that pool of knowledge. But this isn't the end: this is the beginning. It's like learning how to read a map and orient yourself with a compass: a precursor to doing what you really wanted to do in the first place.

Where you go from here is up to you. Enjoy the trip.

Summary

In this chapter, we showed

- ▶ That the same Java code can follow a different branch of the class hierarchy tree to become a browser-based applet, rather than a stand-alone application.

- ▶ That compiled Java bytecodes can come from tools other than a Java compiler.

- ▶ That bytecodes can deliver high-value services, where source code disclosure (as with a scripting language) is not commercially desirable.

- ▶ That the `Applet` class gives a Java program several different levels of control for responding to a user's navigation through a Web page, as well as facilities for communication between several different applets on a single page.

▶ That the launching HTML page can furnish an applet with parameter values that tailor a single `.class` file's behavior to many different situations.

Appendix A
The Java Language

RESERVED KEYWORDS

abstract	double	int	super
boolean	else*	interface	switch*
break*	extends	long	synchronized*
byte	final	native	this
case*	finally	new*	throw**
catch**	float	package	throws
char	for*	private	*transient****
class	goto***	protected	try**
const***	if*	public	void
continue*	implements	return*	*volatile****
default*	import	short	while*
do*	instanceof	static	

The above are class, data declaration, or identification keywords, unless specified otherwise (see below).

* normal flow control or object construction

** exception handling

*** reserved but ignored by Java 1.0.x compilers (*italics* indicate words with specified meanings to be supported in future versions of Java: see Glossary)

RESERVED WORDS (LITERALS)

true

false

null

MARKINGS AND SPECIAL CHARACTERS— COMMENT DELIMITERS

Delimiter	Meaning
/**	Begin documentation comment
/*	Begin indefinite comment
*/	End indefinite comment
//	Comment to end of line

CHARACTER ESCAPE SEQUENCES (FOR USE IN CHAR '' AND STRING "" LITERALS)

Meaning	Literal Representation	ASCII Code (Decimal)	ASCII Code (Hexadecimal)	Unicode
backspace	\b	8	08	\u0008
tab	\t	9	09	\u0009
new line	\n	10	0A	\u000A
form feed	\f	12	0C	\u000C
line return	\r	13	0D	\u000D
double quote	\"	34	22	\u0022
single quote	\'	39	27	\u0027
backslash	\\	92	5C	\u005C

OCTAL AND UNICODE CHARACTER CONSTANT FORMATS

Numeric Format and Range	Meaning
\0 through \377	Octal value of character (<= \u00FF)
\u0000 through \uFFFF	Unicode hexadecimal value of character

OPERATORS AND PRECEDENCE GROUPS—FROM HIGHEST TO LOWEST PRECEDENCE (MODIFIABLE BY PARENTHESES)

Group	Operator(s)	Meanings
Postfix operators	[ ]	Array access
	.	Member access, method invocation
	( )	Method application
	++	Increment after current value return
	−	Decrement after current value return
Prefix operators	++	Increment before current value return
	−	Decrement before current value return
	+	Unary plus (redundant)
	-	Unary minus (multiplies by −1)
	~	Bitwise complement
	!	Boolean complement
Prefix constructives	new	Invoke constructor
	(\<type\>)	Cast to \<type\>
Multiplicatives	* / %	
Additives	+ -	
Bit manipulatives	\>\>\> \>\> \<\<	
Comparatives	\< \<= \>= \>	Relative order
	instanceof	Class membership
Identities	== !=	
bitwise/boolean AND	&	
bitwise/boolean XOR	^	
bitwise/boolean OR	|	
boolean conditional AND	&&	
boolean conditional OR	||	
ternary conditional	?:	
assignments	= *= /= %= += -= \<\<= \>\>= \>\>\>= &= ^= |=	(i) Active assignments have semantics $i = i$ \<modifier\> j: e.g., i += j denotes $i = i + j$. (ii) Multiple assignments are processed from right to left: e.g., a=b=c denotes a=(b=c). All other operators of equal precedence are processed from left to right.

Global Constants (Public Static Values)

Use of these values improves clarity of code and enhances compatibility with future versions of Java or with installations on new classes of hardware. Checking of values against constraints such as `Integer.MAX_VALUE` reduces the likelihood of uncaught exceptions. Defining your own `public static` constants is an effective practice when designing your own classes.

PARTIAL LISTING IN FORMAT CLASS.NAME

Boolean.FALSE	Event.KEY_ACTION	Event.WINDOW_MOVED
Boolean.TRUE	Event.KEY_ACTION_RELEASE	FileDialog.LOAD
Character.MAX_RADIX	Event.KEY_PRESS	FileDialog.SAVE
Character.MAX_VALUE	Event.KEY_RELEASE	Float.MAX_VALUE
Character.MIN_RADIX	Event.LEFT	Float.MIN_VALUE
Character.MIN_VALUE	Event.LIST_DESELECT	Float.NaN
Color.black	Event.LIST_SELECT	Float.NEGATIVE_INFINITY
Color.blue	Event.LOAD_FILE	Float.POSITIVE_INFINITY
Color.cyan	Event.LOST_FOCUS	FlowLayout.CENTER
Color.darkGray	Event.MOUSE_DOWN	FlowLayout.LEFT
Color.gray	Event.MOUSE_DRAG	FlowLayout.RIGHT
Color.green	Event.MOUSE_ENTER	Font.BOLD
Color.lightGray	Event.MOUSE_EXIT	Font.ITALIC
Color.magenta	Event.MOUSE_MOVE	Font.PLAIN
Color.orange	Event.MOUSE_UP	Integer.MAX_VALUE
Color.pink	Event.PGDN	Integer.MIN_VALUE
Color.red	Event.PGUP	Label.CENTER
Color.white	Event.RIGHT	Label.LEFT
Color.yellow	Event.SAVE_FILE	Label.RIGHT
Double.MAX_VALUE	Event.SCROLL_ABSOLUTE	Long.MAX_VALUE
Double.MIN_VALUE	Event.SCROLL_LINE_DOWN	Long.MIN_VALUE
Double.NaN	Event.SCROLL_LINE_UP	Math.E
Double.NEGATIVE_INFINITY	Event.SCROLL_PAGE_DOWN	Math.PI
Double.POSITIVE_INFINITY	Event.SCROLL_PAGE_UP	Scrollbar.HORIZONTAL
Event.ACTION_EVENT	Event.UP	Scrollbar.VERTICAL
Event.DOWN	Event.WINDOW_DEICONIFY	Thread.MAX_PRIORITY
Event.END	Event.WINDOW_DESTROY	Thread.MIN_PRIORITY
Event.GOT_FOCUS	Event.WINDOW_EXPOSE	Thread.NORM_PRIORITY
Event.HOME	Event.WINDOW_ICONIFY	

The ASCII Character Set

In this 7-bit code, with possible values 0 through 127, the first 32 values (0 through 31 decimal, 00 though 1F hex) are used by control characters such as backspace (decimal 8), tab (decimal 9), and form feed (decimal 12).

These control codes, and others, have special literal representations that are tabulated elsewhere in this appendix. Those literal representations should be used for both clarity and correctness. For example, '\n' should be used for a line feed rather than the equivalent Unicode escape sequence, \u000a, since the latter will be translated into an actual line feed at an early stage in the processing of the source code file.

This means that the statement

```
System.out.println('\u000a');
```

will look to the compiler like

```
System.out.println('
');
```

and will produce several error messages. The statement

```
System.out.println('\n');
```

will behave as one would expect.

Other low-group codes, such as 22 ("synchronous idle"), are relics of an earlier generation of communications equipment. The assignment of code 127 to mean "deleted" reflects the use of punched cards and paper tape: In binary, this code consists of seven 1s, represented by punching out all seven possible holes, obscuring whatever was encoded before on that card or in that position on the tape.

The numeric digits, the uppercase letters, and the lowercase letters have the same numeric code values in the 7-bit ASCII, the 8-bit ISO-Latin-1, and the 16-bit Unicode schemes.

ASCII CHARACTER SET

Decimal	Hexadecimal	Character	Decimal	Hexadecimal	Character
32	20	<space>	37	25	%
33	21	!	38	26	&
34	22	"	39	27	'
35	23	#	40	28	(
36	24	$	41	29	)

ASCII CHARACTER SET (CONTINUED)

Decimal	Hexadecimal	Character	Decimal	Hexadecimal	Character
42	2A	*	77	4D	M
43	2B	+	78	4E	N
44	2C	,	79	4F	O
45	2D	-	80	50	P
46	2E	.	81	51	Q
47	2F	/	82	52	R
48	30	0	83	53	S
49	31	1	84	54	T
50	32	2	85	55	U
51	33	3	86	56	V
52	34	4	87	57	W
53	35	5	88	58	X
54	36	6	89	59	Y
55	37	7	90	5A	Z
56	38	8	91	5B	[
57	39	9	92	5C	\
58	3A	:	93	5D	]
59	3B	;	94	5E	^
60	3C	<	95	5F	_
61	3D	=	96	60	`
62	3E	>	97	61	a
63	3F	?	98	62	b
64	40	@	99	63	c
65	41	A	100	64	d
66	42	B	101	65	e
67	43	C	102	66	f
68	44	D	103	67	g
69	45	E	104	68	h
70	46	F	105	69	i
71	47	G	106	6A	j
72	48	H	107	6B	k
73	49	I	108	6C	l
74	4A	J	109	6D	m
75	4B	K	110	6E	n
76	4C	L	111	6F	o

ASCII CHARACTER SET (CONTINUED)

Decimal	Hexadecimal	Character	Decimal	Hexadecimal	Character
112	70	p	120	78	x
113	71	q	121	79	y
114	72	r	122	7A	z
115	73	s	123	7B	{
116	74	t	124	7C	|
117	75	u	125	7D	}
118	76	v	126	7E	~
119	77	w	127	7F	<deleted>

Appendix B
What's Coming in Java 1.1

By the time this book is in a reader's hands, the Java language will already be a richer medium than it was when the book was being written. Web time is like that, and Java's evolution keeps pace with the breakneck advancement of the Web.

Version 1.1 of the Java language was beginning to coalesce as this book neared completion. Some references to these changes are even included in the main body of the book—for example, the warning in Chapter 10 that `private protected` was not invited to re-enlist. It won't be missed.

The latest information available when this book was being completed is summarized here. For updates, check the Web at **http://java.sun.com/products/ JDK/1.1/designspecs/index.html.**

New Gifts in New Wrappers

One group of refinements expected in Java 1.1 are additional simple-type conversion methods, as noted in Chapter 11. The wrapper classes for the simple numeric types will be filled out to a full set, with new classes `Byte` and `Short`.

The abstract class Number will likewise add two methods, `byteValue()` and `shortValue()`, each with a concrete default implementation as `intValue()`: These methods may be implemented more appropriately as needed by a subclass.

Another wrapper class, `Void`, will be added to the API as well.

Teaching Java to Trust

In Chapter 14, we noted that the current tight restrictions on applets are imposed so that users need not fear potentially malicious applet code from untrusted Internet hosts. When trust can be established—for example, through cryptographic authentication—these restrictions can safely be relaxed. To this end, Java 1.1 will implement a subset of a planned Security API, initially including

▶ Digital signatures (cryptographically authenticating source and content of network transmissions)

▶ Class and data signing (authenticating source and content of program elements)

▶ Key management (distributing encryption keys that can be known to be valid)

▶ Access control lists (providing protection of shared resources)

Putting Its Best (Inter)face Forward

The graphics package `java.awt` is "not well liked," as Willy Loman might have said if Arthur Miller had written *Death of a Hacker*. Java 1.1 will address some of the Abstract Window Toolkit's worst deficiencies, beginning the process of adding APIs for

▶ Printing

▶ Clipboard (cut and paste) operations

▶ More abstract handling of user events

▶ Improved presentation of multinational fonts

Additionally, the native layer of AWT will be rewritten for the Win32 platforms (Windows 95 and Windows NT) to make it faster and more consistent with other platforms. This is crucial to maintaining the competitive position of Java and its forthcoming "component" technology, Java Beans, against the native speed and the conformance with Windows conventions of Microsoft's proposed ActiveX technology.

Casting a Finer Net

Abstraction of network operations will become more flexible in the 1.1 version of `java.net`, which will remove the `final` status of classes `Socket` and `ServerSocket`.

Programmers will then be able to subclass these classes. Network anomaly reporting will become more finely grained with new subclasses of `SocketException`. A provisional class, `MulticastSocket`, will move up from the farm team to join package `java.net`.

Building a Stronger (Data)base

The Java Database Connectivity (JDBC) technology will become an API interface in Java 1.1. This will give Java programs a standard way of working with database servers using Structured Query Language (SQL).

Java 1.1 implementations on platforms other than the 68000-family Macintosh will also include a JDBC Bridge module that integrates JDBC into the C-language Open Database Connectivity (ODBC) API.

It's Objects All the Way Down

At the 1988 conference on Object-Oriented Programming Systems, Languages, and Applications, software entrepreneur Mitch Kapor told the story of a Zen novice questioning his mentor: "Tell me, master, if the world sits on the back of the Great Turtle, on what does the Great Turtle sit?"

"My son," replied the master, "the Great Turtle rests on the back of the turtle that is greater still." The novice asked the obvious question, and got the predictable answer; after a few more cycles, the master gently replied, "You're wasting your time, my son: It's turtles all the way down."

Kapor observed that the object technologies of 1988 were a long way from being "objects all the way down," and the early versions of Java have shared that defect. When a Java 1.0.x program reads input from a stream, it doesn't read in objects: It reads in simple types, or even raw bytes, depending on the nature of the `InputStream` that's handling the interaction.

Java 1.1 will take significant steps toward becoming "objects all the way down." It will add object serialization: a uniform API for representing an object as a stream of bytes that can be passed across a communication link and reconstructed into an object at the other end.

When objects can be serialized, they can also be stored to a device such as a hard disk: This will take the first steps toward a facility for "persistent objects." The keyword `transient`, though ignored in Java 1.0.x, labels a field of a class as not requiring storage when an instance of that class is captured in this manner. Details remain to be defined by a future version of the Java Language Specification.

Also coming in Java 1.1 will be the Reflection API, giving objects new tools for asking questions about each others' fields, methods, and constructors. Right now, the operator `instanceof` lets a method ask, "Are you one of these?" By contrast, the Reflection API will allow questions more in the nature of, "Can you do this?"

Serving Up Instant Java

Many advancements in Java 1.1 will be aimed at streamlining Java's use on the Internet and improving the performance of Java applications:

▶ Java Archive (JAR) files will provide a platform-neutral format for aggregating multipart applications into a single file, optionally using compression algorithms, to speed network download.

▶ Remote Method Invocation (RMI) will let Java applications in different virtual machines invoke each other's methods, in the way that applets on a single Web page can do in Java 1.0.x.

▶ Native Method Interface (NMI) will provide consistent packaging for native method libraries on any given platform.

▶ Just-In-Time Compiler Interface standards will promote consistent approaches to various forms of compilation at different points in the process of deployment and execution.

Better Won't Have to Mean Different

Java's developers have committed to maintaining support for the current Java API, even as these new features are incorporated into the language.

You saw how this can be done in Chapter 9, by proper reimplementation of methods to work with new class internals without changing external behaviors. In general, it seems likely that new behaviors will be added through new methods, not by revising the contracts made by the methods of the 1.0.x API. The Java Language Specification states that future versions of the Java language will be distinguished, if necessary, by source code file name extensions so that any future Java compiler can recognize and process any Java source code file of any vintage.

Therefore, while this book will inevitably become less complete as time goes by and Java gains new capabilities, the book should not become any less accurate: The example programs in this book should still work with compilers and other tools for Java 1.1, Java 2.0, and any future versions.

Appendix C
Additional Resources for Learning and Using Java

Because its pace is the pace of the Web, Java almost impels its users to become proficient "surfers."

The authoritative source of current information about Java technology is the owner of the Java trademark and the definer of Java conformance, Sun Microsystems, Inc. Three good Web pages to browse for the latest official news are

▶ http://java.sun.com/

▶ http://java.sun.com/aboutJava/index.html

▶ http://www.sun.com/sun-on-net/java/java.html

But the Java phenomenon is too big for Sun to illuminate all of its corners, and others have emerged as valuable (and independent!) guides to what's going on with Java and related technologies. One alternative view comes from an independent online magazine, *JavaWorld*, located at **http://www.javaworld.com**.

I've found *JavaWorld* a source of both useful and merely interesting information on the technology, opportunities, and people who all make up different parts of the growing Java community.

You Actually Have to Do It

The unique thing about programming, compared to other disciplines, is that it's defined by what you can provably do. In the Media Lab at the Massachusetts Institute of Technology, it's often said that other disciplines can live by the rule of "Publish or perish," while the Media Lab's imperative is, "Demo or die."

For this reason, Web sites with pointers to real Java code are priceless, and one of the best is the Gamelan site. The last time we checked, there were 3,646 items indexed at **http://www.gamelan.com/index.shtml**. These were broken down as follows:

▶ ActiveX Resources (36 entries)

▶ Arts and Entertainment (677 entries)

▶ Business and Finance (92 entries)

▶ Educational (413 entries)

▶ How-to and Help (15 entries)

▶ JavaScript (351 entries)

▶ Miscellaneous (81 entries)

▶ Multimedia (453 entries)

▶ Network and Communications (239 entries)

▶ News (96 entries)

▶ Programming in Java (683 entries)

▶ Special Effects (344 entries)

▶ Utilities (324 entries)

▶ Web Sites (901 entries)

You'd Better Know Beans about Components

Even as "Java applet" becomes an everyday phrase, Java technology is moving toward the next phase that's known as *componentware:* The ability, for example, to drop an object into a word processing document that can update a table or a chart in that document, based on the latest available data, whenever that document is viewed in a connected environment.

The Java-based approach to this goal is currently known as Java Beans. Components based on this standard will be written in Java, making them inherently portable to all Java platforms. The Java Beans technology is planned to embrace the current base of Java applets, while also creating new opportunities for using Java to extend applications based on other technologies. Current information on this still-emerging technology will probably be maintained at **http://splash.javasoft.com/beans/**, with an overview located at **http://splash.javasoft.com/beans/WhitePaper.html**.

Further Reading

Among technical professionals, programmers are infamous for being poorly read in their field. One observer compared the sales of programming books to the population of full-time programmers, and concluded that the average programmer owns only a fraction of a book. If you're not sharing this book with a coworker, you're already on the leading edge of professional self-education.

If you want to go farther with Java, I have four recommendations out of the literally dozens of Java titles on the market.

Books about Java

A professional's Java library should include, to begin with, three books co-authored by Java's creator James Gosling. The first, written with Ken Arnold, is *The Java Programming Language* (Addison-Wesley, 1996, ISBN 0-201-63455-4). The second and third are the two-volume set, written with Frank Yellin and others, entitled *The Java Application Programming Interface* (Addison-Wesley, 1996, ISBN 0-201-63453-8 and ISBN 0-201-63459-7). These are densely written but superbly crafted guides, the essential reference works whose structure most influenced my own presentation of the Java language.

For the developer with advanced network ambitions, I recommend *Java Programming for the Internet*, by Michael D. Thomas and others (Ventana, 1996, ISBN 1-56604-355-7). This 780-page book offers deep coverage of server-side issues, such as using Java in combination with non-HTTP servers or CGI applications. It also gets into the details of native-method extension using C, and provides a thorough discussion of multithread programming.

The graphically oriented developer will quickly come up against the limits of `java.awt`. To leapfrog those limits, take a look at *Graphic Java: Mastering the AWT*, by David Geary and Alan McClellan (SunSoft Press/Prentice Hall PTR, 1997, ISBN 0-13-565847-0). This package is described by its authors as "a product with an accompanying book": That product is the Graphic Java Toolkit, a dramatically more powerful class library than `java.awt` that is provided on a CD-ROM, with extensive discussion and examples making up much of this 600-page book.

Finally, more in the nature of leisure reading or a management briefing is Patrick Naughton's *The Java Handbook* (Osborne McGraw-Hill, 1996, ISBN 0-07-882199-1). Naughton's enthusiasm did much to ignite my own interest in Java, and his 18-page epilogue ("The Long Strange Trip to Java") is a fascinating study in the human side of technology development.

My book skirts the subject of advanced applications of threads. A thorough treatment of this topic, not specific to Java, can be found in *Programming with Threads*, by Steve Kleiman and others (SunSoft Press, 1996, ISBN 0-13-172389-8).

Books about Programming

Finally, I'd like to note that this book is meant at least as much to teach programming (using Java), as it is to teach Java (to programmers). Where this book is used in the former role, either in a class or for self-study, I also recommend the following books to broaden and refine the new programmer's perspective.

Tom Forester and Perry Morrison are already into the second edition of *Computer Ethics—Cautionary Tales and Ethical Dilemmas in Computing* (MIT Press, 1994, ISBN 0-262-56073-9). They address this subject under seven headings:

- ▶ Computer-aided fraud
- ▶ Intellectual property theft
- ▶ Malicious hacking
- ▶ Fragility of vital systems
- ▶ Unauthorized data access
- ▶ Human responsibility for artificial intelligences
- ▶ Workplace issues

An acid-tongued, mildly unfair, but eye-opening critique of program design and usability issues will be found in *The Unix-Haters Handbook*, by Simson Garfinkel and others (IDG Books Worldwide, 1994, ISBN 1-56884-203-1).

But before the new programmer loses faith, we recommend a reviving session with Hans Moravec's *Mind Children: The Future of Robot and Human Intelligence* (Harvard University Press, 1988, ISBN 0-674-57616-0). This is not ethereal speculation, but rigorous analysis and well-supported forecasting of what we'll be using in the next few decades.

It's Not Rocket Science

Java development environments, like the ones on the CD-ROM at the back of this book, are impressive and capable tools. But most of the code in this book was written with only a text editor, and tested with simple command-line compilers and interpreters, under Microsoft's Windows 95.

For quick experimentation with the fundamental elements of the language, this author wrote two short text files and a batch file. The first text file, `TestThis.Top`, looked like this:

```
import java.io.*;
import java.net.*;
import java.util.*;

// edit this file to import other packages as needed

class TestThis
  { public static void main(String args[]) throws Exception
    {
```

The second file, `TestThis.End`, looked like this:

```
    }
  }
```

And the batch file, `TestThis.Bat`, looked like this:

```
@echo OFF
copy TestThis.Top + TestThis.Mid + TestThis.End TestThis.java > NUL
jvc TestThis.java
if errorlevel 1 goto end
jview TestThis
:end
```

From the command prompt, this batch file would take a series of Java statements, wrap them in the opening and closing lines required to turn them into class `TestThis` with method `main()`, and attempt to compile the resulting source file `TestThis.java`. If successful, the batch file would then execute the resulting `TestThis.class` file under a Java virtual machine.

As it appears above, the batch file executed Microsoft's command line `jvc` compiler and `jview` virtual machine, but at various times I substituted other compiler and interpreter invocations to test different diagnostic capabilities or measure competing tools' performance.

That little file `TestThis.End` could hold more, of course, than just those closing braces. Between the first brace, which closes the body of `main()`, and the second brace, which closes the body of `TestThis`, you could insert any number of utility methods: for example, a method for printing values with an invocation less verbose than `System.out.println()`.

Diagnosis of errors is primitive in this arrangement, as discussed in Chapter 2, since there is no convenient linking of error messages directly back to the offending line(s) of code. But the multilevel coloring of matched delimiter pairs in Mansfield Software Group's KEDIT for Windows (a trial version of KEDIT is included on the CD-ROM) is a powerful preventive measure for a large fraction of the errors that occur in writing code.

Many errors in this book's first-draft code, written in text-editing mode, jumped out when the code was viewed with Java parsing enabled. Catching errors before compilation is a habit worth building.

When you get to the point of building graphical interfaces and testing applets, a more advanced environment will be useful. But a minimal tool set can grow with you, without demanding that you climb over the initial hump of defining projects, creating workspaces, and all the other baggage that goes with a big environment on even a tiny little project. It will give you more than adequate performance on any machine that can run an environment like Windows 95, and will continue to be a useful testing environment even when more elaborate tools become a part of your routine.

Appendix D
Using the CD-ROM

It is possible that you're reading this appendix before any other part of this book. The kind of person who buys a book called *How to Program Java* is the kind of person who wants to get started right away. The included CD-ROM will help.

To begin with, the book itself is on the CD, along with Microsoft's Internet Explorer to view the HTML files (if you don't already have an appropriate browser). Screen shots, source code listings (with color highlights), and the full text are here for your reference.

These chapter-by-chapter files can be viewed on both Windows and Macintosh machines, and on other systems that support the same media standards and content formats.

You'll also find on the CD a wide-ranging set of tools for Windows-based Java development. Microsoft's 32-bit application environments, Windows 95 and Windows NT, have attracted many Java toolmakers with their combination of mass-market presence and their adequate implementation of "foundation" technologies, such as threads.

I was pleasantly surprised by the convenience, capability, and performance of both simple command-line tools and full-function integrated environments on Windows 95 during the development of example programs for this book.

Tools for other platforms were still emerging as this CD was being produced. In the week that this CD went to press, *PC Week*'s first page bore the headline, "The Java Juggernaut": The gist is that whether your target platform is a desktop or a mainframe, or some other kind of appliance entirely, someone is developing Java tools to serve you.

In particular, some Macintosh products are shown in Chapter 2. The Web, of course, will be a ready source for the latest information, free beta copies, and trial versions of shipping products from Symantec, SunSoft, Metrowerks, Microsoft, Borland, Powersoft, and many other vendors. See Appendix C for some pointers to promising Web sites.

Note: You may notice, from time to time, a discrepancy between the text of the actual book and the text of the book on the CD. In these cases, you should always consider the text of the actual book the final authority.

System Requirements

This CD and the software on it have been designed to run on Windows 95 and NT systems using a Web browser and Internet connection. Because this CD has been produced in HTML, Windows 3.x and Macintosh users may view the contents using a browser; however, the software on this CD is either Windows 95 or NT specific.

System requirements for the various types of software vary widely depending on what you download from the CD. For more information, read through Chapter 2 and always review all software "readme" files before installing software directly to your machine.

Recommended System

Pentium PC

Windows 95 or NT operating system

4X CD-ROM drive

16MB RAM

KEDIT for Windows (Trial Version)

Though this looks like the most basic tool on the CD, KEDIT for Windows had a lot to do with the quality of the sample code in this book. It has, by far, the most sophisticated syntax highlighting aids that the author has seen in any programmer's editor, making tricky errors (such as unbalanced delimiters) jump off the screen with distinctive colors.

The first draft of this book was written entirely in the OS/2 text-mode version of KEDIT, of which the Windows version is a compatible superset. My installation of KEDIT includes more than 1,600 words of customization code in the editor's embedded programming language, a REXX-like scripting facility called KEXX. KEDIT's editing engine and the KEXX extension language combine to produce a reliable and remarkably capable tool, and I hope you enjoy making its acquaintance.

Café Lite

Symantec kept the best features of their innovative C++ development system, but produced a Java development environment that doesn't look back. Developers accustomed to working with other Windows-based products will learn Café Lite with ease and will quickly absorb the Java approach to programming.

The full-strength Café product has set a fast pace for other Java toolmakers to match, being rapidly upgraded with substantial performance enhancements over the earliest versions. Café Lite will give you a good exposure to the convenience of an integrated development environment, with Café or the client/server Visual Café both worth consideration as your needs expand.

SunSoft Java WorkShop

As noted in Chapter 2, this is the Java development environment most obviously influenced by the look and feel of the World Wide Web. It's an HTML browser that's populated with Java development tools, themselves written in Java.

Java WorkShop provides unusually flexible access to different development options at any point in the development cycle, and lends itself to team environments with its facilities for sharing work across the Net. Its visual tools for constructing a user interface are superb. If you have the capacious memory (at least 16MB) that's needed for good performance, I think you'll like using this unique Java development system.

Microsoft Internet Explorer

The functions of Internet Explorer are on their way into your desktop environment, whether that be Windows, OS/2, or some other operating system. By the time you read this book, the notion of a separate application for viewing local HTML files and remote Net-based resources may already seem rather quaint.

But better safe than sorry: Internet Explorer will give you access to the most sophisticated content options of almost every Web site, and will be a good testing environment for your Java-based Web pages as well as a viewing utility for this CD's HTML files.

CD-ROM Start Instructions

1 Place the CD-ROM in your CD-ROM drive.

2 Launch your Web browser

3 From your Web browser, select Open File from the File menu. Select your CD-ROM drive (usually drive D), then select the file *welcome.htm*.

Glossary

The nature of this book is tutorial, not definitional. The body of the book introduces features of the Java language in the context of the needs that arise when writing programs, rather than presenting them in the formal style of a language specification.

For example, it is in the nature of a specification to lay down rules like, "It is not permitted for an action to follow itself." That's an actual quotation from *The Java Language Specification* (Gosling, Joy, and Steele, 1996), and it's a necessary part of the formal definition of the language. It is not, however, the kind of thing that I've included in the body of the book.

But I want to provide a court of first resort for "language lawyer" questions, without referring all such queries to the 821-page specification. This glossary is meant to cover that middle ground. It elaborates on several aspects of the language, such as the notion of `volatile` values, that did not fit into the narrative thread of the text but will interest readers with more advanced ambitions.

The style of these glossary entries is more formal that that of the main text, which tends to place more emphasis on examples. This glossary also contains many entries that relate to the problem domains in which Java will be used. That charter reaches well beyond the scope of the Java language and API packages. I hope that I have accurately anticipated the new Java programmer's most likely questions about the Internet, some fundamentals of computer science, and related subjects. The connections seemed obvious to me, but it required reference to more than half a dozen different books (as well as the writing of many test programs) to pin down these definitions: I hope, therefore, that the result is valuable to the reader.

Note: Words in italic are explained elsewhere in this glossary.

A

Abstract

An abstract *class* is one that defines at least one abstract *method*. An abstract method is one that is declared, but not implemented. The abstract method *declaration* gives the return type, the method name, the types of the method's *arguments*, and a `throws` clause (if needed), but there is no method body.

329

A program cannot construct an *instance* of an abstract class, but it can *extend* an abstract class with a *subclass* that implements some or all of the abstract methods that the subclass receives by *inheritance*. If any inherited abstract methods are not implemented by the subclass, the subclass is also abstract.

It is common for an abstract class to implement some of its methods: that is, those that define behaviors that must be supported by any subclass. An abstract class might also define *instance variables* that its subclasses will inherit. Contrast with an *interface*, which can define *only* abstract methods, and whose data members can *only* be `static final` members (available as named constants in the methods that the interface requires an implementing class to provide).

Access

By controlling access to an object's data and to the methods of its class, a programmer strikes a balance between two goals: The first goal is that of making a class provide useful services to other classes; the second goal is preserving the programmer's freedom to refine the way that a class does its job. See *extends, package, private, protected, and public.*

Action event

See *event.*

API

An Application Programming Interface is a formal statement of the services that a computer operating environment offers to the application programs that are written to run in that environment. The Java API consists of the language specification plus the descriptions of the standard packages `java.lang`, `java.io`, `java.util`, `java.net`, `java.awt`, and `java.applet`.

An API may deliberately exclude some known capabilities of the environment, typically because the designers wish to keep their options open for future refinements in the details of how those capabilities are provided and used. To write programs using such undocumented features may provide a short-lived benefit in capability or performance, but this is likely to be offset by future costs of revising the program.

If enough programs use undocumented features, however, beyond the published API, then the designers may find that it is no longer practical to make improvements—even much-needed improvements—that would require revision of applications. Java programmers should use Java's *access* control modifiers to prevent such dependencies from hindering the evolution of the classes that they create.

Applet

An applet is a Java program that runs in the context of an *HTML* browser or some other top-level execution environment. Rather than starting with method `main()`, an applet is launched by calling method `init()` of its primary class; the applet's execution is then controlled by other methods whose invocation is usually tied to the applet's coming in and out of view as the user navigates through different HTML pages.

It is currently common for applets to have tightly limited privileges, in particular for applets to be unable to use the local file system or to connect with any resources other than those at an applet's point of origin. Contrast with *application*. A Java applet is typically transferred from an Internet host computer to the user's computer when the user reads an HTML page that contains a distinguishing tag with embedded information on where to find the file that holds the program's *bytecodes*. This process is described in Chapter 16. See also *java.applet*.

Application

Generally, an application is a program that does something intrinsically useful, as opposed to *system software* (such as an operating system or a Web browser) that only exists to reduce the difficulty of writing and using task-oriented programs.

In the specific domain of Java, an application is a program that can be executed directly by the host machine's operating system with the aid of a Java virtual machine, not requiring an *HTML* browser or comparable support environment. Unless deliberately constrained by invoking the method `System.setSecurityManager()`, with an instance of a subclass of `java.lang.SecurityManager` as the argument, an application has full access to the resources (both local and network-accessible) of its host environment.

A Java application begins by executing method `main()` of a Java class. Contrast with *applet*.

Argument

An argument is a piece of information provided as input to a *method*. A method *declaration* states the types of the arguments that the method expects to receive, and gives the name by which an argument will be known within that method. That formal name has nothing to do with the argument's name in any other context.

The number and types of arguments expected by a method, combined with the name of the method, define the *signature* of that method. A *class* may *overload* more than one method with the same name, as long as each such method has a different signature as determined by the number and types of its arguments.

Array

This is a collection of numbered elements, each element being a value of the type that the array is declared to store.

A Java array can be recognized by the postfix operator `[]` appearing in a declaration, as in `int[]` for the type, "array of `int`," or by the square brackets around an expression that evaluates to a number for access to that element of the array, as in `args[0]` for the first element of an array named `args`. Array index values begin at 0.

The size of an array is fixed when the array is constructed. Attempting to access an element number beyond the end of the array will throw an instance of the *Exception* subclass `ArrayIndexOutOfBoundsException`.

ASCII

The American Standard Code for Information Interchange is a 7-bit *code* (defined for numeric values 0 through 127) for commonly used letters, numerals, punctuation, and control characters (such as form feed and new line).
The printable ASCII characters are tabulated in Appendix B.

The ASCII control characters that are not obsolete have been assigned special literal representations, also tabulated in Appendix B. See also *Unicode*.

Assignment

An assignment operation associates a variable with a value. The Java Language Specification equates a Java variable with a C language "lvalue," and describes a Java variable as "a storage location." This can mean either of two things.

If the variable is of a *simple type*, then it names a piece of data. Only one variable is associated with any such value, and the type of the value is the type of the variable.

If the variable is of a reference type, then it names a reference to an *object*. More than one variable may refer to a single object, and the *class* of the value is the class of the variable or any subclass of the variable's class.

awt

See *java.awt.*

B

Binary

Having two possible values, usually rendered as 0 and 1. This can be proved to be the most economical way to represent information, after trading off the cost of representing a larger number of individual units of data against the cost of discriminating between less obviously different values. See *Wiener, Norbert.*

Bit

A contraction of binary digit, usually written using the symbols 0 or 1, representing the smallest possible unit of data or decision-making capability.

Block

As a noun, a block is a group of zero or more *statements*, delimited in Java by {}, that can appear wherever Java normally expects a single statement. A block can serve as a context for local variables. A block (possibly empty) is associated with any `try`, `catch`, or `finally` statement.

Blocking

As a verb, to block in Java is to suspend execution of a thread while it is sleeping or executing a method that is itself blocked. Blocking commonly takes place when a method is invoked that will not return until external input is provided, or when a thread is waiting for all higher-priority threads to become blocked so that the thread can resume execution, or when the `synchronized` keyword has been used to force other threads to wait for a thread to release its lock on some shared resource.

   If a programmer desires to avoid blocking, *stream* methods like `available()` will tell a program how much *data* is currently ready for retrieval: The program can then adjust its request to ensure immediate continuation of processing.

boolean

Named after George Boole, this *simple type* can only assume either of the values `true` or `false` (as described in Chapter 4). Unlike most other languages, Java will not allow numeric values (such as 1 or 0) to be used where a boolean is expected: A boolean is not a *bit*, despite their conceptual similarity.

   With a capital B, Boolean refers to the *class* of that name (described in Chapter 11). This book sometimes uses the capitalized word as an adjective when discussing logical operations in general.

   The difference between `Boolean` and `boolean` will not be ignored by the compiler, which will not use context as a clue to figure out which was meant—though it's possible to *overload* identically named *methods* so that the same method name can be used with either `Boolean` or `boolean` *arguments*.

Branch

The ability to branch is one of the foundations of all programming. This term refers to the ability to choose between two or more paths through a program's sequence of instructions, based on conditions such as the values of data. Java's branching statements are the `if` and the `switch`, described in Chapter 7.

Break

To break is to leave a *block* of code before reaching the end in the normal fashion. Proper use of `break` is essential in `switch` statements and is often useful in a *loop* as well.

This term is also used, idiomatically, to describe aborting a program, typically by pressing a special key or combination of keys such as Ctrl+Break, Ctrl+C, or Command+period.

Byte

A group of eight bits, able to represent 256 different values.

When Java reads and writes bytes during input/output operations, it treats them as having the unsigned numeric values 0 through 255. This range of values is too large to be represented by Java's `byte` simple type, which can only represent the signed values -128 through 127. Many Java methods that work with an external byte use a 32-bit `int` to hold its numeric value.

Bytecodes

This is the term for the output of a standard Java *compiler*, usually packaged in a file with a name like `ThisJavaClass.class`. The same `.class` file can be downloaded and executed in a Java environment, such as a Web browser, on any Java-capable computer.

Normally, these bytecodes are verified, interpreted, and executed by a program called a *virtual machine*. In principle, a computer could be built that used Java bytecodes as its *native* instruction set without a virtual machine's intervention. Such Java chips are planned to be produced at various price/performance points for applications ranging from appliances (such as the canonical "smart doorknob") to workstations.

Bytecodes are also used by other languages, such as Smalltalk, that achieve portability to different types of computer by compiling to a virtual machine and providing a native implementation of that virtual machine on each target platform.

C

Casting

Also called coercion, casting allows the Java interpreter to treat a piece of data as being of a different type—and thereby makes it eligible for operations not normally allowed.

If a 64-bit `long` numeric value is known, for example, to have a value small enough to be representable by a 32-bit `int`, a program may safely cast the `long` to an `int`, and invoke methods that require an `int` upon the result.

Casting is not needed to assign an `int` to a `long`, since this is inherently a safe operation. See *promotion*.

Casting also allows movement down the class hierarchy. For example, if a method will accept an instance of `InputStream` as an argument, then it will also accept any instance of a subclass of `InputStream` in a manner analogous to the promotion of numeric types: The operator `instanceof` can be used to determine if an argument is actually an instance of a more specialized subclass, such as (in this case) `PrintStream`, in which case the argument could be cast to that type so that `PrintStream` methods could be applied to the result.

Certification

This is an alternative approach to ensuring safety when computer systems download applications from remote hosts. Certification uses cryptographic techniques to establish the origin of an application, presumably from some trusted source, and to confirm that it has not been altered during its handling by unknown or untrusted Internet relay nodes. See also *verification*.

class

In Java, or any other object-oriented language, a class is a description of a combination of state and behavior. A class is a central repository for descriptions of behaviors (called methods) of the class, and is a specification for building objects that can carry out those behaviors in ways that will vary according to each object's individual state.

Class method

See *static*.

Class variable

See *static*.

Code

To a programmer, this word has two meanings. Idiomatically, code refers to the written form of a program that is designed to be understandable by a person. This is also called *source code*. When you write a program, you are producing source code, and this process is sometimes called coding.

Code also means, generically, any mapping between two sets of symbols. For example, *ASCII* codes (see Appendix B) provide a standard way of translating letters, numerals, and punctuation marks to *binary* symbols that can easily be stored and processed.

Programmers do not use the word code in the everyday sense of a secret code, designed to obscure meaning. When programmers discuss such schemes, they use the term encryption.

Coercion

See *casting*.

Comparison

Programs perform comparisons to determine if two values have the same meaning (*equality*); to determine if two names refer to the same thing (*identity*); and to place values in rank order, as when sorting words or numbers or when deciding if a *loop* has completed the required number of repetitions.

Compiler

A compiler takes one form of a program and uses it to produce another form that is closer to being directly usable by a computer. A Java compiler takes Java *source code* and produces equivalent *bytecodes*. A *just-in-time* compiler or *native* compiler takes bytecodes (or, when working with other languages, source code) and produces native *machine* codes for the computer to be used for running that program. Contrast with *interpreter*.

Concurrent

Except for computers with more than one actual processor, any computer has only one set of hardware for storing and operating on values. In general, however, computers are so much faster than their users that a computer can turn its attention from one task to another, putting down one state and picking up another, dozens or hundreds of times a second.

The effect is one of doing more than one task at the same time, known informally as concurrent processing even though this is not literally an accurate description. Context switching is a more formal term that captures the difficulty of doing this reliably.

Conditional operator

An operator that defers *evaluation* of one or more operands until it determines whether the value of another operand makes the value of the deferred operand(s) irrelevant. Also known as a short-circuit evaluator, since the process of evaluating the operands may not make a full trip through the *statement*. The Java operators ||, &&, and ?: are conditional.

Console

Console interaction is also known as "glass TTY," where TTY is slang for teletype and refers to the typewriter-style terminals used to interact with early computers. A glass TTY is a computer screen that's providing only text-based, conversational interaction between the user and the computer. DOS and Unix typically provide such facilities, while the Macintosh environment doesn't normally offer this mode.

Constant

A constant is a value that can not be altered by *assignment*. Java reserves the keyword const, which some languages use to declare such a value, but Java does not use this keyword for this or any other purpose. To make a value unalterable, Java uses the keyword *final*.

Constructor

A constructor is a method that returns a new instance of a class. The common form of constructor is a method with the same name as that of the class, requiring no return-type declaration since the return type is the same as the method name. A class can define more than one such constructor, each with a different signature of argument types, to enable construction of objects based on different supplied information.

A class with no explicitly defined constructors will have, by default, a constructor that takes no arguments and returns an instance with default initializations of all instance variables. If a class defines one or more explicit constructors, it will not have a no-arg constructor unless this is explicitly defined as well.

A class may also have other constructors, not sharing the name of the class, but returning an instance of that class: For example, the statement InetAddress iAddr = InetAddress.getLocalHost(); declares and constructs a new instance of the Internet Protocol address encapsulation class by executing a *static method* of that class.

Container

This is the *subclass* of `Component` that serves as the *abstract superclass* of all `Components` that can hold other `Components`. Classes `Panel` and `Window` extend `Container` directly. Classes `Applet` (which extends `Panel`) and `Frame` (which extends `Window`) are the superclasses of most graphical applications.

Cybernetic

Strictly, cybernetic means "measuring differences and applying feedback to reduce those differences." This behavior is found in both natural and artificial systems. Idiomatically, the prefix "cyber" has become a general indicator of any association (however vague) with computers. Where this is used to deceive, mislead, or shift blame from the programmer (or the programmer's employer) to the computer, Ted Nelson proposes the label "cybercrud."

D

Data

Programmers divide the universe into hardware, code, and data. Code makes hardware do things to data. Data is any part of the system that just gets passed around, without being asked to help.

That's not a very formal definition, but data is not a very formalizable term. To the Java virtual machine, bytecodes are data. To the file that gets read by that Java program, however, the bytecodes look like code while the file itself is data.

If that file contains HTTP commands to retrieve a digital photograph from a remote Internet node, then those HTTP commands could be said to be code while the digital photo file is data. If the digital photo file is a self-extracting archive, however, then it contains both code and data.

There is no absolute bottom to this hierarchy, since even a single bit may be either code or data to some part of an information processing system. What something is called depends on whether it's acting or being acted upon at that point in a process.

Deadlock

This is the state that exists when two or more units of program execution (in Java, threads) each acquire control of some resource to perform some task, but each is waiting for access to a resource controlled by another mutually deadlocked entity before proceeding.

Debugger

A programming tool that allows step-by-step execution and internal inspection of the data and behaviors of a program. It does not, unfortunately, detect or remove bugs.

Declaration

A declaration describes a piece of data, or a method, by name and by characteristics such as the data types with which it works. A *compiler* relies on declarations to determine that an *identifier* is being properly used.

Default

A default is any value or behavior that a program supplies unless otherwise instructed. Defaults reduce the number of individual situations that need to be enumerated, making programs easier to write and to understand. In Java, this idea appears in such contexts as the default constructor for a class of objects, the default values supplied by a constructor that takes no arguments or a reduced number of arguments, the `default` case in a multi-option `switch` statement, or the default value returned by a key from a `Properties` data structure

Digit

From a word meaning *finger*, commonly used to refer to a symbol occupying a single position in what may be a multi-digit representation of a value. The binary digits are 0 and 1, the octal digits are 0 through 7, the decimal digits are 0 through 9, the hexadecimal digits are 0 through 9 and A through F.

A digital computer uses internal representations of data that represent, in some way, digital notations. This contrasts with analog computers that use some continuously variable state, such as a voltage or an air pressure, to represent a value. Once preferred for modeling natural phenomena such as the flow of heat in a physical system, analog computers can no longer compete with the price/performance characteristics of digital technology, which has even replaced consumer analog products (such as the LP record) with digital hardware (such as the audio compact disc).

Domain Name System

The mapping between a numeric *IP address* and a more convenient alphanumeric name. For example, the IP address `206.66.184.204` is more easily remembered as `www.pcweek.com`.

E

Encapsulation

This refers to the hiding of low-level data within the controlled access mechanisms of an object. For example, the `Color` class conceals the actual hardware used to control the color that appears on a screen within the encapsulation of the 24-bit representation that the class presents to any program on any computer.

Equality

This is determined by the `equals()` method, which is inherited from class `Object` but should be overridden in an appropriate way by any subclass.

The `equals()` method should return a `boolean` result. It should be reflexive, so that any object equals itself. It should be symmetric, so that the truth of `x.equals(y)` should be equivalent to the truth of `y.equals(x)`. It should be transitive, so that the combined truth of `x.equals(y)` and `y.equals(z)` should be equivalent to the truth of `x.equals(z)`. And it should be existential, so that `x.equals(null)` should always be false.

It is pointless to ask if `null.equals(null)`: `null` belongs to no class, so there is no `equals()` method that can be invoked through this classless reference.

Equality is a less restrictive test than *identity*, since two variables of a reference type (i.e., two different names for what may or may not be distinct *objects*) may meet the relevant test of equality (e.g., two character strings containing the same sequence of characters) while not being identical (e.g., referring to separate *instances* of class String).

Evaluation

This is the process of going through a *statement* and replacing expressions with the values that they return. This may be a *recursive* process if an expression contains operands that are themselves expressions, as for example:

```
aResult = i++ + j++ + (p = q + r);
```

Evaluation, normally an automatic process, can be more precisely controlled with proper use of the operators ||, &&, or ?: (see *conditional operator*).

Event

In traditionally designed programs, the user gets to provide input only when starting the program or when responding to the program's prompts for additional information.

In a graphical operating environment, a program should always be receptive to input, such as commands to resize a window, no matter what else the program is doing at the time.

This calls for an architecture based on capturing events, such as operations of the mouse, and associating those events with particular onscreen components such as a pushbutton or a scroll bar so that the program can take the appropriate action. The standard class `java.awt.Event` defines a vocabulary of descriptive names for integer values returned from event-detecting mechanisms to signal a user's activity.

Exception

An abnormal but foreseeable condition, such as a file being unavailable or a sleeping thread being interrupted. Also, an instance of the class `Exception` that provides a mechanism for packaging information about such a condition and transporting that information for processing by some other part of the program.

Execution

The process of retrieving instructions, determining their meaning, and carrying out the actions that they describe. During this process, the nature of a stream of symbols may shift from being *data* in one part of the process to being *code* in another part. Execution may also be broken into *concurrent* units of control, each called a *process* or *thread* depending on the degree of separation between those units.

Extends

When one Java *class* `extends` another, the original class is called the *superclass* and the new class is called the *subclass*. A class that is declared *final* can not be extended.

A subclass in the same *package* as its superclass can use any instance variables and methods defined by its superclass, except for those declared to be *private* to the superclass. A subclass in a different package than its superclass can use only the *public* and *protected* members of the superclass, and can use those only if the superclass itself is declared as `public`.

A subclass can *override* variables and methods of its superclass, except for those declared `final`, with its own identically named variables and/or methods. These may either replace the corresponding members of the superclass, from the point of view of the subclass, or they may augment the facilities of the superclass by performing auxiliary computations before using the keyword `super` to invoke the superclass version.

A subclass often has an "is a" relationship with its superclass. For example, a Square "is a" Rectangle "is a" Shape; a Circle "is a" Shape. It would be logical for `Circle` and `Rectangle` both to be subclasses of `Shape`, with `Square` a subclass of `Rectangle`.

F

Feedback
A signal or symbol that results from some process and becomes input to the continuation of that process. For example, noise from a speaker that is picked up by a microphone is amplified, detected, and amplified again until the familiar squeal is heard. This is positive feedback. Negative feedback is the process of using a measure of error to guide a system in a way that reduces that error: this is the foundation of any *cybernetic* system.

Final
This keyword denotes something that can not be changed. A `final` value can not be changed by assignment. A `final` method can not be overridden by a subclass. A `final` class can not be extended to create a new subclass.

Floating-point
Any numeric representation that combines a significand (representing the significant figures of a value) with an exponent (representing a scaling factor for that value).

For example, the decimal value 1000 can be represented exactly as an integer, or it can be represented as 1 times 10^3. When represented as an integer, this value is precise to the nearest 1. When written 1×10^3, it is precise to the nearest 0.5×10^3, or +/– 500. When written as 1.0×10^3, it is precise to the nearest 0.05×10^3, or +/– 50.

Finite precision of floating-point formats requires care in making comparisons between values. The identity operator == should be used with care. A class that defines an appropriate version of the `equals()` method may be a more appropriate solution.

Function
In programming, this denotes a named series of statements that may or may not accept some input, but that always returns a value to the point in the program where that name was invoked. Contrast with *procedure*; see also *method*.

G

Garbage collection

The process of identifying data in memory that is no longer accessible by any part of a running program, and that may therefore be discarded. Normally an automatic process, this may be disabled for an entire session to maximize performance, or it may be initiated by calling the static method `System.gc()` before beginning a performance-critical task. See *real-time*.

go to

A famously controversial topic among programmers, the arbitrary transfer of control from one point in a program to another point in the program is either a useful convenience or a nightmare that leads to confusing and hard-to-modify programs. It can be proved that it is possible to construct any conceivable program without this semantic component in a language. Java excludes it.

H

Hashing

The process of generating a "key" value that can be used to determine a storage location for a piece of data. The ideal hashing function results in a uniform distribution of data over all available storage locations. Implications are discussed in Chapter 13.

Hexadecimal

A numeric notation using base 16 to condense binary symbols into a smaller number of digits. A single hexadecimal digit represents four binary digits: the binary symbol for 255 is `11111111`, while the hexadecimal symbol is the more concise `FF`.

HTML

Hypertext Markup Language, the standard notation for describing graphically enhanced files in a format that can be interpreted and rendered on different types of computer.

This notation defines tags that are not displayed, but are interpreted by the HTML display program (commonly called a browser) as instructions to offer services such as jumping to another document when the user clicks the mouse while pointing to underlined text on the screen. See also *applet* and *World Wide Web*.

HTTP

Hypertext Transfer Protocol, the system of commands by which an Internet client computer most commonly requests HTML files from an Internet host machine. The means by which a Java program applies HTTP and retrieves Internet resources are described in Chapter 14.

I

Identity

This is the relationship of either being identical values (when speaking of simple types) or being different references to a single object (when speaking of reference types—i.e., of variables that correspond to objects). See *equality*.

Implements

When a Java class `implements` an *interface*, it means that the behaviors of that class (as defined by its methods) meet a list of requirements defined by that interface. For example, a class that implements the interface `Runnable` must have a method named `run()`, which can be called to begin some activity when an instance of that class is used to construct a *thread*.

Implicit conversion

A value of one type can be used where Java expects a variable of a less restrictive type. For example, an `int` value will be accepted by a method that is declared to take a `float` argument, since any possible `int` value has a valid `float` representation. A `FileInputStream` will be accepted wherever an `InputStream` is required, since every `FileInputStream` is an `InputStream`.

Loss of precision may result when a `long` is implicitly converted to a `double`, since the latter has fewer significant digits even though it has a higher maximum value.

Given this method:

```
static float takeInt(float takeThat) {return takeThat;}
```

the Java compiler will let that method be called with arguments of type `int` or `long`, as well as the specified `float`, as in

```
System.out.println(takeInt(7));    // an int
System.out.println(takeInt(7L));   // a long
System.out.println(takeInt(7.0f)); // a float
```

but it will not accept

```
System.out.println(takeInt(7.0)); // a double
```

because a `double` will never be implicitly converted to a `float`.

Once such conversion takes place, the reverse conversion will never take place automatically even if the values involved make it safe to do so. See *casting*.

Import
This keyword, followed by the name of a package or a packaged class, makes the public characteristics of the packaged class or classes accessible using the name of the class(es) alone, without using the package name in every reference.

The Java keyword `import` should not be confused with the C/C++ directive `#include`, which causes named files to be treated as if they were part of the file that contains the `#include` directive.

Importing a Java package only makes it accessible with a more concise notation, and aids the developer in applying different packages that take different approaches to similar functions. An `import` statement does not place any added burden on the Java compiler or affect the size of the resulting program.

Inheritance
See *extends*.

init()
The method name that is called when an *applet* is loaded by an HTML browser or other support environment. This method is only called once, as opposed to `start()` which is called whenever the applet comes into view—having been halted, when going out of view, by a call to `stop()`. When an applet will no longer be needed, its resources are freed by calling method `stop()` followed by method `destroy()`.

Initialization
The first association of a value with a newly declared variable name. Static final variables must be initialized when declared; others can be initialized, by a statement of the same form as any other simple assignment statement, in a separate statement at any time before the variable's value is first used by an expression. Failure to comply with either of these rules will cause a compile-time exception.

Instance
An object fitting the description provided by a *class*, storing its own value of each *instance variable* defined by that class, and able to use the *static* variables and *method* definitions that are held in common by the class for use by all instances.

Instance variable
A *variable* defined by a *class*, of which each *instance* of that class stores its own value. Contrast with *static* variable.

instanceof
This operator allows a Java program to determine if an object is an instance of a particular class, perhaps allowing the program to make use of specialized characteristics of that object that could not otherwise be assumed.

Integer
This general term is a superset, not a synonym, of the *simple type* named `int`. An integer is any numeric type that counts values discretely and exactly. An integer can not represent fractional values, or values beyond the range determined by the integer type's represented number of bits.

Interface
An interface is a named set of method signatures and/or (implicitly) `public static final` values. When a class implements an interface, it makes a contract to respond to certain method calls. This gives Java multiple inheritance of interface, though the designers intentionally excluded the more error-prone multiple inheritance of implementation.

Internet
A network of interconnected computer networks, accessible to each other using the *TCP/IP* protocol, relying on dynamic routing of data between locations that are each identified by a unique *IP address* or a corresponding *Domain Name System* designation.

Interpreter
A program that takes an instruction stream as its input, and carries out the operations described by those instructions, translating those instructions to hardware operations as they are encountered. Contrast with *compiler*.

io
See *java.io*.

IP address

An IP (Internet Protocol) address is a 32-bit number, usually written as a series of four numbers separated by periods with each number representing a single byte (and therefore having possible values 0 through 255). By convention, the address `127.0.0.1` is a local loopback address that a machine can use to talk to itself without external network hardware. On some machines, the command `host` will take a Domain Name System designation and return a numeric IP address, and vice versa.

Iteration

Repetitive execution of a series of instructions in the form of a *loop*, performed in Java under the control of a `for`, `while`, or `do...while` statement. Contrast with *recursion*.

J

java.applet

The standard *package* providing *class* and *interface* definitions that provide a foundation for constructing *applet* programs.

java.awt

The standard package providing *class* and *interface* definitions that provide a foundation for constructing a graphical user interface and for providing graphical output capabilities in a manner that permits the same Java program to run correctly on any system that provides a Java environment.

java.io

The standard package providing *class* and *interface* definitions that aid the programmer in defining input/output interactions in hardware-independent ways.

java.lang

The only standard package that is automatically imported by every program, providing facilities that are crucial to Java programming though not defined in the core of the language itself. These include the classes `Object`, `System`, `Thread`, `Throwable`, `String`, and `Math`.

java.net

The standard package providing *class* and *interface* definitions that ease the use of Uniform Resource Locators, *IP addresses*, and communication links that let programs communicate with each other and with these network-based resources.

java.util

A standard package providing *class* and *interface* definitions that include data structures (e.g., `Vector` and `Hashtable`) and the `Date` class for abstracting date and time representations. This package also provides the class `Observable` and the interface `Observer` that can be used to implement automatic notification of one object when a change occurs in another. The use of `Observer` and `Observable` is not covered in this book.

JavaScript

A language developed by Netscape and Sun, based on a Netscape language called LiveScript, with a syntactic resemblance to Java and with the ability to access the functions of Java classes.

JavaScript *code* is not compiled: It is embedded in an *HTML* page in *source code* form and executed by an *interpreter* when that page is viewed by a browser, unlike Java programs that are compiled to *bytecodes* that are stored in a separate file and downloaded based on directions embedded in an HTML tag.

JavaScript does not use data typing, it does not have an extensible class hierarchy, and it does not provide exception handling.

K

k (kilo)

Standing alone, abbreviates kilobyte. As a prefix or suffix, denotes a multiplier of 1,024.

key

In the context of a data structure such as the Java class `Hashtable`, a key is a value that is used to store and retrieve some other value. For example, a customer account number might be the key that is used to store and retrieve a customer's address.

L

lang

See *java.lang*.

Libraries

See *packages*.

Lightweight process
See *thread*.

Literal
A value that is represented directly in a program, such as a numeric literal (2), a character literal ('a'), or an array literal ({13, 4, 5}).

Logical operator
A version of a Boolean AND or OR operator that performs *short-circuit evaluation*. See *conditional operator*.

Loop
A repetitive execution of some *statement* or *block* of statements, controlled in Java by a for, while, or do...while statement. See *iteration*.

M

M (Mega-)
Standing alone, abbreviates megabyte. As a prefix or suffix, denotes a multiplier of 1,048,576 ($1,024^2$).

Machine code
The codes that are translated directly by the hardware of a computer into actions for that hardware to perform upon *data*.

main()
The method of a class that is invoked when that class is executed by a stand-alone Java interpreter such as Sun's java or Microsoft's jview. Contrast with *init()*.

Markup language
Any agreed-upon convention for annotating the contents of a file with information to be treated as describing other portions of the contents: For example, a notation that indicates a change of the font to be used when the document is printed or displayed. See *HTML*.

Math
See *java.lang.Math*.

Mega-
See *M (Mega-)*.

Member

A *variable* or *method* that participates in a *class*. This term covers both *static* variables (owned by the class) and *instance* variables (owned as distinct values by instances of the class), and covers both static methods (accessible outside the context of an instance) and normal methods (applied to an instance). Members of a class are always visible within the class, but their visibility to other classes is controlled by membership in a *package* and by the access modifiers *public, protected,* and *private.*

Method

A unit of description of behavior associated with a class. See also *abstract, argument, branch, code, constructor, evaluation, event, execution, function, init(), iteration, loop, main(), member, operator, overloading, procedure, recursion, side effect, signature, statement, static, void, volatile.* Contrast with *variable.*

Module

An identifiable unit of a program with a defined set of mechanisms for providing services to other units. Idiomatically, module suggests ease of understanding the structure of a system with a particular purpose, while object suggests ease of assembling units into new systems with purposes not specifically envisioned when those units were designed. Modules emphasize maintainability; objects emphasize reusability.

Multiple inheritance

See *extends, inheritance, interface, subclass,* and *superclass.*

Multitasking

See *concurrent, deadlock, execution, process,* and *thread.*

Multithreading

See *concurrent, deadlock, execution, process,* and *thread.*

N

Native

An adjective denoting tight coupling between some form of computer instruction and some particular operating environment, such as *machine code* for a particular processor or color attribute settings for a particular video display controller.

The Java keyword `native` denotes a *method* that executes native instructions. Such methods are not subject to Java's usual security protections and can not be called in an *applet*. Native methods are not covered in this book.

net
See *java.net.*

null
The only literal that can appear wherever Java normally expects a reference to an object. This name denotes an entity that is not an instance of any class: It is identical to itself, but has no applicable `equals()` method and does not pass the not equals() test with anything else. A reference to `null` is returned, for example, from an attempt to retrieve data from a `Hashtable` with a key that was never used to store a value in that table.

O

Object
The base class of all other classes, including arrays. Such fundamental notions as `equals()`, `hashCode()`, and `toString()` (for comparing objects' values, for storing objects in data structures, and for providing a printable representation of an object) originate in this class and are overridden in appropriate ways by subclasses. Generically, *object* also refers to an array or any other *instance* of any class.

Operator
A symbol, perhaps made up of multiple characters, that Java understands to direct some action by a program. Java's operators are tabulated in Appendix B.

Overflow
A condition resulting from assigning a numeric value to a variable whose symbolic format can not represent values that large. See also *underflow.*

Overloading
The act of defining more than one implementation of a method or an operator, with the desired implementation inferred from the types of the *arguments* supplied. Java provides overloading of methods, but does not allow programmer-defined overloading of operators. The operator + is overloaded to add numbers and concatenate strings; the operators &, |, and ^ are technically considered

overloaded to operate on both integers and `booleans`, but their meaning is the same in both contexts.

Optimizing

A *compiler* is said to be an optimizing compiler if it does more than minimally translate *source code* into equivalent executable *code*. Possible optimizations, sometimes mutually exclusive, include attempting to minimize memory use and attempting to maximize *execution* speed.

Optimizations performed by a particular compiler may be controlled by various option settings, some of which (called aggressive optimizations) may make assumptions about the relative independence of different parts of the program. It is possible that some optimization settings may cause a program to function differently than was intended by the programmer. Java's object disciplines, combined with proper use of the keyword *volatile*, reduce the likelihood of this.

Overriding

The act of defining a variable or method in a *subclass* with the same name as a variable or method in the *superclass*, modifying the characteristics normally acquired through *inheritance*.

P

Package

When a Java *class* is declared to be part of a package, and the class is not declared to be *public*, then the class is not accessible by classes outside its package; the non-*private* variables and methods of that class are directly accessible to other classes in the same package but not to those in other packages.

If a class is declared to be public, then its public components become additionally accessible by any classes in other packages; its protected components become additionally accessible to subclasses in other packages.

A class with no access modifier, or a variable or method within a class that is declared with no access modifier, is said to have package access. See *private, protected, and public.*

Packet

A unit of data transmitted via a communication link, containing both a messsage or some piece of a message plus additional information such as the origin, the destination, the sequence number, and/or error checking information used to verify correct receipt.

A packet-based network is distinguished from a circuit-based network that opens and maintains a path between two points until an exchange is completed. A circuit-based network need not allow for the possibility that units of data will be received in a different sequence than they were transmitted. A packet network may use different paths, with different transit times, between two points from one moment to the next, and must therefore allow for this possibility.

Parallel processing
See *concurrent*.

Parent
See *superclass*.

Precedence
The rank order in which operands within an expression are processed, in the absence of parentheses. Precedence groups are tabulated in Appendix B.

Precision
The degree to which a symbolic representation of numeric values can distinguish between closely spaced values. A `float`, with 23 bits of precision, can not distinguish between 5.0000001 decimal (about 101.00000000000000000000001101011010 binary) and 4.9999999 decimal (about 100.11111111111111111111110010100101 binary). A `double`, with 52 bits of precision, can distinguish these values from each other.

private
A *variable* or *method* declared as `private` within some *class* is not directly accessible to any other class, regardless of *package* or *subclass* relationships and regardless of whether the class itself is *public*.

Procedure
In programming, this denotes a named series of statements that may or may not accept some input, but which never returns a value to the point in the program where that name was invoked. A procedure is executed to perform some useful effect such as printing. Contrast with *function*; see also *method*.

Process
A unit of control over the process of executing a program, providing a separate address space and separate data contexts from those used by any other process.

Also called a heavyweight process to emphasize the distinction between a process and a *thread*.

Promotion

When a Java expression is declared to use some type of value, it will accept a value of a more restricted type in its place, promoting the supplied value to the more general type (but losing access to more specialized behaviors available to the more restrictive type). See *casting* and *implicit conversion.*

protected

A *variable* or *method* declared as `protected` within some *class* is directly accessible to other classes in the same *package*, and to *subclasses* in other packages if the original class is declared to be *public.* Declaring a class or a class member as `protected` has no effect on its accessibility within a package.

Protocol

A set of data formatting conventions and operational commands used for data communications, as in networking. See *HTTP, IP address,* and *TCP/IP.*

public

A *variable* or *method* declared as `public` within some class is directly accessible to other classes in the same *package*, and to other classes in other packages if the original class is also declared to be *public.* Declaring a class or a class member as `public` has no effect on its accessibility within a package.

Q

Qualified name

The full name of an entity, such as a package or an instance variable, when used to avoid ambiguity.

For example, if a program implements two *interface* definitions named `Inter1` and `Inter2`, and each interface defines a *constant* value named `SOME_CONSTANT`, then these values must be referred to by the qualified names `Inter1.SOME_CONSTANT` and `Inter2.SOME_CONSTANT`.

If two packages, `package1` and `package2`, each include a *class* named `SomeClass`, then a program can not *import* both `package1.*` and `package2.*`, or import both `package1.SomeClass` and `package2.SomeClass`. It can make qualified references to either or both of these classes by using these full names.

R

Radix
The base value of a numbering system. For example, binary numbering uses a radix of 2, hexadecimal uses a radix of 16.

Real-time
When the maximum time to complete a computation is part of the specification of a system, that system is said to be a real-time system. For example, the program that shuts down a power plant if a serious failure is detected may have a required response time measured in seconds; the program that operates a car's antilock braking system may have a required response time measured in milliseconds, or even microseconds. Both are examples of real-time programs. System behaviors such as pauses for garbage collection may need to be specially constrained to meet the needs of real-time programs.

Real-time programs are often characterized by the need to work with data values that are continually being updated by external input such as sensors. This means that a *compiler* may not be correct in making its usual assumptions about which variables are subject to change, for example within a *loop* that continually updates a display. See also *volatile*.

Recursion
When a problem-solving process makes reference to itself, that process is said to be recursive. For example, the process of evaluating expressions includes the need to evaluate terms of the expression that are themselves expressions (see *evaluation*).

A recursive program, the Tak benchmark, appears in Chapter 13.

Reserved word
A word that can not be used as an identifier when writing programs, because the word has a special meaning to the language. Java's reserved words are tabulated in Appendix B.

S

Scripting

The use of an interpreted command language, such as *JavaScript*, to automate some aspect of the behavior of an end-user application. DOS batch files and word processor macros are also examples of scripting.

Short-circuit

See *conditional operator*.

Side effect

A change in the state of the variables or objects accessible to a program, typically resulting from an *assignment*, an increment, a decrement, or an invocation of a *method* that performs one or more of these operations. Also, an external effect such as causing a value to be printed. Contrasts with, but is not exclusive to, the return of a value from an expression.

Signature

The name of a method combined with the number and types of the arguments to the method, used (for example) to determine which of several *overloaded* methods to apply.

Signed

A binary data representation defined for both negative and positive values. Java's `byte`, `short`, `int`, `long`, `float`, and `double` are all signed numeric representations. See *unsigned*.

Simple type

In Java, one of the types `boolean`, `char`, `byte`, `short`, `int`, `long`, `float`, and `double`, that can be represented as values without being contained by an object. Also called primitive types.

Source code

The "human-readable" form of a program. Also known as *code*.

Standard packages

See *java.applet, java.awt, java.io, java.lang, java.net, java.util*.

Statement

Generally, a "sentence" in a procedural programming language. In Java, either an expression statement (such as a simple assignment) or a control statement (such as a `for` loop or a `switch`). A Java statement ends with a semicolon.

static

The modifier `static` indicates that a value or method is associated with a class rather than with an instance of that class.

For example, class `Character` defines the static method `boolean isSpace(char testChar)`, which returns the value `false` from the expression `Character.isSpace('a')`. The method is called outside the context of any Character object.

The same class also defines the method `boolean equals(Object testObject)`, which returns the value `false` from the expression `(new Character('a')).equals(new Character(' '))`. The non-static method is called in the context of a particular instance of `Character`.

A `static` variable or `final static` value is stored only once, in the class. A `static` variable modified by any instance of a class will appear with the modified value to any other instance. Contrast with *instance variable*.

String

An informal name for a character string, which is a composite data entity made up of one or more elementary character entities. Some languages provide this as a built-in data type, while Java provides a predefined class `String` that can hold a character string as a piece of data and can apply various methods to string-type data.

Strongly typed

A programming language is strongly typed if it requires the programmer to declare some kind of data type affiliation for every data entity, and if it enforces rules about the allowable use of data entities based on these declared types. When a Java program can not be compiled because a method is being called with arguments whose types do not match the signature of any method declaration using that method name, this is an example of strongly typed design. Contrast with untyped languages, e.g. *JavaScript*, in which any type of value can be assigned to any variable name.

Subclass
A class that *extends* another class, known as its *superclass*. A superclass may have any number of direct subclasses, each of which may have any number of subclasses in turn.

Subroutine
See *method*.

super
Within an instance method or constructor, or in an instance variable initializer, the keyword super names the superclass of the class of the object within whose context the method is executing. It can be used to gain access to a method or field defined on the superclass that's been shadowed by an identically named member in the subclass.

Superclass
The class named in the optional *extends* part of the declaration of some other class, known as a *subclass* of that superclass. A Java class can have at most one direct superclass, though there may be many levels of superclass above the first.

System software
A piece of software not intrinsically useful, but needed to either enable or improve some aspect of system operation. Obvious examples include an operating system, a device driver, or an antivirus scanner; borderline examples include a disk maintenance utility. A Java virtual machine or applet viewer is system software; a Java applet or application may be system software (e.g., Sun's HotJava browser or the Java WorkShop development system) or it may be an end-user *application*.

T

TCP/IP
Transmission Control Protocol/Internet Protocol. This is the composite name for a virtual circuit connection across the Internet (TCP) using the Net's low-level packet-management mechanisms (IP).

this
Within an instance method or constructor, or in an instance variable initializer, the keyword this names the object within whose context the method is executing. It can be used to gain access to an instance variable that's been shadowed by an identically named formal parameter to a method; to name the object as an argu-

ment to an alternative constructor, after the originally called constructor has modified its arguments or developed additional information; or to name the object as an argument to a method being invoked from some other class.

Thread

A unit of control over the process of executing a program. A Java thread is an object, which receives opportunities to continue execution under a priority-based scheduling scheme.

Thread scheduling behavior may vary in different implementations of the language: Ensuring desired behavior requires explicit attention to assignment of priorities and to yielding of control.

Threads are also called lightweight processes to emphasize their distinction from conventional (heavyweight) processes, which each provide a separate address space and separate data context. Threads share data, reducing the overhead of using them but requiring discipline to avoid unintended interference.

Transient

This keyword advises a compiler that a value is not to be stored as part of a persistent representation of an object.

U

Underflow

A condition resulting from assigning a numeric value to a variable whose symbolic format can not represent values that small. See also *overflow*.

Unicode

A character set defining 16-bit codes (0000 through FFFF hexadecimal), subsuming the ASCII and ISO-Latin-1 character sets (through values 00FF), with additional ranges defined for Armenian, Bengali, Cyrillic, Devanagari, and many other non-Roman scripts.

Uniform Resource Locator

See *URL*.

Unsigned

A binary data representation that is mapped to values beginning with 0. See *signed*.

URL

A uniform resource locator, or an instance of the class URL that encapsulates a URL reference as an input source or output destination.

util

See *java.util.*

V

Variable

As in algebra, a variable is a name for a number or some other quantity that takes part in a computation. A variable can take on different values through *assignment*, unless it is constrained against change by a declaration of *final*.

Verification

The process by which the Java environment establishes the safety of executing a set of *bytecodes*. The verifier is a program of the type known as a theorem prover, able to answer general questions without exhaustively testing all possibilities.

void

When a method is void, it does not return a value. For example, a method could be declared as:

```
void say(String aString
  { System.out.println(aString);}
or it could be declared as:
String say(String aString)
{ System.out.println(aString); return aString; }
```

The first merely has the side effect of sending its argument to the standard output stream; the second does the same thing, but could be invoked in an expression like:

```
String whatWasSaid = say("I said this.");
```

which returns the printed character string and, in this case, assigns it to the variable whatWasSaid.

volatile

This keyword advises a compiler that a value is subject to external change. For example, a *loop* might display a value that is updated by readings from an external sensor or is accessible from an unsynchronized thread. If the loop looks something like this,

```
int sensorReading = 0; // updated by sensorThread
while(true) { sensor.readout(sensorReading);
                Thread.sleep(10000);
                        // check again in 10 seconds
        }
```

then an *optimizing compiler* might assume that `sensorReading` is constant within the `while` loop. Compilers don't read comments.

When it enters the loop, the compiler might store the value `sensorReading` in an on-chip memory (called a register) and use that stored value thereafter. To prevent this, one would declare `sensorReading` as `volatile`.

Note, in particular, that a 64-bit `double` or `long` value that is not declared as `volatile` may be handled in `read()` or `write()` operations by two separate actions on the two 32-bit components of that value. Other operations may intervene. If these operations affect a shared `double` or `long` variable, the variable may wind up with a value that is an implementation-dependent artifact. The current specification encourages, and future versions may require, the more robust treatment of these operations as indivisible ("atomic") 64-bit actions.

W

Wiener, Norbert

Author of *Cybernetics: Or Control and Communication in the Animal and the Machine*, published in 1948 with a second edition in 1961. The following is quoted from the original introduction, written in 1947:

> There is no rate of pay at which a United States pick-and-shovel laborer can live which is low enough to compete with the work of a steam shovel....The modern industrial revolution is similarly bound to devalue the human brain, at least in its simpler and more routine decisions....
>
> [T]aking the second revolution as accomplished, the average human being of mediocre attainments or less has nothing to sell that it is worth anyone's money to buy.

When Wiener wrote this, the world's only real computer took up 1,800 square feet and used about 18,000 vacuum tubes. His prediction therefore showed amazing foresight. His 1950 book, *The Human Use of Human Beings: Cybernetics and*

Society, explores issues that many companies and governments are only now beginning to confront.

Word

A word is a unit of *binary data* that's convenient to handle on a particular type of
computer.

If a processor is built to work with 32-bit values, for example, then its most efficient instructions for storing and retrieving data will generally be those that operate
on 32-bit words, aligned on 32-bit boundaries in the address space of the computer. A *native compiler* for that computer will try to *optimize* programs to operate
in this manner.

Some advanced processors already use a 64-bit word, letting them address
larger amounts of memory and process more complex types of data with greater
speed. Java avoids the potential confusion of differing word sizes by defining its
simple types as specific numbers of *bits*, regardless of the underlying hardware.

World Wide Web

The origin of the World Wide Web was a 1989 proposal by Tim Berners-Lee, a
document and text-processing specialist at Geneva, Switzerland's European
Laboratory for High Energy Physics, also known as CERN (from the acronym of
the center's original French name, Conseil Europeen pour la Recherche Nucleaire).
That proposal can be viewed, of course, on the Web, at **http://www.w3.org/
hypertext/WWW/Proposal.html**.

The Web has been defined as the result of combining the *Internet* with *HTML*.
Tautologically, the Web is what you can see with a Web browser.

This means that the Web is a different thing for every user, since each user's
browser has access to different local files, different firewalled domains, and different value-added services—though all of these are in addition to the shared "public
park" of the Internet, and it is this international pool of accessible resources that
goes by the name of "The Web."

The convenience of the Web is not an unmixed blessing. Think of the relationship between a city and a subway system: Your view of the city is very different if
you go from place to place by walking than if you just go down the stairs, drop a
token in the turnstile, and pop up at the place where you wanted to go.

When you click on an underlined hot spot on a Web page, and see a linked
page appear, you're taking the train instead of walking. The people who run the
trains make it easy to get from one place to another, but the train only stops where
they decide to build a station.

If the only Internet resources that you use are the ones that you can see via HTTP, you can cover a lot of ground—but you may never see some interesting places that lie between the subway stops.

Not all URLs begin with `http://`, and becoming comfortable with other types of Internet-accessible resources can expand your online world. The package *java.net* abstracts the Internet, not just the Web. Don't neglect its other applications.

Index

KEDIT for Windows

VERSION 1.5

For Windows 95, Windows NT and Windows 3.1

Windows Power KEDIT is a full-featured Windows text editor with menus, toolbars, drag-and-drop editing, clipboard access, and Multiple Document Interface (MDI) support. Editing features include sophisticated search and replace facilities, full undo and redo, a sort facility, and regular expression support.

Flexibility Dozens of options let you tailor the interface to suit your preferences, so you can pick the combination of features that work best for you. You can use the mouse, menus, and dialog boxes to access the power of KEDIT or, if you prefer, you can use the keyboard and the command line.

Syntax Coloring KEDIT's syntax coloring facility highlights comments, strings, and keywords in a variety of languages, including HTML, Java, C, REXX, and COBOL. Especially helpful is KEDIT's use of different colors to highlight different levels of parentheses, braces, and nested keywords. Syntax coloring is user configurable, so you can add your own keywords, and even add support for additional languages.

Data Manipulation KEDIT provides a wide range of facilities for working with column-oriented data. Features like column marking, boundary marking, and multiple verify ranges make it easy to view your data. You can move, copy, sort, shift, uppercase, or lowercase columns of data, and you can insert, delete, search for, and replace text in particular columns.

Selective Line Editing This is one of KEDIT's most popular features. Selective editing lets you focus on a subset of the lines in your file, such as all lines containing a particular string, or all altered lines. You can have KEDIT display only this subset of your file, and you can perform editing operations that affect only this subset.

Get Café at a Special Price

The full version of the Symantec Café CD contains the latest Java Development Kit and many exciting new features and tools:

- Debug your Java applets with the Café Visual Java Debugger
- Design your forms and menus with the Café Studio
- Navigate and edit your classes and methods with the Hierarchy Editor and Class Editor
- Compile your Java applets and applications 50 times faster with the Café native compiler
- Just-in-Time compiler let's you build applications that run up to 25 times faster than the previous Java standard

To subscribe or learn more about Café please visit us at: http://www.cafe.symantec.com
By subscribing to the mailing list you can receive the latest information and updates about Symantec Internet Tools

http://www.cafe.symantec.com

Symantec Café includes all the components found in Café Lite, plus a 2-way hierarchy editor, a class editor, a GUI multi-thread debugger, a visual menu and form designer, a native compiler which compiles the .class files up to 50 times faster, a new Java virtual machine for Windows which runs up to 25 times faster than the previous Java standard, 85 samples, a tutorial, and the API docs in help.

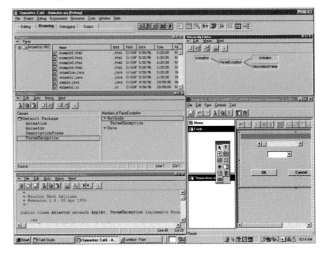

Yes! I want the most advanced Java development tool for Windows NT and Windows 95. Please rush me Symantec Café at this special discount offer!

Available in U.S. only. Offer expires on 6/30/97

(Please print legibly)

Name: _____

Company: _____

Title: _____

Address: _____

City: _____

State/Province: _____

Country (if not USA): _____

Phone: _____

E-mail: _____

You can receive updates on new developments regarding Symantec Café approximately once per month via e-mail. Do you wish to be added to our information bulletin list?

O Yes O No

Upgrade from Café Lite to Café	**$ 79.95**
Priority Code: CAFE97 (Only CD media)	
Number of Units Requested:	$_____
Applicable sales tax:	$_____
Shipping	$_____
$9.95 for each product shipped in USA	
PAYMENT TOTAL:	$_____

Payment Method: O Check O Money Order O Visa

(Please do not send cash) O American Express O MasterCard

Name on card: _____

Expiration date: _____

Signature (required): _____

Mail to: Café Lite Upgrade
P.O. Box 10849
Eugene, OR 97440-9711
Call 1-800-240-2275 24hrs. / 7 days a week
or fax your order to 1-800-800-1438 Priority code: CAFE97